LIFE AND WORK IN POST-SOVIET RUSSIA

LIFE AND WORK POST-SOVIET RUSSIA

Chris Cheang

S Rajaratnam School of International Studies
Nanyang Technological University, Singapore

World Scientific

NEW JERSEY · LONDON · SINGAPORE · BEIJING · SHANGHAI · HONG KONG · TAIPEI · CHENNAI · TOKYO

Published by

World Scientific Publishing Co. Pte. Ltd.

5 Toh Tuck Link, Singapore 596224

USA office: 27 Warren Street, Suite 401-402, Hackensack, NJ 07601

UK office: 57 Shelton Street, Covent Garden, London WC2H 9HE

National Library Board, Singapore Cataloguing in Publication Data
Names: Cheang, Chris.
Title: Life and work in post-Soviet Russia / Chris Cheang.
Description: Singapore : World Scientific, [2020]
Identifiers: OCN 1204206795 | ISBN 978-981-122-797-4 (paperback) |
    ISBN 978-981-122-676-2 (hardcover)
Subjects: LCSH: Diplomats--Singapore--Biography. | Singapore--Foreign relations--Russia. |
    Russia--Foreign relations--Singapore.
Classification: DDC 327.59597047--dc23

British Library Cataloguing-in-Publication Data
A catalogue record for this book is available from the British Library.

For any available supplementary material, please visit
https://www.worldscientific.com/worldscibooks/10.1142/12005#t=suppl

Desk Editor: Karimah Samsudin

Typeset by Stallion Press
Email: enquiries@stallionpress.com

This is a remarkable book. First, it is very rich in details and reveals much about what is Russia and on how to survive living and working there — in earlier times and at present. Secondly, it is written in a reader-friendly way with a minimum of intellectual and theoretical language. Most importantly, in the context of today's intensive geopolitical and strategic competition between China and the United States of America (USA), the roles of Russia's separate relationships with China, Europe and the USA, and their impact on global security and stability are well explained. This book is a gem!

Ong Keng Yong
Executive Deputy Chairman,
S. Rajaratnam School of International Studies /
Nanyang Technological University, Singapore
Former Secretary-General of ASEAN

I was Permanent Secretary in the Ministry of Foreign Affairs when Chris served his second tour of duty in Russia. During my two visits there, he showed me aspects of Russia which he writes in great detail in his book — Russia's rich culture, Russia's history, complicated politics, pride in its role in world affairs, and its "Near Abroad", its people and aspirations. He is a diplomat who walks the ground with a good pulse of the country. His anecdotes about his varied experiences over 3 postings in post-Soviet Russia show his empathy and deep understanding of the country. It is written from the viewpoint of a diplomat, with a keenness in observation, helped by his experience as a journalist as well.

Tan Chin Tiong
Senior Advisor, Institute of Southeast Asian Studies (ISEAS)-Yusof Ishak Institute
Former Director, ISEAS-Yusof Ishak Institute
Former Permanent Secretary, Ministry of Foreign Affairs
Former Ambassador to Japan

Life and Work in Post-Soviet Russia is a readable and engaging account of a Singapore diplomat who served three stints in Russia, altogether 15 years in all. Although a personal account, it is well-researched. Cheang paints a detailed picture of changes in the country at a granular level, as felt by its people and outsiders like himself, with interesting insights. His analysis of the direction of Soviet foreign policy and its relations with the US and the West and with China is balanced and thoughtful.

Chan Heng Chee
Ambassador-at-Large, Ministry of Foreign Affairs
Former Ambassador of Singapore to the United States

For many, Russia is a vast and foreign place, somewhat strange and separated by language, culture and distance. This book unveils Russia, through the personal encounters of a foreign diplomat travelling across the land. His tales are told plainly, but not without wry humour. Mundane matters, like common superstitions or driving habits, are related with a lively curiousity and an observant eye. But a broader picture also emerges, as he pieces together his encounters that have stretched over two decades, and journeys across the country to places less travelled. This is a book which provides both acolytes and seasoned observers of Russia an earthy and ground up account of a land and people not that strange or different from the rest of us.

David Lim
Former Member of Parliament for Aljunied Constituency
(1997–2006)
Former Acting Minister for Information, Communications and the
Arts (2001–2003)
Former Group Chief Executive Officer of Neptune Orient Lines
Limited and Chief Executive Officer (CEO) of the Port of Singapore
Authority

My very first visit to Moscow, Russia, was in June 2006. In June 2007, I went to St. Petersburg for an Energy Conference. There, I had the luxury of visiting the fabulous Hermitage Museum. I was invited to Yaroslavl for three days in September 2010 for a Conference on Economic Development chaired by President Medevev. In March 2011, together with Chris Cheang and my economic development colleagues, we visited the immense Russia Far East. With each visit, my knowledge of Russia increased a little. I turned to several books on Russia to learn the history, culture, and political evolvement. Chris Cheang's book here will enhance my appreciation of Russia.

Philip Yeo
Chairman, Agency for Science, Technology and Research
(Feb 2001–March 2007)
Senior Advisor for Economic Development, Prime Minister's Office
(April 2007–August 2011)
Chairman, Standards, Productivity and Innovation for Growth
(April 2007–March 2018)

Russia is a major power and will always be. Russia is, however, a puzzle to most of us. I thank Chris Cheang for helping me to be less puzzled by this important country. I hope that in the coming years, Russia will play a more active and positive role in its engagement with ASEAN.

Tommy Koh
Professor of Law, National University of Singapore
Ambassador-At-Large, Ministry of Foreign Affairs, Singapore

Reading Christopher Cheang's fascinating book, I experienced with him all those reverberating years of my country, which he has skillfully depicted.

His book is a profoundly deep analysis of post-Soviet Russian history. He spent three tours of duty in Moscow since 1994 and witnessed the dynamics of developments. His pen is highly professional and the stories are so vivid. I was overwhelmed by his delicate approach and reverence to his readers.

He succeeded in describing genuine life in Russia. Of great interest is his presentation of the political, economic and social fabric of Russian society.

His contacts covered a broad variety of people from numerous walks of life. That gives additional authority to his analysis. I also read with great pleasure the preface written by my dear friend Bilahari Kausikan, former Ambassador to Russia, who gave an excellent panorama of the contemporary international scene.

Igor V. Khalevinski
Chairman, Russian Diplomats Association
Co-Chairman, Eurasia Peoples Assembly
Former Minister for Labour and Social Development, Russian Federation
Ambassador-at-Large, Ministry of Foreign Affairs, Russia

This masterly book presents an unbiased picture of Russia, immune from any ideological dogmas and prejudices. Deep and broad knowledge of the country's history and visionary talents allows the author to stay above them and impartially assess the problems facing the country. It makes reading the book exciting – both for those who were never interested in Russia and who were actively involved in it. This book represents an overview of developments in Russia over the past few decades, or as thought-provoking research. It raises many questions and offers readers to come up with their conclusions, particularly about Russia's geopolitical role.

Readers are also acquainted with the author; his roles as an unbiased outside observer and participant in events in the country (being a high-ranking diplomat) allow him to act as an independent thinker.

Evgeny Gavrilenkov

Partner of GKEM Analytica (Business and Economics Consultancy)
Editor-in-Chief of the Moscow Higher School of Economics Journal
Member of the Russian International Affairs Council

Chris Cheang's *Life and Work in Post-Soviet Russia* is a unique survey both in style and in substance, as the author sought to convert his long-term personal experience of exploring the enigma of former communist empire into a profound academic research — both timely and inspiring. His recollections and thoughts on the twists and turnarounds of Russia's independent development — from the turbulent time of former communist apparatchik, Boris Yeltsin, known as "Tsar Boris", to the era of ex-KGB spy-turned president, Vladimir Putin — put together, are more than just facts written by Chris Cheang when he was a Singapore diplomat posted to the country in one of the most dramatic moments of its history. Obviously, this is something much more.

The book gives deep insight into the intricacies of the Kremlin's Byzantine-type politics after the collapse of the Soviet Union and explains how Russia's national idea was shaping up, making the new independent Russia a rising Eurasian power between the East and the West.

The book is frank, objective, unbiased and full of perspective. This makes Chris Cheang's book a curtain-raiser in a time of information wars and fake news.

Sergei Strokan
Observer, Kommersant Publishing House, Moscow, Russia

Chris Cheang has written a marvellous book. It should be read by anyone looking to grasp and understand Post-Soviet modern Russia. These memoirs are a wide-ranging and pleasantly personal account — from the turbulent 1990s through the stabilization of the Putin era. In addition, there is plenty of professional analysis. Through Chris Cheang, and a powerful foreword by Amb. Bilahari Kausikan, we hear the calm, confident, and experienced voices of diplomats from Singapore — voices the wider diplomatic and political world are advised to hear. Timely… and important."

David Edic
Past Presi
San Diego World Affairs Cou

Chris Cheang's *Life and Work in Post-Soviet Russia* is an insightful highly enjoyable memoir. Written from Chris' unique perspective foreign diplomat from Singapore whose first assignment to Russi shortly after the dissolution of the Soviet Union and chaotic econo and political landscape through its rapid rise during the commo boom of the early 2000s, to the post-global financial crisis of 20 Chris takes the reader from his initial stay and learning the challer that the country and its people faced after everything they knew trusted changed with the collapse of the central government. Ch unbiased yet candid observations are astute and bring the reader b to the point and time of major events, how they impacted relati between Russia and the West, and he finishes with a thought assessment of the current situation. All in all a very enjoyable, w written assessment of Russia over the past 25 years told through Ch personal experiences of living and working in Russia during t fascinating time.

Tim O'Br
Former Regional Director for Russia and the Commonwealth
Independent States (CIS) from 2008–20
Financial Services Volunteer Co
Moscow, Rus

Contents

Foreword

Why Think About Russia?

Singaporeans generally do not pay enough attention to Russia. And if Singaporeans do think about a country that is a Permanent Member of the United Nations Security Council (UNSC), a nuclear weapon state, and a major energy producer that occupies about an eighth of all the land on this planet, their sources of information are usually western and, in particular, American. That is only one side of a complicated story.

Post-Soviet Russia no longer plays much of a direct role in Southeast Asia. But for half a century during the Cold War, the Soviet Union's relationship with the United States (US) fundamentally shaped the international order. In our region, the Cold War was 'hot' in Indochina. The Cold War, and in particular how it ended, still exerts an influence we cannot ignore. Christopher Cheang served in Moscow for three tours of duty between 1994 and 2013, just after the crucial transition from the Soviet Union to the Russian Federation.

Christopher and I have been friends and colleagues for decades. He is a talented political analyst, and I have always valued his insights and learnt from him. He is one of the unsung legions of underappreciated and largely anonymous foreign service officers without whose professionalism and dedication to duty, our foreign policy could not succeed. He tells the story of this seminal period in post-Soviet Russia's evolution through his everyday personal experiences. Any Singaporean with an interest in international affairs will benefit from Christopher's sharp and original observations. He has a point of view Singaporeans will not find in western accounts.

Why should we be interested in Russia? We commonly and loosely speak of the 'American century'. Yet, for half the 20th century, global order was divided and contested between the US and Soviet Union. If there was ever a period when America alone defined the international order, it was historically exceptional and very brief — the 20 years or so from 1989 when the Berlin Wall came down to circa 2008–2009 when in the eyes of many around the world, including many Americans, the global financial crisis discredited US-led globalization and the so-called liberal international order.

Brief as it was, that brief period was nevertheless crucial, although not in the way the US and its allies thought at the time. Mistakes made in dealing with Russia at that time still bedevil contemporary international relations. The primary error was to misinterpret the meaning of the end of the Cold War, and view that event in terms of 'defeat' and 'victory' as conventionally understood.

The Soviet Union clearly failed. 'Containment' and western pressures certainly played a role in increasing stresses on the Soviet system contributing to its failure. However, the Soviet Union essentially collapsed under the weight of its own economic inefficiencies and Gorbachev's belated and clumsy efforts at reform. This made the meaning of 'victory' more ambiguous than the US and its allies were prepared to admit.

The Soviet Union was only one state-form of an older Russian civilization. States come and go; civilizations are enduring. The US treated the Soviet Union as a defeated country whose legitimate interests could be brushed aside and disregarded. After the Soviet Union imploded and Russia plunged into a decade of instability and weakness, understandings reached as the Berlin Wall came down were denied or ignored.

The most central of these understandings was that NATO would not expand further than the former German Democratic Republic's eastern border. However, NATO today extends as far east as Poland and the

Baltic states, and as far southeast as the Balkans. Any successor to the Soviet Union would have found this threatening. Objectively, over-extension was not even in the West's own interests. It could not but degrade NATO's deterrent credibility: is an attack on, say, Estonia or Montenegro, really going to be regarded as an attack on all NATO members, warranting a response that could risk nuclear war?

The dénouement came in 2014 in Ukraine. I was in Kiev in

human rights, in effect, encouraging Ukraine to 'join the West'. He did not quite promise the crowd milk and honey, but that was the impression he created.

The mainly young crowd responded enthusiastically. But the thought that flashed through my mind was Hungary in 1956, when the US had encouraged Hungarians to rise against the Soviet Union, and then watched with folded arms when Russian tanks crushed the revolt. In 2013, it was the EU that took the lead in Ukraine and dragged in a reluctant US. The young crowd had forgotten the troubled history of east central Europe which had seen more blood than milk or honey.

No Russian government can stand idly by and see Ukraine lost to the West. The heart of Russian culture lies in *Kievan Rus* and Moscow has legitimate geopolitical interests in Ukraine. Among the Maidan demonstrators were a number wearing the uniforms and waving the flags of organizations that had collaborated with the Nazis to fight the Soviet Union. Were these *agents provocateurs*? We will never know. But the fact is they were there. The young crowd probably did not notice or if they did, did not understand what bitter memories these shadows from the past evoked. But Moscow surely noticed. With 20 million or more dead during the Second World War alone, no Russian government can ever forget the repeated threats from the west: from Napoleon, Imperial Germany, and Nazi Germany.

A Russian reaction was inevitable. The pretext, if one was needed, was at hand. One need not approve of President Putin's response to conclude that it was utterly feckless of the EU to encourage Ukraine to move into the western camp without either the capability to deter a Russian reaction or respond effectively when Russia reacted. One of the most foolish statements I have ever heard is Secretary of State John Kerry's condemnation of Russia's annexation of Crimea as 19th century behavior in the 21st century. It assumes that every country shares or ought to share your values. In international relations, to make such an assumption is to invite ambush.

Singapore joined the international criticism of the annexation of Crimea as a matter of principle. As a small city-state in a less than salubrious neighbourhood, we cannot view unilateral changes of international boundaries with equanimity. Also, as a matter of principle, we did *not* join the sanctions the US and EU unilaterally imposed on Russia. Of what use were those sanctions except as a salve for western *amour propre*? Did sanctions reverse the fate of Crimea? Western sanctions only drove Russia deeper into China's embrace, not a posture that many Russians find particularly comfortable.

The post-Cold War western response to Russia was not so much the result of clinical calculation of interests, as symptomatic of the hubris that infected US and European foreign policies after 1989. The dangers of the Cold War had imposed a certain discipline, acceptance of limits, and balance, mental as well as material. Absent that discipline, some — and not just eccentric academics — were unable to resist the temptation to regard the end of the Cold War not just as one, albeit major, geopolitical event in a process that would continue as long as the state system existed, but as the End of History itself.

The idea is patently absurd and was never without critics. It is now clearly overtaken by events, and the author of the phrase shrouds his idea in discreet silence. But the no less sweeping, if somewhat superficially more plausible, claim that the western definition of certain values and political practices were universal, resonated widely at the time and has still not been entirely discredited.

Hubris eventually led the US to war in the Middle East, war waged not for limited goals but in the name of universal values. Yet, the proximate cause of those wars — 9/11 — was itself stark proof that those values were not only far from universal, but so repugnant to some as to invoke a lethal rejection. That those who resorted to violence were a tiny minority of Muslims was irrelevant. In fact, the rejection of violence by the vast majority may have masked the extent of discomfort throughout the world — across a diversity of ethnicities, faiths, and political systems — with western insistence on the universality of its values.

regard for the interests of other countries. Occasional doubts about the geopolitical implications of a rising China were largely soothed away by comforting post-Cold War delusions of a permanently ascendant West.

Today, the characterization of Russia as a 'revisionist power' skirts over an inconvenient fact. After the Soviet Union collapsed, Yeltsin, Russia's first post-Soviet President, and even Putin during his first term, wanted nothing more than for Russia to be accepted by the West as an equal, and accommodated many western interests. Moscow's overtures were met with rejection or worse. In his memoirs, Robert Gates, former Director of the CIA and Secretary of Defence, admitted that the West badly underestimated the extent of Russian humiliation at the end of the Cold War, and how the "arrogance" of western officials, academics, and businessmen in telling Russians how to conduct their domestic and foreign affairs "led to deep and long-term resentment and bitterness."

The West today demonises Putin. This is short-sighted. Putin's fundamental achievement was to stabilise post-Soviet Russia and keep it a coherent polity. The West has chosen to forget that in the early 1990s as the Soviet Union disintegrated and its successor state, the Russian Federation, struggled to control its vast territories, the primary western concern was not Russian revisionism, but the dangers arising from the collapse of a nuclear-armed superpower. At the time, I asked a western defence attaché what he most feared. "Control of nuclear mines" was his reply.

My father had been Singapore's Ambassador to the Soviet Union from 1971 to 1976. I had often visited Moscow and travelled in the Soviet Union in the early 1970s. That period was seemingly the height of Soviet power with communism on the rise globally. Conditions in Moscow and other cities were not as comfortable as in the West, but not at all bad. Moscow was safer than most western cities, street crime was almost unknown — the KGB made it so!

No one who did not experience Russia in the immediate post-Soviet era can imagine conditions then, or the potential threat that only vaguely accounted for tactical nuclear weapons might had posed if post-Soviet Russia had not been stabilized. When I was posted to the Russian Federation in 1993, I was profoundly shocked by the contrast with what I had experienced in the 1970s. As I rediscovered Moscow on foot and by metro, the security services thought it necessary to send discreet word through one of my officers to be careful. "Tell your Ambassador", they said, "Moscow is not the same and we cannot guarantee his safety as before". They meant well, but the stark changes were obvious.

The Russian federal government was then, to say the least, uncoordinated. Its writ did not seem to run very far beyond Moscow's inner-ring roads. The outer districts were dilapidated and felt unsafe. Crime was rife. Gunfights between rival gangs in the streets were not uncommon. Nightclubs and casinos required customers to check their weapons at the door. Inflation was high. Poverty and even starvation among old-age pensioners was a reality, even in Moscow, the capital city.

There was deep bitterness among ordinary Russians over their country's sudden loss of status, made harder to endure by the evaporation of state benefits they had taken for granted. One day, as I stood by the side of the road waiting for some demonstrators to pass (protests were then common and I remember that the banners had something to do with pensions) so I could cross, I overheard an old woman angrily tell her husband gesturing toward me, "Look at that Japanese, they are laughing at us now". I had enough Russian to understand and tell her I was not Japanese and not mocking anyone, but I doubt she was assuaged.

Corruption was pervasive and open. Everything seemed up for grabs. One day, a friend of a friend of a friend asked if Singapore would be interested in developing Cam Ranh Bay, then still a Russian naval base, as a civilian port. I asked my interlocutor to identify his *krysha*. The word means 'roof' but in the slang of the times meant his principal, the guy with the muscle to make the deal. He was reluctant but finally named a Deputy Prime Minister. I was sceptical and refused to proceed [illegible]

he asked me to turn up at a particular office in the Russian 'White House', the seat of the Russian Federation's government, the next day.

I duly presented myself at the appointed place and time, and was indeed ushered into the presence of a Deputy Prime Minister whom I recognised from his media photographs. Without any preamble, he matter-of-factly and without embarrassment, told me what it would cost us, assured me that his cut would be taken care of by the Vietnamese and Russian militaries so we need not worry about that, and bluntly asked if we had a deal. I replied that I needed to consult, and asked for a few weeks to get a decision on such an important matter. He impatiently dismissed me, but not before making clear that my share, if I wanted one, was up to me to extract for myself from whatever I told my government. I never heard anything more from the Russians. He had obviously concluded that since I could not settle on the spot, I was not serious.

Putin's methods in restoring coherence and order were not the gentlest. But could other methods have worked in a Russia that had fallen to this level? I doubt it. And I think my doubts — whatever their other grievances or disappointments — are shared by most Russians whose history, and certainly their experiences in the immediate aftermath of the Soviet Union's collapse, has led them to fear disorder — *bespredel* — far more than authoritarianism.

During Soviet times, the West paid too much attention to dissidents. In the immediate post-Soviet period, the West paid too much attention to those who spoke fluently of 'democracy' and not enough to the day-to-day needs of ordinary Russians. I sometimes wonder what relations between would be like today if the US had then been as generous to Russia as it was to Europe after the Second World War.

I paid a call on Gorbachev out of sheer curiosity. Since his relations with President Yeltsin were strained, I had sounded out contacts in the Kremlin, in the Russian foreign ministry, and even in the intelligence service before doing so. Their reply was all some variant of "if you want to waste time, go ahead". Gorbachev spent most of the meeting musing aloud about running in the next presidential election and how he could win given the mess Yeltsin was making. Gorbachev was oblivious of the fact that he was probably the most hated man in Russia at that time, held responsible for the Soviet Union's break up and the hardships ordinary Russians were enduring. As he showed me out, an embarrassed aide apologetically said with unconscious irony, "Mikhail Sergeyevich is a little out of touch".

Gorbachev confused western praise with domestic political support. Consequently, the once mighty Secretary-General of the Communist Party of the Soviet Union (CPSU) now appears in advertisements touting Louis Vuitton. This was not a mistake that Putin will ever make. It is not a mistake the Chinese, who have almost obsessively studied the Soviet Union's experience, the better to avoid its fate, are likely to make. And it is not a mistake that I hope Singaporeans will ever make.

Much of the chaos of Russia in the immediate post-Soviet period was due to an extremely ill-considered attempt to reform the Russian economy by so-called 'shock therapy'. This was a theory of western academics whose advice was detached from any Russian reality that anyone not blinded by love of their own theories could see. I could not understand how anyone could believe that a 70-year-old system could be changed in 500 days into a functioning market economy. When I asked one former Russian leader why he had agreed to such a hare-brained scheme, he shrugged his shoulders and said, "We didn't know better". I used to joke with Russian friends that all their troubles were due to trusting three foreigners too much — Karl Marx, Fredrich Engels, and Jeffrey Sachs.

Mao Zedong did not personally get along with Stalin but deferred to him as one of Lenin's original comrades. Once Stalin died, Mao never showed as much deference to any Soviet leader, but he never renounced Marxism-Leninist as the Chinese Communist Party's (CCP) legitimating ideology. Mao's criticism of the Soviet Union was

results. So much so that there have been increasing concerns in the West that China may present a challenge to western development models.

This is illustrated by the over-reaction to a minor theme in Xi Jinping's speech to the CCP's 19th Congress in 2017. China, Xi boasted, was "…blazing a new trail for other developing countries to achieve modernization. It offers a new option for other countries and nations who want to speed up their development while preserving their independence; and it offers Chinese wisdom and a Chinese approach to solving the problems facing mankind."

These two sentences in an extremely long speech were taken as an almost existential challenge to the West, and spawned a disproportionate amount of excited commentary, as if Xi had said something of extraordinary or exceptional significance. However, in pointing out that there were alternatives to western development models, Xi was only stating, albeit in somewhat grandiose terms, what had been obvious for a long time.

The essential issue confronting the non-western world for the last three centuries or so has been adaptation to the challenges of a western-defined modernity. Traditional societies were not static and could innovate. However, they had no sense of modernity as we now understand the term. The most successful examples of adaptation or — to call the process by its proper if politically inconvenient name — westernization, have all been in East Asia, beginning with Meiji Japan in the 19th century.

Contemporary China is the most important example of successful westernization. But Japan, South Korea, Taiwan, and Singapore, among others, had also adapted and developed in their own ways. Xi's boast that the experience was somehow uniquely 'Chinese' is historically inaccurate. China's experience was unique only in the trite sense that every country's experience is unique.

After the failure of the Qing dynasty to reform itself and the 1911 revolution, all China's experiments in search of the wealth and power that would enable it to stand up to the West — first republicanism, then communism of different variants — have been with western doctrines and ideologies. Communism is a western ideology which China borrowed from Russia. To participate in the global process of westernization is of course not to lose all identity, culture, or history. No country ever does. The process was always one of adaptation and never wholesale adoption. However, there is no denying that Socialism with Chinese Characteristics, the most recent and successful of China's post-Qing experiments, is rooted in a blend of western ideologies, facilitated by the restoration of relations with the US after 1972.

Russia's trajectory has followed a broadly similar pattern. In the 18th century, to hold its own against the West, Peter the Great dragged a reluctant Russia into modernity, building a new capital, St. Petersburg, on European lines as a symbol of this effort. Russia became one of Europe's great powers. Russia nevertheless still lagged behind and by the early 20th century, this Tsarist-led effort at modernisation had run out of steam. This was underscored by Imperial Russia's defeat by Japan in 1905, the first time any European power had suffered military defeat at Asian hands. Only slightly more than another decade later, Imperial Russia collapsed, and the Bolsheviks seized power to start a different phase of modernization.

Lenin famously said "Communism is Soviet power plus electrification of the whole country". It was left to Stalin to brutally industrialize the country and collectivize agriculture, turning a peasant society into a modern industrial state. However, by the time Brezhnev took office in 1964, this effort was peaking. Thereafter, the Soviet economy was increasingly in trouble as defence absorbed an increasing share of a stagnating GDP and Soviet power began to over-extend itself globally. None of this was evident at the time. Only an obscure dissident, Andrei Amalrik, published a book in 1970 asking *"Will the Soviet Union Survive Until 1984?"* Nobody paid much notice, but his timing was off

Soviet Union collapsed, and to muster the political will and courage to change course to save the CCP from the limitations of Marxist-Leninist economics and Maoist excesses. Deng, however, did not abandon Soviet-style political structures. China is still a Leninist state led by a vanguard party that insists on its absolute control over all aspects of politics, economics, and society.

It is highly improbable that US–China strategic rivalry will have as clear-cut a dénouement as did US–Soviet rivalry. China is a far more successful economy than the Soviet Union ever was. China and the US are integral and irreplaceable components of the global economy. The Soviet Union was peripheral. But by 2012, the CCP itself had openly acknowledged that China's growth model of the 1990s and first decade of the 2000s was unsustainable over the long-run. A new model with a 'decisive' role for the market in the allocation of resources was needed. The adjective describing the role of the market is one that the CCP itself chose.

It is a delusion to think that economic reform must necessarily lead to western-style political arrangements. There nevertheless is a fundamental contradiction between the imperatives of a Leninist state in which the over-riding value is political control, and the market which by definition means less control. The choice is of course not absolute but a matter of balance between the two elements. Still, the trade-offs are not obvious and require difficult — and risky — political choices.

The Soviet leadership from Brezhnev onwards chose to pretend that the contradiction did not exist. They lied to themselves. By the time Gorbachev came to power, the system could not be saved. Deng Xiaoping was not inclined to self-delusion and bought valuable time for the CCP. However, China may now be reaching the limits of economic reform within a strict Leninist political framework. By the early 2000s, the CCP itself seemed to recognise this and was cautiously experimenting with more flexible political arrangements at the local level. The intention was to promote 'intra-party democracy' and bottom-up input in the selection and promotion of local party officials.

Xi Jinping stopped this. The lesson Xi seems to have taken from the collapse of the Soviet Union was the necessity of a strong party based on 'democratic centralism', or in plain language, a party totally subordinate to the will of its top leader. Xi is not wrong. Gorbachev overlooked the elementary point that in a Leninist state, the party *is* the state and the leader in large measure defines the party. By unleashing *glasnost*, Gorbachev sealed the Soviet Union's fate. However, by strongly asserting party discipline and control, and significantly weakening if not totally abandoning collective leadership, Xi has also sharpened the fundamental challenge of economic reform within a Leninist framework.

I do not know how this will play out. The Soviet experience is that things work until they do not. Having seen the consequences in Russia, I can only hope that China will succeed in navigating the contradictions of a Leninist system. I doubt that China will fail as did the Soviet Union. The CCP is a more adaptive institution than the CPSU. But we should not be too surprised if black swans are quietly breeding in China and may suddenly appear as the CCP circles around rather than confronts the fundamental issue.

Under Xi, the CCP has increasingly resorted to an assertive ethno-nationalism to hold the system together in the face of slow growth and patchy reform. In Russia, Putin also legitimates his rule by a strong emphasis on ethno-nationalism. Russian and Chinese ethno-nationalisms are not naturally compatible. Chinese ethno-nationalism is infused and animated by a strong sense of victimhood and implicitly claims that China is owed a heavy historical debt by its oppressors during the 'hundred years of humiliation'. The 'China Dream' is, at its core, revanchist.

It has not been lost on Russia that it is counted among China's oppressors. In 1964, Mao told a Japanese delegation, "About a hundred years ago the area from east of Baikal became Russian territory, and since then Vladivostok, Khabarovsk, Kamchatka and other points have ~~been territories of the Soviet Union. We have not yet presented the~~

the Sino-Russia border has since been mutually demarcated and agreed. However, that does not mean that the Chinese have forgotten that an unpaid bill exists. In July 2020, the Russian Embassy in Beijing celebrated the 160th anniversary of the founding of Vladivostok, built on lands seized by Imperial Russia after the Second Opium War. This aroused attacks on social media by Chinese netizens which included some members of state media and 'Wolf Warrior' diplomats. It should be no surprise that a sense of insecurity nevertheless persists on the Russian side.

In 1993, I asked an FSB[1] general how many illegal Chinese there were in Siberia and the Russia Far East. "I don't know", he bitterly replied, "we lost control of our border". This was clearly an exaggeration, but he was not so much stating a fact as exhibiting the streak of Sinophobia that lies deeply buried in Russian political culture, the lingering, subconscious racial memory of 300 years of 'the Mongol yoke.'

In 2000, speaking at Blagoveshchensk on the Amur River along the border with China, Putin said, "If in the short-term we do not undertake real efforts to develop the Russian Far East, then in a few decades the Russian population will be speaking Japanese, Chinese, and Korean… The real issue is about the existence of the region as an inalienable part of Russia." Two years later, Putin described the

---

[1] Successor service to the KGB.

development of the Russian Far East as "the most important geopolitical task facing Russia."

We should neither place too much emphasis on such statements nor ignore them. The Sino-Russia relationship is not just an 'Axis of Convenience' as one academic had dubbed it. He later changed his mind and called it 'A Wary Embrace.' Russia and China share deep suspicions of the US-led global order and do what they can singly and together to challenge and undermine it. Still, China and Russia were brought together as much by western mistakes as common interests. After Stalin died, Mao accused Khrushchev of 'big-power chauvinism' and this was one of the underlying causes of the Sino-Soviet split. Now that China is the stronger and ascendant partner, assertive Chinese ethno-nationalism may be in danger of making a similar mistake.

Heightened US–China strategic competition will characterise international relations for decades to come. Assertive Chinese ethno-nationalism has aroused misgivings in Europe, Britain, Canada, Australia, Japan, India, and other countries. As the 19th century ended, Bismarck said that the most important fact in the 20th century would be that Americans, like the British, speak English. Referencing Bismarck's statement, the late John Lukacs, an American–Hungarian historian who fled to the US in 1946 just as Hungary was absorbed into the Soviet sphere of influence, wrote in 1970: "It is not impossible that the most important condition of the next hundred years might be that the Russians are, after all, white." We shall see.

Preface

September 2017, I had pondered over whether I should write a book about my professional life and personal impressions of Moscow and Russia. In 2016, I commenced writing in cursive the first few hundred words in a journal, only to cease after a few days, thanks to a loss of interest and an almost complete lack of motivation. I was not certain whether the effort would be worth my while and would be of interest to anyone, outside my immediate circle of family members and close friends.

Impetus for writing this book came after I entered the employ of the S. Rajaratnam School of International Studies (RSIS) a month after my retirement, when its Executive Deputy Chairman (EDC), Mr. Ong Keng Yong, encouraged me to undertake this task.

Other factors spurred me towards writing this book.

Being the only Singapore Foreign Service Officer (FSO) to-date to have done three tours of duty there during a momentous period in post-Soviet Russian history (1994–1997, 1999–2004, and 2006–2013), I felt that my experience there should be recorded.

I have always had a keen personal interest in Russia, stemming from the developments presented below.

I joined the SFS in July 1980, the year that marked the beginning of a decade of momentous events in world history, which to a large extent had a profound impact on Singapore's foreign relations and on shaping my worldview as well.

First, the Soviet invasion of Afghanistan in December 1979 heralded the beginning of an almost decade-long engagement, which weakened its power and arguably was one of the major factors which led to its collapse in 1991. I vividly recall watching Singapore's television station broadcasting a statement from the then Foreign Minister of Singapore, Mr. S. Rajaratnam, criticising the Soviet action. Singapore was one of the first Southeast Asian states to openly express disapproval of the Soviet move.

Second, the election of Ronald Reagan as the US President in 1980 and his pursuit of policies like the Strategic Defence Initiative (popularly known as Star Wars) and support of missile deployments in the then West Germany (Federal Republic of Germany, or FRG), the focus of the US–Soviet Cold War, to counter Soviet missiles, was another contributory factor to the Soviet Union's undoing.

Third, Mikhail Gorbachev's rise to power in 1985 and his twin policies of *perestroika* (restructuring) and *glasnost* (openness), inextricably weakened the hold of the Communist Party of the Soviet Union (CPSU) on the country. Having to conduct a costly conflict in Afghanistan, while supporting its Cuban ally in Angola and Vietnamese ally in Cambodia and maintaining its hold over the growing restiveness in Warsaw Pact countries (symbolised by Solidarity in Poland), and satisfying its own people's material needs, all based on the inefficiencies and weaknesses of the Soviet economic system, proved to be a burden the Soviet Union could not bear.

Fourth, Deng Xiao-ping's crackdown on the students' movement on Tien An-Men in 1989 was no less a momentous development in the Asia-Pacific and in China's own socio-political and economic development, in contrast to the chaos that accompanied the Soviet Union's collapse.

His visionary socio-economic policies provided the stimuli for China's rapid development in the subsequent decades and its rise to global power.

Finally, Sino-Vietnamese hostilities which began with China's "punishment" war against Vietnam in February 1979, (essentially a response to Vietnam's December 1978 invasion and occupation of Pol

Pot's Cambodia, China's close ally), pressure on Vietnam by ASEAN (Association of Southeast Asian Nations) and like-minded countries of the international community, as well as Vietnam's own calculations, led ultimately to its withdrawal from the country in September 1989. (Sino-Vietnamese hostilities then were perceived as a Sino-Soviet "proxy war" and a reflection of their regional/global rivalry). That paved the way to Vietnam joining ASEAN in 1995; the other two ... in the Indo-Chinese conflict during the Cold War period,

of my overseas assignments during my career. Unlike Bonn (1985–1987) and San Francisco (2013–2017), Russia to me was (and remains) the most fascinating. It was, to quote Churchill, "a riddle wrapped in a mystery inside an enigma".

Coming from a very small island with no natural resources, I was fascinated by its immense size and wealth in terms of natural resources, and its tortured but challenging history as the birthplace of the world's first Communist state. While Communism was a failed ideology, in its heyday, it managed to bring about much socio-political and economic disruption in the world.

As a boy, I was amazed by the historic and unprecedented exploits of cosmonauts, Yuri Gagarin and Valentina Tereshkova. The country and society which produced these individuals had piqued my boyhood curiosity. (Little did I expect that I would meet Tereshkova years later in Moscow, together with members of a Singapore parliamentary group; she was and remains a parliamentarian).

My interest in Russia was also connected with my boyhood fascination with the events that led to the rise of Nazi Germany, and World War II in Europe and Asia. I developed a keen interest in the Soviet Union's major role in the defeat of Nazi Germany. Operation Barbarossa, which sought the dismemberment of the USSR, ended with disastrous consequences for Nazi Germany itself (the division of the country till 1990); it redrew Europe's borders and led to the rise of the Soviet Union as a world power and the Cold War with the West.

In Bonn, the Russian "connection" for me was palpable. I was one of the many keen observers of the tension within the FRG, between it and the Soviets regarding Bonn's support of NATO's *Doppelbeschluss* (dual-track decision) to station US Pershing II and Cruise missiles, in response to the Soviet deployment of its SS-20s. It was a period when domestic tensions were high because many Germans were really afraid the *Doppelbeschluss* could lead to war with the USSR. (Quite a number of acquaintances and friends of mine there had made their fear known to me.) East–West relations as a whole underwent severe strains.

The Russian "connection" was also evident when I predicted to a number of my German contacts and friends that the reunification of the country would take place before the end of the 20th century. Expectedly, my prediction was scoffed at. Above all, the Soviets, I would be told, would never allow it, while the US and the rest of the West would not support it. My belief was based simply on the assumption that ties of kinship, history, and culture would prevail over Marxist doctrine and even Soviet and Western reluctance and fear of a reunified Germany. Moreover, the FRG was the stronger and more dynamic part of the country; it was only natural that it would not only dominate a united Germany but was an attraction to many East Germans who led lives deprived of many creature comforts, in comparison to West Germans. My wife and I personally knew an East German lady who had fled the German Democratic Republic (GDR) and lived in the FRG; her touching stories of life's difficulties there were confirmed by what I had observed in East Berlin during my own visit there in 1984 as part of an official delegation of foreign diplomats. What I observed in my day-trip to East Berlin was a vindication of my belief that eventually, the GDR would be absorbed into the FRG.

The final Russian "connection" was my chat with an elderly gentleman whom I met at a party of a friend of my wife, in the country's south. Being the only non-white, I stood out in the small crowd, whereupon this gentleman approached me, politely asking whether I was one of the Vietnamese "boat people" who had found refuge in the country (the term used in the mid-'70s to the '80s to refer to the South Vietnamese refugees who fled the country after the fall of South Vietnam to the North in 1975; many ended up in the West).

Admittedly, I was not thrilled to have been associated with any refugee and replied matter-of-factly that I was a Singaporean diplomat, to which he exclaimed, "Singapore fell to the Japanese in '42 while I was fighting Bolshevism in Russia at the same time." It turned out that he had served on the Eastern front in one of Nazi Germany's elite enemies. Captivated by his tales, I wondered whether I would ever get the opportunity to visit Russia myself.

These factors account for my deep interest in Russia.

Since local interest in Russia is limited, I hope to engender it with my book. Moreover, since much commentary, analyses, and information on Russia in the English language are dominated by American and British standpoints, a Singaporean perspective would be in order. If my book broadens the outlook of its readers, especially Singaporeans, on Russia, then it would have served its purpose.

My life, work, and personal experience between 1994 and 2013, and my personal assessment of major developments there, are described, less so in my capacity as a retired diplomat but more as an individual who remains very interested in developments in Russia. The standpoints of my coevals there with whom I was closely acquainted are also included, to expose readers to other viewpoints.

If the reader tires of some repetitive points, the fault lies at my door. My purpose in repeating them is simply to reinforce an observation about an event, development, or impression.

I neither kept a diary nor noted in writing in any way, the events/incidents described in this book. At the time, the thought that I would one day put my experiences in Russia onto paper, did not occur to me. However, I was able to recall all the events and incidents described in this book, as my life in Moscow was really an unforgettable experience.

My wife too helped to jog my memory of a number of events. Nevertheless, I take full responsibility for any errors of omission or commission.

I have tried to remain as detached as possible in recording my observations and experience, but like all observers of human events, my words cannot be totally value-free.

Acknowledgements

pen to paper. To him I extend my gratitude for his full support and boundless patience, without which I would not have been able to devote the time and energy to writing this book. His valuable suggestions were also taken into account in the final draft of my book.

To Bilahari Kausikan, who served as Singapore's Ambassador to Moscow in the mid-1990s and for whom I worked at the beginning of my first tour of duty, goes my appreciation for writing the Foreword. Bilahari was the former Permanent Secretary (the highest-ranking official) of the Singapore Ministry of Foreign Affairs (MFA) and above all, a treasured friend. I thank him also for his indisputably relevant and thoughtful insights to make this book readable.

I also stand in debt to another former Permanent Secretary of MFA, Mr. Tan Chin Tiong. His pinpoint observations helped me to re-orient some chapters which required rewriting.

The late Ms. Viji Menon, Visiting Senior Fellow in RSIS, provided me with much-needed suggestions to improve the book's quality. I was fortunate to have been her colleague and friend in RSIS and to have benefitted from her advice, before her untimely death. She herself worked in the Singapore Embassy in Moscow between July 1983 and July 1985, and hence had experience of life there, albeit during the Soviet period.

To write about Russia, requires some level of expertise, experience, and insight into the country. All this I fortunately acquired during my stay in Moscow, with the help of all whom I met and worked with there all those years.

My thanks go to all the individuals with whom I became acquainted in Russia between 1994 and 2013. It goes without saying that the Singapore Embassy's Russian staff members were crucial in helping me grasp and appreciate what their country is all about; they were my constant and daily interlocutors, not only about work in the Embassy but also about developments in their country. My fellow MFA colleagues who served there had also been helpful to me and my gratitude to them is expressed here.

My publishers are also thanked, for without them this book would never have seen the light of day.

Finally, this book is a tribute to the Singapore Ministry of Foreign Affairs (MFA) where I spent a long career.

July 2020

Chapter 1

Initial Impressions of Russia

My first contact with a Russian/Soviet person of some standing, was the late Mikhail Voslenski, whom I met at a security conference in Kiel, the FRG, in 1981. Voslenski, a Soviet academic, who had defected to the West, had become a critic of the Soviet system. I had it on good authority that he was an accomplished individual. One of my sources was the organiser of the conference, the late Professor Werner Kaltefleiter, then Vice-President of Kiel University. (He was an influential figure in the German educational arena at the time). Other participants with whom I chatted, echoed Professor Kaltefleiter's view.

Voslenski had made his name with his book, *The Nomenklatura: The Soviet Ruling Class*. Fluent in the English language, his thoughts and insights on the Soviet Union which he shared with me personally as well as other participants of the security conference, certainly made a discernible impression on them and me. Needless to say, they were not very positive viz his exposé of how well members of the nomenklatura lived compared to the average Soviet citizen.

They only served to confirm my already-ingrained prejudices about life in the country and the very nature of the Soviet system. He spoke about the nomenklatura's access to "special shops", where one could purchase most of the craved-for Western goods, to the best medical care and housing in the country, and of course, to the "right" to travel abroad, especially to the West — all of which were either denied to the man-in-the-street or to which access was made difficult. Essentially, he was quite critical of the Soviet leadership's apparent lack of a sense of *noblesse oblige.*

(Indeed, when I chatted about these very issues with Russians, whose acquaintance I had made, including the Embassy's Russian staff members, during my first tour in Moscow (1994–1997), all of them, without exception, were glad that they now had the same "rights" as members of the nomenklatura a few years before. However, they bemoaned the fact that these "rights" were of no real consequence, unless one had the money to exploit these "rights").

The slogan of the Kiel conference was "*einseitige Abrüstung nein, danke!*" (unilateral disarmament — no thanks!) was a sign of the times. The FRG was then in the throes of Soviet attempts to scuttle the NATO *Doppelbeschluss.* Kaltefleiter, I believed, was close to the then opposition CDU (Christian Democratic Union) which supported the *Doppelbeschluss.* Unsurprisingly, he criticised the Soviet position. The controversial security debate on the *Doppelbeschluss* was not only exciting but also eye-opening. My conclusion was that real and durable security cannot and must never be based solely on the expressed good intentions of one's opponent but must be backed by credible means of retaliation and just as important, the political will to resort to them.

The second Russian/Soviet individual whom I became acquainted with, was an official of the Soviet Embassy in Singapore in 1983. I was invited by him, with other MFA colleagues to an event, during which he proceeded to "enlighten" us on the Soviet position on the arms race with the US. I felt compelled to reply that I was neither familiar with the issue nor was competent to discuss it. For good measure, I stressed that as a small country far away from the Cold War's focus in Europe, Singapore's interest in Soviet–American arms control issues was quite minimal. His impassive face showed that he must have posed me this question not with any real wish to extract some credible answer but only because it was his job to do so.

Subsequently, during my assignment in Bonn, I did not have any contact with Soviet diplomats, not because I had intentionally shunned them but more so as my work had nothing to do with the Soviet Union.

Negative Views of Russia — Assignment to Moscow

I had no experience of Russia or its people to form an opinion of the country, one way or another, when I was informed that I was to be sent there. Based on what I had read about Moscow and Russia in the media (all negative) in the years and months preceding my posting order to Moscow (MFA parlance for written order for an overseas assignment), trepidation, bewilderment, frustration, dismay, shock, and even anger were sentiments which took hold of my very being when I was informed that I should discount rumours and the perception that Moscow was a "difficult and dangerous place", and that I did not have much choice in the matter, in any case. Moreover, it would have been impolitic of me to reject this "opportunity". When one is faced with such a Hobson's choice (which was what I perceived it to be), one naturally must know what answer is expected of one. I sank into the slough of despond. I did not know whether I would emerge from it, but succeeded in hiding my state of mind from my colleagues. On the other hand, I was determined not to let my feelings get the better of me, for I desperately wanted to secure an overseas assignment, and if it was to be Moscow, then so be it.

My concern about the assignment revolved around the then widespread perception of post-Soviet Russia as a country riven by lawlessness. My views on Russia had been shaped by media reports on the country. Images of unchecked organised crime gangs controlling the organs of state and thugs running amok on the streets of Moscow began to fill my imagination. Poverty and social deprivation and the lack or absence of basic items like toilet paper were said to have been the norm. My wife and I had to purchase rolls and rolls of toilet paper in Singapore, having been told that this very important item (especially good quality paper) was in very short supply in Moscow! While I had a keen interest in Russia's history and development from an intellectual standpoint, that positive sentiment was not enough to counteract the negative news revolving around the trials and tribulations of life in post-Soviet Russia. Hence, I did not jump for joy about my posting there.

I was also seized with an element of unjustified prejudice and preconceived notions about the country. In the mid-1980s, I had occasion to visit Poland a number of times, East Berlin for a day, and spent some time in Prague and Budapest on holidays. Having observed socialism first-hand in these countries, I did not have any illusions about the bankrupt nature of the Communist system. And now I was being assigned to Moscow! Although it was plain to me that Russia was no longer run by Communists, I could not help thinking that the country was still gripped by its ideology.

I was at my wits' end over the fact that I could not argue my way out of the assignment. The only positive sentiment I had then was the fact that I would be working for Ambassador Bilahari. I knew him well and had the greatest confidence that he would guide and teach me how to navigate the difficulties of life and work in Moscow.

Hence, a sense of dread and unease filled me as I prepared to set out for the Russian capital in April 1994 to attend a three-month language course in Moscow State University (MGU), the country's best, scheduled to commence in early May 1994. My wife and daughter spent these three months in Europe, with her family and friends.

My unpleasant sentiments were further compounded by my not-so-pleasant memories of my first trip to Moscow in 1979. On my way to Frankfurt-am-Main for a holiday in the FRG, I flew Aeroflot, the cheapest airline from Singapore, with stopovers in New Delhi and Moscow.

The flight to Moscow from New Delhi in 1979 was unforgettable. An Indian gentleman seated next to me pressed the button for the stewardess, who appeared after a few minutes, in a surly mood. Upon being told by the gentleman that he would like some water to drink, she abruptly and curtly replied that there was none on board! I recall her as a rather overweight and far-from-beautiful individual, unlike the many examples of feminine pulchritude serving on Aeroflot whom I had occasion to set eyes upon in the post-Soviet era, during my many trips across the immense country. Needless to say, the Indian gentleman, cowed by her rather dismissive tone of voice, did not make any further requests! I myself was rather intimidated by the whole incident but luckily, I had the presence of mind to have bought some drinks in Singapore before my departure.

The stopover in Sheremetyevo Airport (SA) lasted more than a few hours. The airport was bedecked with large banners of Misha, the Russian bear mascot of the 1980 Summer Olympics in Moscow. SA

the airport transit area; the fact that most of the items listed on the menu were not available as well as the absence of toilet paper in the airport loo, certainly did not make a good impression on me.

Returning to 1994, advised by my colleagues in the Embassy to bring as much cash as had been permissible, since the local banks then were not very plugged into the global system, I carried on my person a small fortune in US dollars. This was meant to tide me over for quite some time. Cash was king in those days, as the use of credit cards was very limited. This only added to my reservations about my coming life in Moscow. How could it be that one could not just remit money to Moscow like what I would do when I was in Bonn, I asked myself? I would simply deposit a Singapore bank cheque in Singapore dollars into my German bank account and after its clearance (in a week or so), I would have the equivalent funds in deutsche Mark. What kind of a country had Russia become in the wake of the Soviet collapse, with no proper banking system as I knew it? How could one live a normal life in the absence of a normal, functioning, and reliable banking system? These questions *inter alia*, would plague me the first few months of my life in the Russian capital.

I was therefore on pins-and-needles even before my flight landed in SA on a cold, damp, and dark night at the end of April 1994. I was greeted by a colleague from the Embassy. SA had physically changed for the better in comparison with 1979. However, the morose-looking immigration officials whom I had encountered that April night in 1994 reminded me of my 1979 experience (when they expressed doubts about my identity as my passport photo of a hairless face did not match the thick beard which I grew later) — I was initially refused permission to enter the transit area! Thankfully, I finally managed to convince them that I was not an impostor.

Fortunately, unlike in 1979, this was now post-Soviet Russia of 1994 and I had become a diplomat — they did not treat me like the student I had been 15 years before. In fact, the immigration officials were rather polite, to my surprise and delight.

The long drive to the students' hostel in MGU was not one to brag about. I had no choice but to stay in a hostel; while I carried a diplomatic passport, I was not yet accredited to the country since officially, my responsibilities as a diplomat were scheduled to commence only in August 1994. However, I did not have a problem with having to stay in a hostel. It would offer me more opportunities to mingle with fellow students and learn the language fast — that was my reasoning. It was just as well that my family was spending time in Europe for the duration of my language course; they would not have been able to live comfortably with me in the hostel.

The broad avenues and wide streets which led to MGU were dark, and whenever they were lit, only cast slight rays of light (for the most part, the lampposts were either out-of-order or simply turned off). My Embassy colleague enlightened me on the situation, remarking that the country had found itself in a political and socio-economic crisis and could not spare the necessary funds for street-lighting — that comment only added to my sense of gloom and doom about my new "life" in Moscow. Thoughts raced through my mind — was this what Russia had become, so bankrupt that it could not even afford to light the main streets of its capital? If that was the case, then its people were probably not living lives of ease and plenty. My family and I would live better but rather isolated lives in the midst of poverty, a thought which was rather uninviting to me.

Conditions in my hostel also caused me to question my presence in Moscow. My small room was dirty while the common loo (rather malodorous) was situated perhaps 30 yards from my room. Added to that was the fact that the food in the cafeteria was neither to my taste nor attractive to bestow one's eyes upon (my ingrained prejudices were expressing themselves, not any sense of objectivity, I admit). Not having any cooking skills meant that I was dependent on the cafeteria. However, I was blessed with probably at the time huge monetary resources, compared to my fellow Russian-language and students from other disciplines, not to mention the average man-in-the-street. With my salary and allowances, I could afford to eat out often in the then few reasonably-priced restaurants in town. That I did. Whenever I ventured out of the hostel to par[...] the *дежурная* (invariably a matron[...] a hostel), would warn me of the dar[...] streets after dark. Street crime rates were high in 199[...] years thereafter but thankfully, I did not fall victim to any things. Once-in-a-while, some kind South Korean students with whom I shared the common kitchen, would take pity on me and invite me to share their well-cooked and tasty meals.

As luck would have it, my immediate next-door neighbour, an Israeli gentleman, left the country after a month or so, and I took over his room, having to pay extra of course. I did not mind that for I now had his *en-suite* room as well as my own. My life from then onwards, began to take a clear turn for the better.

Learning the language and about the country

My whole attitude and sentiments towards Moscow underwent a change as soon as my Russian language course started. It started with the fact that I had the luxury of being the only student in my "class". My teacher (let's call him Mr. P) who told me he had commenced his *métier* in Algeria, was a bespectacled, slight-of-built chap in his early 40s. He was kind, understanding, mild-mannered, and on-the-ball. Between May and the end of July 1994, he devoted his full attention and energy to drill into me the basics and subsequently the nuances of the language.

Compared to the German language, I found Russian difficult. The Cyrillic script, the language's grammatical structure, declension of its nouns, pronouns, adjectives, numerals and particles as well as its six cases — nominative, genitive, dative, accusative, instrumental, and prepositional, were complicated to me. German was an easier language to learn and master, and I say that with as much modesty as I can muster that even today, after 37 years since I finished my intensive 10-month German language course in the Goethe Institut in Mannheim and Munich (April 1982 to February 1983), I am still very fluent in the language and am more at ease reading, writing, and speaking the language than Russian.

Age was also a barrier. Yours Truly was already 39 going on 40 in 1994. It was nevertheless patently clear to me that I had to apply myself to the task of learning and hopefully, mastering as much as I could of the language, come what may.

Mr. P was patient with me; he himself told me that being then in my fourth decade of life meant that learning a difficult language by any measure, was not going to be as easy as ABC. He took care to explain the finer points of the language in a deliberately slow manner (in Russian, for he did not speak English). It was remarkable how he could make himself understood to me in a language which was to me totally foreign. That was a testimony to his abilities as a language teacher.

He was also a very dedicated fellow — he would literally knock on my room door whenever I was really late for class! A few times, I would sleep-in and "forget" about class. To my dismay and surprise, Mr. P would be at my door, politely as was his wont, but firmly insisting I turn up at his class within the following hour! Fortunately for me, he did not have to turn up at my door often, for I had by then resolved to be punctual.

Thanks to him, by the time the course ended, I had, more or less, grasped the fundamentals of Russian grammar, although my command of its many verbs, nouns, pronouns, and adjectives, as well as vocabulary, still left much to be desired. The fact that he and I were chatterboxes by nature certainly helped — practice makes perfect!

Being an FSO meant that my interest in Russia inevitably and understandably revolved around mainly socio-political and economic developments in the country. Therefore, my questions to Mr. P always turned on the Russian expressions for these developments — the issues and challenges that Boris Yeltsin, post-Soviet Russia's first President had to manage, resolve and overcome. Mr. P was my first source of information. While he was obviously not authoritative, he believed that he represented the man-in-the-street's standpoint, and would not cease to remind me of that "fact".

His opinions are worth noting. He made it plain that he had to dissimulate his thoughts and feelings during the oppressive Soviet era. Now freed from the fear and constraints of chatting freely with foreigners, he was very candid about his life, that of his friends and colleagues, and how the tumultuous changes had a deep impact on all of them. I would find that Russians were/are very warm and open people who would not hesitate baring their souls to anyone whom they trust and who would listen sympathetically.

First, he felt many of his countrymen had become paupers as a result of "shock therapy", the socio-economic reforms that had been undertaken. Whatever little or, for some, small fortunes that they had saved during the Soviet period, became either worthless or had lost a substantial amount of their original value, given the freeing-up of hitherto controlled prices in the Soviet command economy and the concomitant monetary reform.

Second, people had to either live hand-to-mouth or find second, third, or even fourth jobs just to "survive", as he chose to put it. Even with multiple jobs, the majority of the "common people" as opposed to the "Novi Russki" or "New Russians"[1] was living hand-to-mouth.

Due to the existence of a weak and inefficient government, the bane of the "common folk" included high inflation and rising levels of corruption, the lack of or low levels of basic government services like

---

[1] "New Russians" was a term that gained notoriety in the early 1990s to refer to the nouveau riche of the then chaotic and relatively impoverished post-Soviet Russia.

providing law-and-order, health, and education, and other trappings of the "civilised world".[2] The Novi Russki, with their ill-gotten gains, could dispense with government services and live comfortably with inflation and corruption — they were dyed-in-the-wool capitalists of the corrupt and dishonest kind, he argued passionately.

I must stress that the popular conception and association in the Russia of the early and late 1990s that Novi Russki and all wealthy people were "crooks" or dishonest, persists to this day. According to a joint study undertaken in August 2018 by the Carnegie Moscow Centre (a well-known think-tank) and the Levada Centre, an independent non-governmental and sociological research organisation, two-thirds of respondents believe it is probably impossible to become rich while remaining honest. The implication to me is that wealth is associated with thievery. I would hear that refrain being expressed mainly by what one might describe as "common folk" — and even some officials and small businessmen, I might add — all through my long sojourn in Moscow and elsewhere across the vast country. I would always engage in conversation whenever and wherever and with whomever I could, about the challenges the country faced.

Third, health and educational standards fell, in the train of the reforms which Mr. P rather scathingly termed "criminal". It was difficult to secure affordable and reliable health services; ditto for education. (I was to find out myself after I assumed my post in the Embassy the outrageous charges for good health services; I could afford them, thanks to my insurance and MFA coverage, while the average Russian could not).

Fourth, socio-economic hardship had led to high crime rates, which he had never thought he would experience in his lifetime, given the relatively safe and secure environment of the Soviet era.

Fifth, the gap between the rich (many of whom he termed "vory" or thieves who "stole from the Soviet state") and the poor, was widening

---

[2] I would hear the term "civilised world" many times being uttered by Russians of all stripes, in public and private, between 1994 and 2013, and even today. Russians then and even now think of the West as the "civilised world".

by the day. It was sad and ironic that despite its vast natural resources and mineral wealth, the common people did not live well. His observation would be one of the consistent refrains I would hear from many a Russian, even till my final assignment ended in 2013.

Finally, societal mores with respect to sex and attitudes towards the elderly were beginning to change for the worse.

His sentiments, expressed in a passionate tone, came across like a *cri de coeur* to me, to try to understand the difficulties the man-in-the-street had to undergo in post-Soviet Russia. I also got the impression that he believed foreigners felt that post-Soviet Russia's difficulties were nothing more than a prosaic matter. Hence, his rather emotionally-laden narration of his country's situation.

Being a born sceptic, my initial reaction was to discount his views. Of course, I had already seen Moscow's backwardness in comparison with the FRG. However, at the time, his observations appeared too unbelievable. Thankfully, with the passage of time, I could take the measure of them, with my own observations and increased interaction with Russian or foreign students whom I met in MGU, and my colleagues in the Embassy (i.e., Russian staff members and fellow diplomats), as well as my daily perusal of the English-language daily, the *Moscow Times*.

Thanks to Mr. P, I also absorbed all the Russian language terms for those monumental changes in the society and as a result, my command of the language grew in leaps and bounds, although it was still far from fluent. Today, I can read, write, and comprehend it at the advanced level, having taken part-time lessons in the language during my first, second, and last tours of duty in Moscow. For this, I must thank Mr. P, as he provided me the basis for all that.

The need to focus and learn the language meant that I had to rid myself of the prejudices and preconceived notions of my host country. And when one learns a language, one also absorbs the culture of that language and, in the process, appreciates its richness and qualities. Moreover, my three-month stint as a language student gave me insights into and an experience of life in the Russian capital through contact with Russian and foreign students in MGU, where Russian was the lingua franca. Truth be told, I had little contact with other foreign students for I did not think I would improve my command of the language by communicating with non-native speakers of the language. Hence, almost from the start of my stay in Moscow, I tried to have more contact with Russians or foreigners who spoke the language fluently viz. those from the former Soviet republics.

Since my teacher was assigned to me by MGU on a one-to-one basis, my contact with other students was also not to be taken for granted. Fortunately, the hostel would organise regular parties which I would attend as often as my mood and my schedule would allow. At this party (whose dates were not fixed and occasionally, no party was organised at all), one would meet one's fellow students from Russia, the former Soviet republics, South Korea, China, and Europe as well as North America, not only to socialise but more so to practise one's command of the Russian language with its native speakers. From the Russian and former Soviet republics' students, I would also learn some of the subtleties and nuances of the Russian language as well as Russian social mores.

The then Ambassador, Bilahari Kausikan, would thankfully have me over to his Residence to meet his contacts, Russians and non-Russians. They would answer all my questions about the country and with the Russian guests, also provided me the opportunity to practise the language.

Moreover, I took the opportunity to see and experience as much of Moscow as possible. Being a student on a generous MFA allowance meant that I did not have any work responsibilities and hence, more than enough time and more important, the means to indulge myself in the large city's many distractions, principally eating out in restaurants which, at the time, were quite limited in number. All-in-all, I certainly must have been one of the very few financially-blessed students in MGU that summer of 1994. Being in that very unenviable financial position, I became to some extent, the cynosure of the less fortunate students (financially-speaking) with whom I became acquainted while at MGU.

Chapter 2

Moscow Becomes More Familiar

Умом Россию не понять, Аршином общим не измерить: У ней особенная стать — В Россию можно только верить.

You cannot grasp Russia with your mind
Or judge her by any common measure,
Russia is one of a special kind —
You can only believe in her.

(Translation found on the website of Russkiy Mir Foundation, dated 10 December 2012).

This poem, by one of Russia's greatest poets, Fyodor Tyutchev, was brought to my attention by one of the first Russians with whom I became acquainted in Moscow. He was an academic who was a close friend of Ambassador Bilahari. Let me address him as Mr. O. We were invited to his flat for dinner in the summer of 1994. He related this poem to me in reply to my question about the difficulties I had trying to grasp what made Russia tick. Looking back, to a large extent, he had hit the nail on the head.

Further Impressions and Observations

I arrived in Moscow about half a year after President Boris Yeltsin's October 1993 confrontation with members of the State Duma (the

Russian parliament) ended in violence and death (when he ordered the storming of the parliament building) and victory over those political forces that had opposed his socio-economic policies. I did not expect to see any visible and open signs of the instability which preceded this confrontation, for Yeltsin essentially had by then, succeeded in neutralising his political opponents.

In the December 1993 parliamentary elections, the first election in post-Soviet Russia, some semblance of stability returned to the country. However, an astute observer of Russia, Michael McFaul, correctly pointed out "the actual balance of power within the State Duma was divided relatively evenly between supporters and opponents of Yeltsin".[1] McFaul, who was the US Ambassador to Russia (2012–2014), had been working in the Carnegie Moscow Centre, a US think tank in the early 1990s, and is an insightful observer of post-Soviet Russia.

Hence, stability in Russia in early-1994 was of a qualified and limited nature. I was therefore not surprised to observe some level of *bespredel* or *bardak* which Russians I had become acquainted with, were wont to use to describe the state of the country (both nouns denote "chaos" or "a mess").

This became immediately obvious to me in the first few days of my stay in Moscow. Watching the behaviour of motorists on Moscow's grand avenues and boulevards as well as on its wide side-streets from a bus or taxi or while walking on its broad street pavements, I would be struck by the virtual absence of law-and-order on these vital arteries of Moscow, now and then.

One could observe vehicles driving against the traffic on smaller roads or streets and occasionally, even on the wide boulevards and avenues themselves. Drivers would even reverse not just a few yards but quite a distance against the traffic or mount the wide pavements to beat the traffic. Such behaviour was in obvious disregard for the safety of pedestrians, not to mention the fact that such acts were irresponsible and dangerous, and showed utter contempt for the law! (The pavements of most boulevards are wide enough for cars to drive on.) I would

---

[1] Source: *From Cold War to Hot Peace: The Inside Story of Russia and America*, p. 35.

observe this kind of behaviour even until 2013 before my departure, although, such instances were markedly fewer in number or regularity when compared to the 1990s or early years of this century.

I was also struck by Moscow's wide boulevards and avenues with their 10 to 15 lanes. Moscow's wide streets and roads corresponded to the vastness of the country. I would often wish that we could have, in Singapore, such wide spaces! Obviously, these were musings of an unrealistic nature; I envied the immense size of Moscow and Russia itself.

I considered myself to be professionally and personally lucky to be in Moscow. It was not *hauteur*. Observing and analysing the Russia of 1994 was interesting and challenging for any diplomat. I considered myself lucky personally, because I had the opportunity to compare my own fortunate lot and that of Singapore with the unfortunate lot of the people of Moscow and Russia. Had I been born in Moscow or another part of this vast country, I would be out of work or if I had a job, I would have to struggle to make a decent living. Mind you, Muscovites then were not starving but the majority, for sure, did not live totally free of want or worries about whether and when the next decent meal would come from or how one would have to pay the rent or utility bills. I do not think anyone then (apart from the relatively small number of relatively well-off and wealthy people) even thought about when and where they should take their next holiday! On the other hand, I was already planning my first holiday to be taken in Western Europe.

I discerned overt signs of poverty in MGU, on the streets of the city, even in the so-called better districts, on the bus, and in the trains (viz. the metro or MRT in Singapore parlance). All that was evident in the shabby and unfortunately even dirty clothes and unpolished or worn-out shoes of many Muscovites, and on the tired faces of many commuters of the city's public transport system. (By the way, its metro was one of the best in the world. The trains would arrive on time, and importantly, very regularly every few minutes.)

Poverty was also evident in the queues of people who would line the inside of metro stations or out on the nearby streets and who would hawk everything from a comb to World War II (WW II) medals of war veterans. Yes, a comb — an image which will forever remain embedded in my memory is that of a man, perhaps between 35 and 40 years of age, standing in a queue of people in one of the metro stations in the city centre (Arbatskaya station), holding a comb for sale! I noticed him a few times over a week at least, in the same spot with the same object (perhaps he had many combs to sell) while I was on my way to and from the Embassy. I would visit the Embassy often after my language lessons in MGU.

WW II war medals were also on sale, but whether they were genuine, I could not tell; however simply judging by the age of the chaps who were trying to sell them, they must have been genuine, I thought to myself. It was sad for me to think that WW II veterans saw no other way to feed themselves but to sell their war medals, awarded to them for defending their country in the most brutal war in history, the 1941–1945 contest of wills between Hitler and Stalin.

Other individuals would be hawking all manner of clothes, gadgets like old Soviet and foreign-made cameras — I once even spied a very old Leica. Household items like kettles, cutlery, and even expensive-looking crockery were to be seen. Not all, but most of these individuals were pensioners (the spending power of their already small pensions had been reduced by high inflation). It was a sight I will never forget. To me, this was the market economy gone wild and built on a *pasar malam* model (literally night-market in the Singapore context where all sorts of items would be for sale). The ordinary men and women of Russia and the country which had given the world Tchaikovsky, Rachmaninoff, Prokofiev to name a few and had sent the first man and woman into space, not to mention played a vital role in the defeat of Nazism, did not deserve this cruel fate.

A third sign of poverty was discernible in the fact that many Russians had to *khalturit* (to moonlight) to supplement their meagre wages. They would use their personal vehicles or even those of their employers to serve as taxis! I personally had occasion to use the services of a "pirate taxi driver" (the Singapore term for unlicensed taxi drivers in the pre- and early days of Independence) in the person of an ambulance driver who drove his ambulance as a "taxi"! He told me he could take me home as it was on his way to pick-up a patient, in response to my expressed concern whether it was permitted for me to even ride in his vehicle.

One could and did bargain with the driver over the fare before getting into his vehicle. On another occasion, I sat in the vehicle of a chap who claimed to have been a retired colonel in the Soviet Armed Forces. When I politely asked why he saw it fit to drive for a living, he nonchalantly replied that "*mne nado simyu kormit*" (I must feed my family), adding that his pension was miniscule. On a third occasion, the driver politely stressed he was a physician, in answer to my questions. Like the ex-colonel, he complained about the high cost of living, high inflation and low pensions and his low salary as a physician, which had forced him and them into the "taxi profession". One need not have bothered to wait for any of these "taxis" on the streets; they would always appear if one just stood on the street. If a driver either refused one's counter-offer of the fare or one's destination was not to his liking, a line of other "cabs" would be waiting behind his vehicle.

I would avail myself of the services of these "cabs" in all the cities I had occasion to travel in Russia during my three tours of duty. Such "cabs" could be found all over the country at the time, as I was to discover when I visited the many towns and cities all over Russia. Those were the days of Uber, Lyft, and Grab without today's technology when the passenger was really king!

It was a lesson to be learnt, namely that one's level of education would not count for much in an unstable economy and society. Many of the Embassy's Russian staff members were also qualified individuals — there were engineers among a number of them. One of them, a handyman, claimed to have been trained as a nuclear scientist in a research institute and once said to me, half in jest, that were Singapore interested in building a nuclear weapon, he and his former colleagues could assist us in the endeavour! Another, one of our maids, told me she had been working in the Soviet space programme as one of its many engineers! While I was neither in a position to verify their claim nor was interested in doing so, I did not have any reason to doubt their word.

Educated people simply took whatever jobs which were available and which paid a decent wage — they did not, in many cases, represent the profession for which these people had been trained. What a waste of their talent, was my first thought.

Academics and even scientists were said to have had second or third jobs. A leading academic whom I got to know, told me matter-of-factly while we were chatting about the socio-economic situation, that the combined savings of him and his wife came to a grand total US$5,000. While that sum of money at the time was not small change, I was nevertheless taken aback, for it was not an amount I considered large at all. The academic however appeared to be satisfied that at least, he and his wife had this spare cash on hand. Not many individuals at the time could claim to have such an amount of money. He was one of the country's leading experts on the Asia-Pacific region.

It was really sad for me to know that educated men and women had to moonlight to supplement their low salaries which regularly went unpaid in many Russian state bodies, enterprises and nascent small businesses. In that regard, our Embassy staff members were happy to have had the chance to work for us as their salaries were not only decent but were always paid on time. Not being paid on time was a challenge in many workplaces which did not go bankrupt. The widespread practice of *khaltura* (moonlighting) touched almost all sectors of the working population.

To me, unbelievably low wages for civil servants are a clear sign that a country is not stable economically or politically. If any government cannot afford to pay its officials a decent wage, corruption will inevitably become second nature. In that regard, a Russian official nonchalantly told me over dinner one evening with his wife, how low his salary was, while we were chatting about many issues, including the state of the economy. He cited the ridiculously low figure of US$50 a month, which I could not believe! He also volunteered the information that he did not have a choice but to charge a "small fee" for advice on this-or-that matter. I had neither coaxed him into revealing his salary nor was he embarrassed about doing so. In those days, I did not get the impression that Russians (acquaintances, contacts or even strangers in a bar) were embarrassed about discussing the state of their country or their own personal financial circumstances, whenever I raised the issue or whenever the conversation veered towards such an issue. After all, one could observe oneself the reality of the situation. In short, highly-educated people were not spared the ravages of poverty in post-Soviet Russia.

At the time, there was no real middle class to speak of. My private drivers also held two to three different jobs. And they were educated and qualified people. I had four drivers during my three tours of duty in Moscow; they would send and pick-up my daughter from her school in their own vehicles or in my personal car.

The one was a teacher, the other had held a clerical job in a small firm, the third was a mechanic while the last was a paediatrician (based on what they told me; I could not and did not double-check on their backgrounds but certainly believed their open declarations that they had to have other jobs "to survive" as all of them would put it). A Russian musician friend of mine (who prefers anonymity) related to me that not only talented musicians but all those whose livelihoods depended on the state, for example, teachers, physicians, academics, and who had to subsist on very low wages, did not have a choice but to moonlight and literally have two to three other jobs.

A fourth sign of the dire state of the country was clearly seen on some of the streets where women would ply their trade. Post-Soviet Russia was not only going through unprecedented economic, political and social changes but its morals and values were also being turned upside down. I was told and had read that during the Soviet period, sex was a taboo subject for the outwardly prudish Soviet leadership and the people at large. Unfortunately, the Soviet collapse released all that pent-up and repressed sexual energy. Prostitution must have become one of the ways to make a quick buck to "survive" during those difficult days. These unfortunate women would occasionally even appear on a side-street, over a hundred yards from the Embassy. However, with the growing prosperity as the new century began, street-walkers would become less of a fixture on the streets.

Many of Moscow's nightspots and casinos were also magnets for ladies-of-the-night of a "higher order". Unlike the street-walkers, these "ladies" would continue their trade into the new century and beyond, in the myriad of night-clubs and established casinos (casinos were banned in 2009 and restricted to four special zones across the country). The prudish sexual norms of the Soviet era yielded to a libertine lifestyle in which *Wein, Weib und Gesang* appeared to have become the order of the day.

A fifth sign of the country's difficult economic position was evident whenever one encountered visibly poorly-fed conscripts on the streets, even on two of Moscow's fashionable pedestrian thoroughfares (like Novi Arbat and Stary Arbat), approaching strangers for money and/or cigarettes. I too had been approached quite a number of times for money/cigarettes and never once would I reject the pleas of any soldier. A smoker (like I was then) would never decline the request of fellow smoker for a fag. It was a sign of the times that even the Russian Armed Forces could not remain untouched by the momentous and chaotic changes in the country's political, social and economic life.

The sorry state of the Russian Armed Forces made an indelible impression on me. It had become a shadow of its previous Soviet self. It was badly-led, lowly-paid, not well-trained, staffed by disillusioned officers and poorly-fed conscripts, and had suffered untold losses in Chechnya, according to media reports and some Western military attaches whom I knew. (I wore many hats in the Embassy; apart from being the number two man, I was the officer-in-charge of politico-economic affairs, military matters and (until our trade promotion authority, the Trade Development Board (TDB) opened an office in the Embassy), trade and commercial issues).

Unfortunately, children, especially orphans, are always among the helpless and innocent victims of any momentous changes in a country's socio-political or economic situation. If I may digress a little, with my wife and daughter, I visited an orphanage not far from our flat, in the summer of 1995, thanks to the suggestion of Mr. C, a diplomat neighbour of mine. He brought our attention to the plight of orphans in Moscow and in response to my request, recommended that my wife and I visit an orphanage. No sooner had my wife, my daughter and I stepped into the orphanage's common room than we were literally embraced and hugged by many children ranging in age between 5 and 15. I was moved to tears when the children who clung to me screamed out "papa, papa". So were my wife and daughter. My ethnicity was obviously not important to them (all the orphans and staff members there were ethnic Slav Russians). The orphans whom we encountered that day were not starving but their very shabby clothes made it clear that their lives were far from comfortable. Moreover, it was obvious that their premises were, like most state institutions then, in very dire need of repair. My family and I were so glad to have been there, having brought some, if only temporary joy to the children, with our company as well as food, clothes and of course, toys.

One of the officials of the orphanage who acted as our escort, told us that the Soviet collapse a few years earlier had made the situation for the orphanage much worse. She assumed all other orphanages in Moscow and elsewhere in the country must have gone through and were still going through the same experience. I could only speculate whether this was indeed the case. However, I assumed that this was within the very real boundaries of the possible. The diplomat, Mr. C, whose work revolved around charity as well, was also of the same opinion.

Despite the sorry state of the country, I had never encountered any ragamuffin on the streets of Moscow or the many Russian cities I had visited from the time I set foot into the country in April 1994 till my departure in mid-2013. I believe it must have been due to the deep Russian love of children that would not allow waifs to wander on the streets without supervision.

The fact that the US $ was de facto legal tender was another reflection of the severity of Russia's socio-economic difficulties. One could purchase this-or-that with US $ (I had brought over US $ in cash when I arrived in Moscow in April 1994). Wages in many firms were also paid in US $. If my memory serves me right, this practice was made illegal in the late '90s. However, it was widely ignored, as far as I could ascertain. It was only when the country's politico-economic situation stabilised in the early years of the century that the US $ gradually began to lose its lustre. Nevertheless, even in 2013, when

I left the country, the US $ was still an attractive currency to Russians to have at hand, and I had the impression, they would prefer it to the ruble. Whether that has changed since, I cannot say for I have not been back to the country.

Finally, the market economy in the early post-Soviet years was really quite primitive, at least in the retail sector. The following example illustrates my point. Many shops had a very archaic payment system. One had to secure a piece of paper for an item(s) one wanted to purchase from the sales clerk; the piece of paper would display the item(s) to be purchased. Thereafter, one had to proceed to the cashier to pay for it/them; armed with the receipt, one would have to return to the first counter to pick-up the item(s). This archaic practice did not totally end with the passage of time. Even as late as 2013, there were at least two mini-markets on a street not far from my flat (which was situated on a side-street off Stary Arbat, a very fashionable neighbourhood) in which this practice was still in force.

My wife and I were regular customers in both of them; I once casually asked the sales clerk, a matronly woman in her fifties the reason for this continued practice to which she nonchalantly replied that the staff members were "used" to it and did not plan to change it. These mini-markets also used the abacus together with a normal cash register, to my surprise. In answer to my question, the sales clerk emphatically replied that the abacus was more accurate than the cash register and would never break down. I was fascinated by the use of the abacus in many grocery shops in Moscow and Russia; my recollection of the use of the abacus in Singapore's provision shops was confined to my boyhood and early youth days.

That post-Soviet Russia was undergoing tremendous changes to its politico-economic and social structures, for which its people, especially the common folk, were paying an unnecessarily high price, was more than obvious.

It is not a cavil to argue that the speed at which "shock therapy" (as the reforms were then known), was undertaken, was totally unavoidable. My own observations at close-quarters convinced me that Russia could have undertaken reforms at a tempo commensurate with its people's history, traditions, culture, and (relative lack of) experience with the complex ways of the market economy. However, political expediency dictated the unnecessarily fast pace of the reforms, without much or little consideration to society's relative immaturity to adapt to them. There were fears and concerns that unless market reforms were introduced and implemented fast, the Communists and nationalist forces opposed to the reforms, could seize power at the next elections.

The question for me at the time and since, was whether the Russian people's great suffering was worth the impact that shock therapy had wrought on the country. Moreover, like people everywhere when faced with economic adversity, the Russians could and did circumvent newly-enacted laws on the nascent market economy. My contacts would often cite as an example, the quick privatisation of state assets which was considered a socio-economic and political priority; it had been implemented with apparently little or no regard for other factors or circumstances necessary in a privatisation programme. In the process, it was said that quite a few state assets fell into the hands of organised crime groups or speculators, and was not considered a success in the planned equitable distribution of state wealth.

Apart from the obvious signs of poverty mentioned above, my other observations about the consequences of shock therapy were the following:

(a) The conditions under which the average educated person (like an academic) lived came as quite a shock to me. They were very far from what I had observed and experienced in the FRG. Germans in the 1980s lived well and much better than many other people in the world, including Russians. The first flat/abode of a Russian or Muscovite I set eyes upon was that of the academic, Mr. O, in the summer of 1994. His flat was not located in the city centre but almost on the outskirts. It took me and Ambassador Kausikan more than an hour to get there — first on the Moscow metro and then on a bus. The block of flats in which Mr. O lived was in a sad state of disrepair; one could not have been proud of the façade. The foyer and lift certainly were in need of renovation and repair respectively. His flat's condition, however, was in a decent condition but I was quite surprised that he did not live better (being new to the country, I had mistakenly believed an academic would have the means to live much better). Indeed, in the course of my work in the next few years, I visited another academic who received me in his flat on at least two occasions, to chat about socio-economic and/or foreign policy issues. I must say the state of his flat too was far from decent. Of course, by then, I was no longer new to the country and was aware that academics, among others, were not well-paid. Hence, it was not their fault they had to live that way. I would visit the flats of other Russians, not only in Moscow but also in other cities and, in general, the conditions there were not that much different. When one compared the state of our HDB flats[2] like the façade, lifts, and public areas, one could not say that those in Russia could match ours at all. I assumed shock therapy made an already bad situation even worse in this regard;

(b) Many Russians had to literally live off the land, by growing vegetables and raising poultry where possible, as money was short, and wages were low and not paid regularly. Many though not all, had *dachas* (loosely translated as country homes) which were not necessarily large or comfortable but provided the average Russian a place to relax on weekends and, in the 1990s, to tend to the growing of vegetables and raising poultry. The Embassy's Russian staff members also engaged in this very Russian practice, although their salaries were decent and always regularly paid. That was their way of living then during a difficult time in their country's history. One of them, our handyman, would present me and my wife a bottle of preserved vegetables almost every year from 1995 till his retirement in the first decade of the century. They were quite tasty and as he had never failed to remind us, were free of preservatives, additives, and other "chemicals". My Russian contacts, including

---

[2] The HDB, or Housing and Development Board, is Singapore's public housing body which built, still builds, and maintains the flats in which most of Singapore's population live.

my part-time Russian language teacher, had also narrated to me their *"dacha* life" and the Russian and Western media were reporting on this aspect of Russian life as well;

(c) The savings accounts of people were wiped out by runaway inflation and monetary reforms. I read many accounts of this unfortunate state of affairs and would also be told about it by many Russians I got to know;

(d) Pyramid schemes had assumed some measure of popularity as well as embodied some hope for many desperate people. A very well-known case was that of MMM, run by one Sergei Mavrodi. The *Moscow Times*, a leading English-language daily, reported widely on the case. I recall my private driver a few years later telling me how he had lost most of his life savings in the scheme. He must have been one among many who fell for this fraud;

(e) The drawn-out, tired, and generally not-too-happy faces of many Russians whom I would observe on the street, in the train, and on the bus — in short, anywhere and everywhere — were clearly signs of the impact of their country's socio-economic reforms on them. Many also appeared older than they actually were. Quite a number of chaps I met were younger than I, but their faces showed a different and harsh reality. We all know that stress ages the body prematurely; as many Russians at the time were living very stressful lives, due to the momentous changes in their country, it was not surprising that their faces bore signs of old age well before their time.

It should have been plain to anyone that more than seven decades of Communism meant that the Russian people would not be able to assume, adapt, and accept the responsibilities that free enterprise and a market economy would bring, especially at the fast pace of shock therapy. Russia's socialist system was incapable of adapting to the ways of capitalism, which an observer, James Sherr, described as "the introduction of free-market liberalism to a country without liberal institutions or a rights-based, effective legal order".[3]

---

[3] See his observations in *Hard Diplomacy and Soft Coercion: Russia's Influence Abroad*, p. 46, Chatham House.

No less a personality than President Putin himself also made the same point but in a different context in *First Person: An Astonishingly Frank Self-portrait by Russia's President Vladimir Putin*, by Nataliya Gevorkyan, Natalya Timakova, and Andrei Kolesnikov (2000: 102).

Referring to the St. Petersburg authorities plan to introduce control over the gambling business and derive revenues for the city, he noted that "the casino owners showed us only losses on the books. While we were counting up the profits and deciding where to allocate the funds — to develop the city's businesses or support the social sector — they were laughing at us and showing us their losses. *Ours was a classic mistake made by people encountering the free market for the first time.*" (Emphasis mine). According to his personal website, in June 1991, he began work as Chairman of the Committee for International Relations in the St. Petersburg City Hall, and from 1994, concurrently held the position of Deputy Chairman of the St. Petersburg City Government.

An open sign of Russian immaturity (no offence meant to my Russian friends and acquaintances) in the ways of the market economy was evident in the fact that Western advisers and consultants were employed in Russian official bodies associated with the privatisation programme and in organs associated with economic planning and policy-making.

After my assignment began in mid-1994, I met one of these advisers, who told me that his job was, *inter alia*, to provide advice and guidance to Russian officials on financial and fiscal matters. This fact rankled at the Russian consciousness and pride, as I was to ascertain subsequently. A prominent Russian journalist emphasised to me a few years later that many Western advisers had behaved towards Russia as if it were a Third World country. However, Russia was never, was not, and should never be considered as part of the Third World, he passionately argued. This comment was reiterated often enough by many other Russian contacts as well.

If indeed it had been the case that Western advisers had been condescending towards their Russian colleagues, then one could not blame any Russian who resented such behaviour. I am, however, not in a position to say that had indeed been the case.

While it was true that Russia then was a poor country, its achievements and progress up till then meant that it was not a Third World state. It had sent the first man and woman into space. Moreover, unlike many Third World countries, Russia could boast of high literacy rates as well the excellent quality of its engineers and scientists, not to mention its cultural contributions to the world.

Yet, all was not totally doom-and-gloom. There were always exceptions to the despair of the man-in-the-street. The Russian entrepreneurial spirit and ability to adapt to the fast socio-economic and political changes was evident in the fact that open-air and street markets of sorts opened and thrived in the immediate post-Soviet era, and by the time I arrived in Moscow in the spring of 1994, many more had sprung into life.

One of these markets my wife and I enjoyed visiting in the first few months of our arrival in Moscow was that by the Moscow river, opposite Gorky Park; there, one could find all sorts of works of art on sale by budding artists. Another was in Filevsky Park, where one could purchase items from World War II war medals (and even Nazi memorabilia!) to souvenirs, and old books, etc. (In the winter, one could cross-country ski there, which we did in our first winter in Moscow in 1994/1995). Finally, another of our favourite places to visit was the world-famous Izmailovsky Park where, apart from being able to find souvenirs and antiques, one could also get a hearty Russian meal at a reasonable price.

Despite or in spite of the Soviet system, many Russians developed increasing levels of entrepreneurial skill. In the late 1970s and early 1980s, I recall seeing quite a few of them on Singapore's High Street where they would be shopping for bargains (consumer electronic goods and computers being their main items of interest). They were known as *chelnoki* or shuttle traders who would purchase such goods in Singapore and elsewhere in the world; as they were in short supply in the Soviet Union, the *chelnoki* could make good money. Some of the *chelnoki* would become wealthy.

According to Wikipedia, Oleg Tinkov, one of Russia's wealthiest men, "began wholesale electronics trade from Singapore in 1992, and to simplify the registration of documents he registered a limited liability partnership Petrosib in St. Petersburg, and then regional companies Petrosib-Kemerovo, Petrosib-Novosibirsk and Petrosib-Omsk and others. Goods arrived in St. Petersburg and from there went to the regions, where they were sold with a larger markup. He started with calculators and went on to office equipment, televisions, VCRs and even artificial flowers and trees. In the beginning, Oleg himself flew to Singapore, then began to use air transport, but the turning point came when an Indian dealer Ashok Vasmani shipped him half a container of TVs on credit."

Unfortunately, not everyone in the country had talent, skill, determination, and plain guts to engage in trading, or establish any form of business activity. Hence, shock therapy turned out to be a long-drawn ordeal for the majority of the people.

While the majority had much difficulty in making ends meet, a very small minority became wealthy beyond imagination. They would flaunt their wealth in casinos and expensive restaurants, which only grew in number as time distanced Russia further from the Soviet collapse. One would see their luxury cars on the streets, much to the dismay but concealed anger of the majority. I recall overhearing a conversation of a middle-aged couple one afternoon while waiting at a bus stop near my hostel in MGU. Although my command of the language then was still rudimentary, I could understand enough of what they were saying, and it was obvious the target of their angered tone of voice was a young chap sitting in a latest Mercedes model (illegally) parked not far from the bus stop. Constant references to the "mafia hooligan" in the car were made by the couple, in clearly incensed tones. Envy was prevalent among the majority of the (impoverished) people, and it was irrelevant whether their assumptions that the rich were "bandits" were based on fact or fiction. Society was so divided that anyone with money who flaunted it would be labelled a bandit or a *vor* (thief).

Political figures such as Yegor Gaidar and Anatoly Chubais associated with the introduction of shock therapy[4] into the country were reviled as

---

[4] The late Yegor Gaidar was the Acting Prime Minister from June to December 1992; shock therapy is associated with him. Anatoly Chubais is considered to have been the

"*vrag naroda*" (enemy of the people, a very Soviet term). This term was freely used by many disparate individuals I spoke to about the process. I recall how a "pirate" taxi-driver in whose car I was riding as a passenger, became very passionate when chatting about the unprecedented reform processes in his country, in response to my questions. In a choleric outburst, he called for a full-scale re-nationalisation of assets acquired "illegally by bandits"!

Having matured intellectually as a university student in the late 1970s and professionally as a diplomat in the 1980s with the Soviet Union as a superpower, I just could not fathom how Russia, the Soviet Union's successor state, could have fallen so deep into an abyss of political, social, economic as well as moral and physical decay.

I did not derive any joy from being an observer to these changes in the life of a great country, especially the harmful impact they had on the man-in-the-street with whom I would jostle on the metro or bus for a seat or standing place and whom I would see on the street daily. I saw in him and his fellow citizens only people, individuals who certainly did not deserve this fate. The cost of shock therapy and its accompanying effects on Russian society was unjustifiably high — according to David Satter, an American journalist with a long history of writing on the Soviet Union and then Russia, "by various estimates, 5 to 6 million people died prematurely during the Yeltsin period".[5]

The first six to 12 months of my stay in Moscow also opened my eyes to the Russian character. I came to the conclusion that Russians are very generous, hospitable, and kind even to strangers/outsiders to whom they take a liking. What they then lacked in material possessions, they more than made up by their high degree of friendliness, kindness, hospitality, and basically human touch. I experienced that first-hand in MGU in the persons of two Russian students — unfortunately, I cannot recall their names. They were poor students, a young married couple, who lived in a small one-room flat in the hostel, while Yours

---

father of the privatisation process and was an influential member of Yeltsin's administration.

[5] Source: *The Less You Know, the Better You Sleep*, by David Satter, pp. 75–76, Yale University Press.

Truly had two rooms, one of which was an en-suite. They invited me once or twice to their room for dinner, and shared with me their meagre portions of meat and vegetables. I would naturally respond to their kindness but since I do not know how to cook, would invite them to restaurants. They would always express their gratitude but would not accept my invitations. They became my first acquaintances in Moscow; they would correct my command of spoken Russian and answer all my questions about politics, their lives, Russia's history, and so on. To this day, I regret not having continued my contact with them after I started work in the Embassy.

My Russian language teacher, Mr. P, was also a paragon of Russian hospitality, kindness, understanding, and openness. He would often insist on paying for a cup of tea or coffee during our breaks between lessons, although his salary was a pittance. Unfortunately, I lost contact with Mr. P as well after assuming my post in the Embassy. I regret that to this day as well.

Finally, thanks to Ambassador Kausikan, I had the opportunity to visit a Russian household (my first) and partake of its owner's hospitality — Mr. O was an old friend of Ambassador Kausikan, an academic whose expertise was China. (He had learnt Mandarin in the 1970s in Nantah, Singapore's only Chinese language university at the time.) This kind and gentle individual went to great lengths to provide his two guests with more than enough food and drink. It was a very touching experience for me which I shall never forget.

The figure of US$50 to US$100 as the average wage for teachers and educated people were cited frequently by Russian acquaintances and contacts as well as by my Russian staff members, not to mention the long-resident Singapore businessmen, and Western diplomats and expatriates. I believe Mr. O must have earned that little as well; I recall his educated wife had to supplement the family income by working as a nanny.

During the course of the subsequent three years of my first assignment, and my second and third assignments stretching into 2013, these traits came to the fore in all the Russians I encountered personally and professionally, independent of their social status or financial position. That surely is a virtue of the Russian people.

My Damascene moment about Moscow in particular and Russia in general came with the end of my three-month language course. It was time well-spent for I was no longer the frustrated FSO who had felt that my assignment to Moscow was a "mistake".

Chapter 3

Life as a Diplomat in the Yeltsinite Era

Challenges to Work

Any diplomat wet-behind-the-ears who had to serve in post-Soviet Russia barely three years after the Soviet collapse would have been intimidated. Without wanting to sound as if I am blowing my own trumpet, I was not in that state of mind.

I was over-confident and over-enthusiastic about my work, when I commenced duty as First Secretary in the Embassy in August 1994. Armed with just three months of Russian language training but firm in my knowledge of Tsarist Russia, Bolshevik Russia, and the Soviet Union (I had started reading about the country's history and that of Germany under the Hohenzollerns and Hitler at the tender age of 10 in 1965), I fell under the (mistaken) impression that I would not have any problem becoming very productive in my work. My self-confidence was rather misplaced for the following reasons.

My Russian contacts at the time were not as open as the Germans and Westerners whom I had met in Bonn. Seven decades of Communism had led to a mindset that did not value openness towards strangers, including foreigners. Meeting and chatting freely with foreigners was still a novelty for many, though not for all. Even academics and journalists were still feeling their way into what was for them, still a new world. Being candid and open about an issue had yet to become second nature. However, in their own way, my Russian contacts were as frank as they could have been, considering the fact that only a few years before, direct, personal, and unsupervised meetings with foreigners were rare and infrequent, as I had been given to understand.

Therefore, one had to be careful not to fall into the trap of absorbing the "party line" from Russian official sources. For the sake of balance, I had to broaden my contacts to the academic and journalistic community, as well as Western diplomats and expatriates. I had to work that much harder to separate the wheat from the chaff when it came to evaluating information and assessments of significant events or developments.

Russia's latent distrust of and disappointment with the West, which less than a decade later would become entrenched, meant that one expected to be told a version or assessment of developments/issues with a rather jaundiced eye. Details on post-Soviet Russia's complicated relationship with the West are found later in this book.

On the other hand, I also did not wish to rely solely on Western sources (businessmen, diplomats, or journalists) for their reading on this-or-that issue or development. I believed that there was some bias in their approach and assessment of Russia. One could even detect a sense of *Schadenfreude* on the part of some of them. I could not fault them though, for Russia in the form of the Soviet Union had, just a few years before, posed an existential threat to the West and had been an adversary and a formidable military opponent since the end of the war.; I assessed that while the West might have "forgiven", it certainly had not forgotten or could not forget the "sins" committed by Russia's predecessor state.

A challenge to my work also came in the form of more sophisticated media technology. The 1990s were the days when cable TV had already made its mark and one could hardly compete with it when it came to ensuring the timeliness of one's report. Yet one was forced to do so, in some aspect. I shall cite an example. By 1995, President Yeltsin's re-election in the 1996 Presidential Elections was not a foregone conclusion; he faced in Gennady Zyuganov, the leader of the KPRF (Communist Party of the Russian Federation) a formidable opponent. Indeed, shock therapy, which was associated with Yeltsin's presidency, had impoverished the majority of the Russian people who were perceived as likely to support Zyuganov. Moreover, quite a few people I knew, saw Yeltsin as a Falstaffian character which they felt also reduced his chances at re-election.

Western print and electronic media were reporting almost daily on the Yeltsin–Zyuganov rivalry and likely election outcomes, and Yours Truly naturally was under self-imposed pressure to assess the situation and report on it too. Yeltsin won by a small majority with widely-believed help from the oligarchs' media outlets; they naturally feared a return of Communism.

A number of my acquaintances had even speculated that many a meeting had been held, *sub rosa*, between representatives of the oligarchs[1] and Yeltsin's staffers, to discuss strategies and actions to ensure his re-election. Whether they actually took place, I cannot say.

Finally, securing open and above all, reliable information, on basic matters proved to be frustrating. If one required the address and/or telephone number of so-and-so, one could not consult the "Yellow Pages" for there was none, I had been told.

While enterprising Westerners published a much-needed handbook of addresses of Russian and foreign companies, diplomatic representatives, and Russian official bodies, it alone was not sufficient to secure basic information on the address or telephone numbers of an individual's office or organisation, let alone his home address or telephone number, if that individual, organisation, or company was not large enough or if he/it did not subscribe to the handbook's services. In this regard, without the hard work and versatility of my Russian staff members who always managed to secure the addresses of many a Russian I had to meet, I would not have been able to meet the many people I had to in order to discharge my responsibilities as a diplomat.

Even if one had managed to secure the address of a required contact by hook or by crook, finding it on a reliable map of Moscow would be another issue. I was given to understand that during the Soviet era, the authorities did not freely provide information on roads and streets (on

---

[1] The oligarchs was a term used to describe Russian tycoons who became extraordinarily wealthy in post-Soviet Russia, thanks to the privatisation of the command economy.

maps) in an effort to control and monitor the movements of suspected foreign spies. Secondly, quite a number of streets had been renamed after the Soviet Union broke-up. (Those were the days when GPS would certainly have come in handy). Finally, being a very large city with many side-streets and alleys, many a time, even my experienced drivers had difficulties getting to the right place on time. Hence, there were quite a few occasions when I arrived late for appointments, much to my embarrassment; I would always blame the traffic!

Ambassador Kausikan also proved to be very understanding, supportive, and encouraging. He gave me the confidence to soldier on and acted as a fillip to my morale in the initial few months of my assignment. With great sadness on my part, he left Moscow for New York in early 1995 to become our Permanent Representative to the UN there.

Between his departure and the arrival of the next Ambassador, in November 1995, I assumed the position of Chargé d'Affaires *ad interim* (CDA a.i.). The relatively long period of time in this position proved fortuitous for me.

First, it provided me the opportunity to gain the experience of running the Embassy. The only other time prior to that when I had assumed the position of CDA was in Bonn, where I served in this capacity for short periods of time whenever the Ambassador went on leave or was out of the host country on official business.

Second, as CDA a.i., I had more access to high-level events (one of which was attending a Kremlin event at which President Yeltsin was the Guest-of-Honour), and in the process, helped me to widen my network of contacts. Indeed, at an event meant for Ambassadors, I made the acquaintance of the assistant to a leading member of the State Duma (Parliament), the late Stanislav Govorukhin, one of the Soviet Union's and post-Soviet Russia's leading filmmakers. In 2011–2012, he was the head of Vladimir Putin's campaign office in his successful presidential re-election bid. Thanks to him, I paid a call on Govorukhin to chat about developments in the country. (He enjoyed President Putin's respect; the President attended his funeral in 2018).

I would remain in contact with Govorukhin's assistant till my departure from Moscow in 2013. He and his wife became quite close to me and my family. We had the honour and pleasure to have been invited to his modest flat a number of times. His insights into the country's developments proved invaluable to me.

Third, the position caused me to speed-up the process of getting to know my host country better, in preparation for the arrival of the new Ambassador.

By relating the above-mentioned difficulties I faced, I do not want to give the impression that life as a diplomat in those early days of post-Soviet Russia was totally miserable and daunting. Far from it. One must take matters in their stride.

On a professional level, I did not have much of a problem operating in Moscow and making good friends out of a number of my contacts.

First, I spoke enough Russian to break the ice. Second, Russians are, by nature, very friendly and open once one gets to know them well. Finally, my extrovert nature made a huge difference at events and receptions when one had to make the first move to get to know people. While I always made it a point to chat with my fellow ASEAN diplomats at a reception or event, I also made sure that I set aside some time to get to know as many Russians as possible. After all, my job was to make as many local contacts as possible.

Making the acquaintance (which might lead to friendship) of a cross-section of different people also required that one had to be tolerant of their personal habits with respect to tobacco and alcohol consumption. In those days, it was not uncommon to meet quite of number of people who partook of tobacco and of course, alcohol. In that respect, I did not have any issue with smoking and drinking, mainly red wine. Not being an inveterate smoker, I had quit smoking in 1984 after 16 years, only to resume it in 1994 in Moscow. At the time, smoking and drinking were *en vogue* with many people in Moscow. Not all my contacts, however, were smokers or drinkers.

Today, with the advent of a younger and more health-conscious generation, these habits are gradually losing their attraction. Alcohol consumption indeed has decreased with increased prosperity and stability as well as growing interest in sports and exercise. A *Reuters* report dated 1 October 2019 cited a World Health Organisation (WHO) report (issued on that day) that stated that alcohol consumption in Russia had fallen 43% from 2003 to 2016. President Putin himself had set and still sets an example by his well-publicised engagement in sports like skiing and judo, and his well-known aversion to alcohol and tobacco.

Moscow's Distractions

In the 1990s, indulging in sports and exercise were not on the list of priorities of the Russian who was more concerned about making a decent living. Indeed, between 1994 and 1997, I must have been one of the few foreigners who during summer, would cycle almost every weekend on Moscow's many side-streets, wide boulevards, and large parks, almost always accompanied by stares from the pedestrians many of whom I assumed, had not often caught sight of such a colourful mountain bike as mine (it was a striking yellow), let alone owned one! Ditto for my next two tours of duty — I got to know Moscow's streets better on my bike than sitting in a car, which would be invariably trapped in its many traffic jams.

However, unlike in the 1990s, by the 2000s, I was pleasantly surprised to observe that many Russians, young and old, would be on their bikes in parks and on the smaller streets. Joggers too as well as roller-skaters were always to be spotted in Moscow's large parks.

On a personal level, the long and cold winter did not bother me and my family members in the least since we have been keen cross-country skiers since the 1980s. Thanks to my wife who taught me (when we were in Bonn) and later, my daughter, how to cross-country and downhill ski, winter represented a magical period of time. The long winter must have been unbearable and unpleasant to my fellow Southeast Asians. Indeed, quite a number of my colleagues in the ASEAN embassies made that plain to me. Not surprisingly, they did not appear keen on cross-country skiing at all; however, I found in Geoff Ward, the NZ Ambassador, a ski partner.

My family and I always looked forward to spending our winter weekends in Moscow's many large snow-filled parks, indulging in miles and miles of cross-country skiing and occasionally, embarking on long walks in the forested winter wonderland or on the frozen and ice-bound rivers. We would frequent parks in Serebryany Bor, Yasenovo, and occasionally Filevsky Park. Muscovites too were avid cross-country skiers but were not that good at downhill skiing, in my opinion. There were a few hills for downhill skiing in the large city and its environs but obviously, they were not the right places to perfect one's downhill ski skills. Nevertheless, my wife, my daughter, and I had the pleasure of engaging in downhill skiing on these little hills.

There was a larger and higher hill outside Moscow for downhill skiing. My family skied a few times there, and a couple of times with Sergei Markov, a political observer who became a good friend. He himself was new to the sport.

As the decade progressed, I also noticed that there were many more cross-country skiers in my favourite haunts, enjoying the delights of Moscow's long and cold winters. What struck me was not only the fact that there were many more skiers, but that they were better dressed and no longer used wooden skis but modern, Western-made skis. (In the 1990s, the not-so-many skiers I encountered were more often than not dressed in drab ski jackets and plodded on the snow on wooden skis.)

If we were bored with Moscow's parks, we would fly to Finland's Arctic Circle to indulge in both cross-country and downhill skiing. When we first skied in Yllas, in Lapland, the far north of Finland, in 1996, we did not encounter any Russian on the slopes during our two weeks there, or in the queue for the ski-lift, not to mention in the restaurants and shops in the ski resort. However, just a few years later, we would encounter many all over the place, and I assumed, this was a tangible sign of Russia's growing prosperity and the increasing popularity of trips abroad. During our last ski trip to Yllas in 2012, the whole resort appeared to have been dominated by the presence of Russian skiers!

An encounter one cold winter day during a ski holiday in Finland remains in my consciousness. In the winter of 2003/2004, while cross-country skiing alone or so I had thought, at minus 35 degrees Celsius, I came across a Finn who claimed to be working in Singapore and a lone Russian on the ski trail, at different times on that day. Skiers would normally greet each other on the trail. On that day, my whole face was protected by a ski-mask against the cold — ditto for these other two skiers with whom I exchanged greetings at different points on the ski trail. While I love the frost, skiing at minus 35 degrees Celsius was not a walk in the park. For the Finn and the Russian however, it was child's play. Two members of two countries whose harsh climate made them hardy people. Whoever chooses to fight Russia in any conventional war should not forget the fate which befell Napoleon and Hitler, was my main thought as I watched the Russian ski away from me, after our short chat on the ski trail. Ditto for the Finn. I also recalled the just-as-hardy Finns who fought the numerically larger Soviet army in the winter war of 1939–1940.

Moscow was and remains a cultural paradise. I would say its cultural life was and still is one of the best in Europe and in the world. My wife, who loves the theatre, opera, as well as ballet, would visit them as often as possible on her own or with her newfound friends and acquaintances, Russians and foreigners. I was of course not afforded this luxury for I had to discharge my responsibilities. She and my Russian and foreign contacts introduced me into the world of Russian culture by way of invitations (or suggestions) to attend this or that concert, opera or play. My wife and I would also attend a concert, play or opera on our own.

I had never really believed I would enjoy the magnificent performances of the Bolshoi or any other theatre of culture for that matter. But enjoy them as well as visits to the many great museums I certainly did.

My favourite museum is that devoted to the Great Patriotic War (GPW) as World War II (WW II) is known in Russia and the former Soviet Republics. Situated in Victory Park, it is really impressive for the attention its exhibits pay to portraying the Russian/Soviet role in history's most disastrous conflict. I encouraged all my visitors to Moscow to visit this museum, and most did so. I must have walked its massive halls no less than 15 times during my long stay in Moscow and was never bored. This museum covered all aspects of that struggle in its magnificent exhibits and photos.

Children too had very good distractions in the circuses, and animal shows (like the Cats' Theatre) and dolphin park as well as the zoo. There were two main circuses — the one had the usual animal and clown performances while the other featured gymnastics and acrobatic acts. My wife and I have never been particularly keen spectators of any animal circus but our daughter, like most children, loved it. I preferred going to the gymnastic and acrobatic circus, not least because of the superb performances of its acrobats and gymnasts. Needless to say, both circuses were very popular with Muscovites and foreigners. I might add that tickets were very low-priced, when compared to what one might have to pay in the West for the same level of entertainment. I encouraged most of my visitors to Moscow to attend the circuses, and they were never disappointed.

Moscow also had much to offer in terms of nightlife. The end of the Soviet period had let loose many inhibitions. One could spy many a rakish character in the night clubs and bars as well as cafes. Moscow in the 1990s, in the words of Singaporean Edwin Tham, a long-standing resident of the city, "was pretty decadent". Tham accurately described the nightclubs as "wild, since the Russians really enjoy partying and are pretty uninhibited". Today, in Tham's view, "the nightlife is still good, although not quite as decadent". I surmised that the prudish norms of the Soviet era had given way to the unfettered hedonism prevalent in the nightlife scene.

In the early to mid-1990s (and well into the early 2000s, even when many more restaurants, nightspots, bars, cafes, etc., came onto the scene), for most expats, two nightspots were popular. The first was incongruously named "The Hungry Duck" (THD). It was owned and managed by a Westerner with whom, like most expatriates, I was remotely acquainted. A watering-hole, one would and did meet Western self-employed businessmen, representatives of almost every Western company, the media, diplomats, *et al.* It was seen as "wild" for women could and did dance and strut their stuff on the bar, sometimes in quite skimpy clothes, to the obvious amusement and delight of the predominantly male crowd. Russians were also regular patrons. There, one would not have been surprised to encounter patrons engaging in Rabelaisian behaviour, now and then. But I myself had never witnessed any saturnalian-like behaviour there. It was closed in 1999, reportedly due to complaints by members of the State Duma.

The other nightclub, "Night Flight" (NF) was both a restaurant (one of the best in Moscow in the 1990s) and a bar/disco, run by Swedes. Elegantly-dressed ladies-of-the-night made up the dominant female guests; occasionally, decent women would pop into the club with their boyfriends or husbands. Unlike the THD, NF's clientele were expected to be members of the "genteel" and "educated" crowd, and hence to comport themselves accordingly.

In NF sometime in 1997, over some beers, I made the acquaintance of a Western gentleman who would, years later, work in a Russian television network. He had then only just arrived in Moscow from Eastern Europe where according to him, he had worked in the financial sector. On another occasion, I caught sight of a correspondent of one of the major Western cable news networks in the nightclub. He obviously could not really have expected to remain *incognito* in an establishment whose regular clientele must have assuredly been regular viewers of his network. Yet when I tried to start a casual conversation with him, by politely suggesting, *sotto voce*, he closely resembled this well-known correspondent, he beat a hasty retreat!

Both establishments had "face-control", which essentially meant their bouncers could decide whom to admit and whom to deny entry. THD's policy was not as strict as NF's. Unfortunately, many Russians were not admitted into NF in its early days, to their understandable chagrin. I was given to understand that the Russians were seen as impecunious, unlike expatriates and foreigners. Given the dire state of the economy in the 1990s, that assumption was not entirely baseless.

However, well-to-do Russians had their own exclusive clubs and restaurants to which no outsider, let alone a foreigner, could gain access, unless he or she had an invitation. Besides, these unusually high-priced establishments would probably not have attracted foreigners in any case. Unlike foreigners, wealthy Russians then did not bat an eye about paying more than the norm. I assumed then that when one comes into big money too fast after being deprived for generations in an inefficient command economy, one's marginal propensity to consume would not be dictated by considerations like high prices. Moreover, the "deficit economy" of the Soviet period had led to a high pent-up demand for goods and services; high prices did not deter conspicuous consumption in Russia at the time. In short, it was easy come, easy go. I would say most, if not all the wealthy Russians in the early to mid-1990s became very rich much faster than many Singaporeans or, for that matter, many Europeans, Japanese, or Americans.

In the years that followed, Moscow would see many more such bars and restaurants in its nightlife scene. And Russians, not only the rich ones, were finally allowed to partake in enjoying the nightlife in their own city and country.

First Out-of-town Work Visits

Our relations with Russia during my first assignment were insubstantial for three reasons. First, Singapore was focused on strengthening its links with its region and China. Second, Russia itself was feeling its way in its relationship with Southeast Asia. Finally, Russia was too preoccupied with domestic issues, developments in its "Near Abroad" (the term used then to describe the former Soviet Republics), and above all, its relations with the West. Nevertheless, we sought to broaden our commercial and economic links which would logically provide the basis of any sustained relationship.

To that end, a Singapore trade mission to St. Petersburg, Vladivostok, Khabarovsk, and Yuzhno-Sakhalinsk in autumn of 1994 was organised. I joined the delegation at Ambassador Kausikan's instructions. I was not to regret it; apart from the obvious need to cultivate contacts in other parts of the huge country, the trip also gave me a lesson in the dos and don'ts of socialising with Russians which I shall never forget.

Allow me to recount this lesson. During the delegation's visit to Vladivostok, the usual evening reception was held during the visit.

Hosted by the Russian side, it was a generous spread of food and drinks, and most reflective of generous Russian hospitality. Since I was the only Singaporean diplomat in the delegation, I was called upon to make toasts and respond to the toasts of our Russian host; he stressed that as I "represented" the delegation members, I had to drink on their "behalf" as well. Not wanting to offend our host but also because at 39, I naively believed I was still young enough to keep up with our host's many toasts, I did not hesitate to down at least six or seven small glasses of vodka, perhaps a glass or two of brandy, all within less than half an hour and not on a full stomach to boot!

I subsequently woke up in my hotel room and rang Ambassador Kausikan to share my horrid experience, to which he remarked that I must have been drunk for my speech was a wee bit slurred! He was right. I subsequently learnt from my fellow delegation members that I had passed out after all those toasts and they had to help me onto the bus which brought us back to our hotel. Since then, I have never sought to "compete" drinking with a Russian. I obviously forgot this "lesson" for some three years later, during a farewell dinner party in my flat, at which some of my closest Russian friends were present, not wanting to be outdone, I drank as much as my Russian guests and paid the price.

No sooner had the last guest, the astute political scientist and observer, Sergei Markov shut the front door behind him at around two in the morning, than I fell onto the floor, to my wife's obvious dismay! Sergei, who would go on to work with the Putin administration in one capacity or another, when told a few weeks later by me about my effort to become the cynosure of the party, laughed it off, adding that foreigners should never underestimate the Russian capacity for drinks. Years later, Sergei himself would no longer partake of alcohol as he had in the 1990s. In that regard, he, like many of his countrymen, would take to sports and exercise with a vigour and passion that one would not have believed had one been told of it in the difficult decade of the 1990s in Russia.

What also struck me about this trip was the immense size of the country and its bountiful natural resources. The flight from Moscow to Vladivostok, our first stop, took almost nine hours, if my memory serves me right. To know that Russia is the largest country in the world by looking at a map is one thing; to experience its vastness on a long flight is another. Vladivostok at the time was a dirty and undeveloped city with an overly expensive hotel! I was not impressed by it at all, and its drab buildings only added to my negative feelings about it. However, when I revisited the city just before it became the host of the Asia-Pacific Economic Cooperation (APEC) Summit of 2012, it was a very different and much better place; it looked and felt like any modern city.

Russia's natural resources wealth does not lie only in the ground in the form of oil, gas, metals, etc., but also in its internal waterways and in its water sources. In its many waterways like rivers, one finds abundant supplies of fish. During a *shashlik* (skewered meat) barbeque organised by our hosts by a river not far from Yuzhno-Sakhalinsk,[2] I came under the immediate impression that the river was in spate. It was not; upon closer inspection, I was astonished to see in its fast-flowing waters thousands, perhaps millions of fish — salmon. I was informed by a member of our host's group that its dark "colour" emanated from the fish massed in the river!

Unfortunately, like most cities in Russia, I could not help but notice the sorry state of many buildings there, including and especially the massive high-rise blocks of residential flats, a common feature of Russia, many having been built during the Soviet era. This scene repeated itself in Vladivostok and Khabarovsk.

Like the three other cities in the Russian Far East, quite a few buildings in St. Petersburg required massive renovation. Upon taking a stroll one late afternoon on one of its main boulevards, one could not but notice the fine facades of many majestic buildings. However, were one to enter them or proceed to their rear, one would encounter another reality, indeed a stark reality. Invariably, one would see that the façade and its background surroundings were as different as day-and-night — the one might be grand and even clean, the other decrepit and dirty. Needless to say, I was really shocked to have come across such

---

[2] Yuzhno-Sakhalinsk is the capital of Sakhalin Oblast, the administrative term for a federal subject of Russia.

contradictions, but soon realised that the situation represented what one might describe as a Potemkin village. However, I concluded that the country had other more pressing problems to worry about and deal with, and little or no energy, let alone resources, to devote to the upkeep of its myriad of public buildings.

In any event, our trade relations grew on the strength of increased Russian demand for foreign goods and services.

Singapore's Trade Development Board (TDB) subsequently opened an office in the Embassy to promote bilateral trade — I worked with the TDB to develop contacts and links with nascent Russian business organisations and Russian officialdom. A visible sign of Singapore's growing trade relationship was evident in the growing, yet small presence of resident Singaporeans who represented a number of companies, most of which were engaged in trading.

I worked with Mr. Rajinder Sethi, the head of Agio, a trading company incorporated in Singapore, to establish an informal Singapore business club, an initiative begun by my predecessor but completed by me and Mr. Sethi. The club's representatives would meet as often as they could, most of the time on Agio's premises, to discuss issues of common concern like the impact of ever-changing and contradictory customs regulations on their businesses.

Despite Sethi's hard work and commitment in terms of time and energy as well as ideas, the club did not exist long, due to lowered levels of interest on the part of its members and changes in its membership composition thanks to staff rotation to and from Singapore. Sethi was subsequently appointed Singapore's Honorary Business Representative, in recognition of his well-deserved and long-standing efforts to boost our economic links with Russia. His long residency as well as wide network of contacts and experience of running a business in Moscow, with offices in other parts of the country, were indispensable to our efforts to develop our trade links with Russia.

Alongside our interest in increasing our trade links, we also sought to establish and promote links with Russian scientific bodies and Russian scientists and scholars. In the immediate few years after the Soviet collapse, scientists and scholars were not spared the negative impact of the tremendous changes on the country's socio-economic and political system, and most found themselves in dire financial straits. Hence, they were more than willing to work with foreign scientific institutions. We naturally responded to this trend and organised visits to scientific bodies in Moscow, St. Petersburg, and Novosibirsk, in Siberia.

I vividly remember a visit to Akademgorodok, the scientific centre of Siberia, situated not far from Novosibirsk, in the summer of 1996 as a member of a Singapore delegation; it was and remains the centre of scientific activity in that huge region. Our host was the Siberian Academy of Science, which is a branch of the Russian Academy of Sciences. We were very well-treated by our host and visited a number of scientific institutes. I could not help but notice the poor quality of the equipment used in the institutes we visited. Ditto for the quality of their staff members' clothes and the physical state of their offices and buildings. They were apologetic about the state of their equipment, and candid about their meagre salaries and research grants, and expressed the hope that our visit would lead to mutually beneficial cooperation.

Despite their obvious lack of funds, they organised a sumptuous dinner for the delegation, again a testimony to the generosity and hospitality of the Russian. I felt a tinge of sadness to have seen very talented people having to work and live under such trying and demanding circumstances. I was privileged to have learnt that Russia's wealth lay not only in the earth but more importantly in its talented but relatively-impoverished scientific manpower.

What I also remember from this visit to Novosibirsk was the huge mosquitos which found refuge in my hotel room! Thankfully, they are not malaria-carrying creatures found in the warm regions of the world, but with their wing-span, are as large as a small butterfly! I could not get much slumber, not only because the mosquitos did not allow me that luxury, but also because trying to sleep during the long days of a Siberian summer in my room (which did not have any heavy and dark drapes) was quite impossible. One did not have a choice though for our hotel, we were told, was one of the best in Novosibirsk. I could only imagine what it would have been like had we stayed in a cheap hotel.

Moreover, there was no regular stream of hot water; one had to literally wait to be told by the receptionist when it would come onstream.

This was also the case in Moscow and across the country; I was told that the water-pipes had to be repaired, maintained, or cleaned and that one could do that only in the summer obviously — the outcome being one could not take showers as often or whenever one chose and, on occasion, not at all for a day or two. As a student in MGU, there were at least three occasions during which I had to forego a shower as there was no hot water at all in the student hostel. I compensated for that by making use of the shower facilities in the Embassy during my regular visits there as it had its own water heater. I was thankful though that the Moscow summer was neither hot nor humid.

Another out-of-town visit is also fresh in my memory. Soon after I became CDA a.i., I was invited by the local authorities in Ivanovo to visit their city, about a six-hour drive from Moscow. One of the Embassy's staff members had roots in Ivanovo and helped arrange my visit. The importance the local authorities attached to my visit was made obvious by the appearance of local police escorts, on the outskirts of the city, to my complete surprise. Treated like a dignitary, I met high-level officials who organised a press conference and local TV coverage, also to my surprise. I could not of course, make any commitment to their questions about Singapore's interest in investing in the city and region's mainly textile industry or other sectors. The visit was well worth it from my standpoint, as it provided me with another opportunity to assess the state of this huge country's economy outside the relatively prosperous settings in Moscow. What I saw in Ivanovo was not encouraging, as I encountered quite an economically depressed city and region. I would be told that many of the country's regions found themselves in a similar situation.

Chapter 4

Issues of Professional Interest

Organised Crime

In the early to mid-1990s, there was literally a handful of Singaporean businessmen or representatives of Singaporean companies resident in Moscow.

Mr. A was one of the pioneers of Singaporean businessmen who took chances and risks to enter the very volatile and risky Russian market in the immediate pre- and post-Soviet era. He was, like most Singaporeans, engaged in trading.

The dearth of consumer goods, characteristic of the Soviet era, meant that pent-up demand in post-Soviet Russia rose on an unprecedented scale. Mr. A ran his own small company and like representatives of other Singaporean companies there, saw these opportunities early and set-up operations in Moscow and some other Russian cities. They had to undergo many trials and tribulations. Apart from having to deal with difficult and corrupt officials, one had to manage relations or have links with people who could deal with organised crime figures or anyone who claimed to have links with them. In short, one had to have a *krysha*.[1] I cannot say with certainty that all Singapore companies which operated in Moscow and other

---

[1] *Krysha* literally means roof; it basically means connections or links to someone who could protect one's business from the predations of rival organised crime groups. In later years, with the ebbing of the power of organised crime groups, they were said to have been replaced by corrupt law enforcement officials.

cities had a *krysha*. Mr. A however did not seek to hide that fact he had one.

Mr. A's office was headed by a Russian, Mr. F. He told me he could speak Dari and Farsi and claimed to have been a veteran of the Afghan war. He also claimed he had connections to the "security services". Mr. F was Mr. A's *krysha*. Mr. F's claim of who he was, had a ring of verisimilitude — he always exuded charm, was full of confidence and exhibited composure when dealing with people, traits which were foremost in a *krysha* (in contrast to the popular film version of a *krysha* which might portray him as a short-tempered, violent and aggressive individual).

Messrs. A and F would regale me with stories about members of other *kryshas* coming by their office to offer their "services"; they would leave when told that it already had its own *krysha*. Violence was always expected but thankfully had never taken place because of their polite but firm refusal of any "offer".

Mr. A was also a good source of information on the business environment in Moscow which I had been given to understand, was more or less similar to the situation across the country, with of course adaptations to the specific regional and local peculiarities. For instance, from him I learnt for the first time that one had to keep two or three sets of books, the "real" one for oneself and another for the tax authorities, and perhaps a third for the *krysha*. One could not have just one set of books as the nascent tax system was not only contradictory, but also predatory. One would go bankrupt sooner than later were one "honest". This refrain I would hear many a time till my departure in 2013, from those engaged in business, especially SMEs (small- and medium-sized enterprises).

Our regular meetings and consequent banter would also yield bits of information like the need to become and remain good "friends" with officials, in particular customs officials if one's business involved imports/exports. By that, Mr. A meant one had to bear gifts on a regular basis. He would hint, once in a while, that large sums of cash had to change hands as well. Mr. A left Russia in the 2000s, having made his money there.

Mr. D, a Singaporean who spent time in Moscow as well as in a city east of the Urals also became a close contact of mine. He provided me a wealth of information on the challenges of doing business in Russia. Apart from having to deal with corrupt officials, another major problem was collecting payments from customers and clients. Mr. D would stress that the opaque and contradictory regulations with respect to business operations of local and foreign entities, were making things difficult for many businesses and this had led to cash-flow issues. Mr. D also confirmed that it was not uncommon for many businesses, local and foreign, to keep two or more account books — one for the taxman and the other "real" book for one's bosses!

The pernicious effect of *krysha* extended beyond businesses; its targets could include any visible activity in the marketplace, even those which were not a going concern or did not have any direct commercial dealings.

A telling example was the experience of *Newsweek*. Its then bureau chief, Andrew Nagorski, a friend of mine whom I had met in Bonn a decade earlier, related to me the following incident. In the early 1990s, two armed and burly men literally forced his office car[2] off the road and threatened the driver with harm if he refused to lead them to the office. While there, as one of the men waved around a gun, both offered their "protection" and insisted on speaking to the "boss" (Nagorski was out of the office then, on an interview). They left after some time; however, upon returning to his office, Nagorski found his staff members pale-faced and worried. After hearing from them what had happened during his absence, Nagorski, in consultation with his head office in the US, called a press conference (with foreign and local journalists in attendance) and emphasised that *Newsweek* would not be blackmailed into paying any protection money. This action worked, for thereafter nothing more was heard from the thugs.

---

[2] In the 1990s and up to the early 2000s as far as I can recall, the vehicles of all foreign entities like news bureaus, businesses, etc., had distinctive licence plate numbers which distinguished them from those of the locals.

Let me illustrate another example of organised crime's effect on a business with which I and Ambassador Kausikan were personally familiar. One of the top bars and restaurants at that time was situated in a large building on Novi Arbat, one of Moscow's premier thoroughfares. It was owned by a German, we were told. We became acquainted with one of the bar's staff members. One evening, as soon as we set foot into the bar, this staff member told us, *sotto voce*, that his German boss had abruptly left the country after being bought off by a local businessman. The local businessman, a serious and threatening-looking chap, had apparently appeared with a large suitcase (presumably stuffed with cash) and passed it to the German. It amounted to all intents and purposes, to an offer the German apparently could not refuse, *a la* "The Godfather." Neither I nor Ambassador Kausikan doubted the word of this staff member that the German must have been threatened with physical violence were he to reject the "offer". The "takeover" of a business, local or foreign, involving threats of this nature was common in the 1990s and would assume a somewhat different form in the 2000s.

One could spot rather obvious "mafia-like characters" in the casinos on Novi Arbat, the most well-known of them being incongruously named "Cherry Casino"! Ambassador Bilahari and I would drop by, once in a while just to observe these colourful personalities. On one occasion, I recall watching in disbelief how one of them passed a US$100 tip to a waiter; these chaps indulged in what in Russian is termed "*brosayet dengi na veter*" (literally to throw money to the wind viz. spending money like there's no tomorrow). They would almost always be accompanied by tall, invariably blonde, outstanding-looking molls — I would think to myself that these larger-than-life characters closely resembled what I had up-to-then seen only on the cinema screen!

Quite a number of these colourful characters were not ethnic Russian but hailed from the Caucasus, judging by their physical appearance and rather swarthy complexion. That is not to say there were no ethnic Russians in this milieu but I must admit, I would see more non-Russians in that casino on every occasion I stepped into it.

A few years later, I would get to know a Caucasian businessman who was a regular patron of another large casino in Moscow where one would see many non-Russians too. He invited me on two occasions to join him there. I did not stay long for I am not a gambler, but I observed the same behaviour among its many patrons with their towering *inamoratas* holding onto their arms for dear life. It was very entertaining to observe all of them interacting with one another, cheek-by-jowl, in the casino.

After less than a year in Moscow, it became patently obvious to me that *radix omnium malorum est cupiditas* must have become one of the cardinal forces behind the actions and motivations of most, if not all "businessmen" in the country. One had to be strongly motivated if one was prepared to risk life and limb to run, let alone promote and maintain one's business under the very trying and dangerous circumstances then. The very weak or practical absence of the rule of law provided untold opportunities for the strong-hearted to exploit. Organised crime had become a festering sore on the body politic of Russia and businessmen were often the first victims of the weak rule of law or its practical absence. Some examples suffice to make my point.

Vladislav Listyev, Ivan Kivelidi, and Paul Tatum come to mind in this regard for their murders were highly publicised in the mid-1990s. The first was a television journalist, the second a banker, and the third an American hotelier.

Listyev was a popular journalist and television anchor in Russia in the early 1990s. His murder in March 1995 was believed to have been linked to his decision to support a ban on advertising on a state-controlled television channel that he had been appointed to run, according to an article dated 2 March 1995 in the *New York Times*. The article went on to quote Aleksandr Yakovlev, chairman of the board of the channel, as telling the *Itar-Tass* news agency that he himself had begun receiving telephone threats after the decision to stop showing advertisements. Yakovlev said that Russian public television had changed its methods of selling advertisements, creating an in-house agency that multiplied the company's advertising revenues seven times, from US$1.1 million a month to US$7.8 million. "The difference must have ended up in the pockets of some moguls," Yakovlev was quoted as saying.

Listyev's killing would be one in a series of high-level murders which gave the impression that Russia was becoming a lawless state or one controlled by organised crime groups.

A few months later, in August 1995, banker Ivan Kivelidi was poisoned in an apparent contract killing. His funeral was attended by the Prime Minister, Viktor Chernomyrdin, and members of the country's business and political elite. An article dated 8 August 1995 in *The Independent* quoted Vladimir Shcherbakov, the deputy head of the Russian Business Round Table,[3] as saying that there had been 90 attacks on businessmen in the previous year, in which 46 were killed. Nine of the Round Table's own senior members were among the murder victims. "Not one conviction has been made," he said.

Kivelidi had been the most prominent businessman to have been killed in Russia in 1995. He led both Rosbiznesbank, a leading bank, and the Russian Business Round Table. The 5 July 2006 edition of the *Moscow Times* reported that Vladimir Khutsishvili, a business partner of Kivelidi, had been arrested for his murder; according to Wikileaks, he was subsequently convicted for the killing.

Unlike the other two individuals, Paul Tatum was an American who founded the Americom Business Centre, and became part-owner of the Radisson Slavyanskaya Hotel, a luxury hotel in Moscow. In 1995, a dispute over control of the hotel became public knowledge and one of the items of gossip and chit-chat at dinner parties and other events where diplomats and businessmen as well as Russian officials would meet. Ambassador Kausikan himself said, half in jest, that Tatum was playing with fire by going public with his dispute and feared that he might pay a high price for it; his observations proved prescient for in November 1996, Tatum was gunned down in a metro station close to the disputed hotel. Speculation and allegations of high-level involvement

---

[3] The Russian Business Round Table, which represented the 200 largest businesses in Russia, was said to have been the country's most influential business organisation, and had close ties to Chernomyrdin.

in his murder case were bandied about but no proof was ever forthcoming. Tatum's murder only added to Russia's negative image in the West.

Targeted assassinations of businessmen were not confined to wealthy Russians or Westerners. A Singaporean businessman of Indian origin was also a victim. In November 2002, Sudhir Gupta escaped an assassination attempt in Moscow, which took the life of his driver, according to a report in the *Straits Times* dated 19 November 2002.

I first met Gupta with Ambassador Kausikan in the summer of 1994 — he was then in the food business but later went into the production and distribution of tyres. He was one of the pioneers of Singaporeans who saw the potential of the Russian market and took great risks to explore and exploit the "market" in the early post-Soviet era.

Post-Soviet Russia appeared to domestic and foreign observers to have fallen into chaos with a weakening, if not great loss of governmental authority at the local, regional, and federal level. High-level murders of top businessmen and the state's seeming inability to bring the culprits to justice, only served to confirm and entrench already widespread views among sections of the international media and even a number of Russian journalists that Russia had become a "mafia-state".

I had the dubious privilege of becoming an observer to these unfortunate developments in post-Soviet Russia and sought to ascertain whether there was any grain of truth to this growing perception. Being a politically-charged, and sensitive subject, it was not a simple matter to pinpoint who authoritative sources were and even if one could do that, one could not assume they would be willing to chat about the issue with a foreigner, let alone a diplomat. Nevertheless, I managed to secure some sources over the few months as I worked on the matter. Apart from live sources, I also read widely quite a few Western and Russian media reports on this issue.

The fact that the West then (and now) had a keen interest in developments in Russia meant that Western assessments of this sensitive and controversial issue had to be sought. Officials dealing with this matter in key Western embassies were therefore consulted.

I was most fortunate in being able to meet a high-level official in the Interior Ministry's department dealing with organised crime. He dismissed suggestions that organised crime groups controlled the state or that their influence was on the rise. The state's determination to fight organised crime groups was seen in its measures against them. Arrests had been made of organised crime figures and actions had been undertaken against their illegal activities. This would not have been possible if they had been in control of the state or its organs, he maintained.

To me, what he had said was not as significant as the fact that he had agreed to meet me at all and devote some time to discussing this very delicate subject. This showed that Russian officialdom must have been concerned about the country's image abroad as a "mafia state" and was keen on correcting that image, even with a small country like Singapore. (This official in subsequent years assumed a very high-level position in the government and other organs of power).

The rest of my sources (like journalists and businessmen) came to more-or-less the same conclusion, viz. that while organised crime was powerful, it did not run the state as such. Some placed more emphasis on the extent of organised crime's power in the state while others believed its influence over and in the state was exaggerated and over-estimated.

I was and remain chary of arguing that Russia then was in the hands organised crime groups. My own impression was that the Russian state faced a real challenge to its authority by organised crime groups but no one could argue without any doubt, backed by indisputable evidence, that they were in actual control of the state and directed its courses of action. Indeed, with the rise of President Putin to power, organised crime's hold on society was seen to have been broken. President Putin was not a leader who would brook the continued existence of powerful and independent non-state groups like organised crime within the strong state he had sought to establish.

Quite a few observers will not share my standpoint; perhaps, they had or have access to very authoritative sources who have incontrovertible evidence that organised crime groups controlled the Russian state at that time. I can only reflect here my own conclusions.

I must admit nevertheless, there were few times during my first assignment, between 1994 and 1997, that I was (unduly) concerned about the possibility of organised crime groups turning up at the Embassy to offer their "*krysha*" services. What would or could we do should they turn up? Ring the police for help? Policemen then were seen as weak, corrupt, poorly-paid, and said to have been in the pockets of organised crime groups. I had occasion to speak a few times to the Embassy's militiamen (police) who were on duty round-the-clock, all year round, about my concerns. They would reply, in jest, that "bandits" (the term widely used for organised crime groups) were unlikely to turn up at the Embassy as they knew what to expect from them! (What they exactly meant by that, I neither asked nor saw the need to.) My concerns proved to be totally unfounded. Diplomats were thankfully spared being offered this "service".

Corruption

Corruption appears and will thrive when a society finds itself under the cosh; Russia was then in such a situation, with a weak economy, political instability and generally ineffective institutions. Many figures were bandied about in the 1990s, in the early years of Putinite Russia and even today, about the high level of corruption in Russia. I do not see any sense in quoting any figure, for it can only be estimates. However, there was no doubt that corruption was and remains a real challenge to the Russian economy and the country's institutions.

While it did not directly affect my life, there were two incidents which brought this issue into sharp relief.

The first took place when an official claiming to represent the Moscow city authorities met me and suggested that I make known to Singapore companies the investment opportunities in the city, including in the then planned Moscow City, a huge commercial development. He hinted that I too could "benefit" from them, to my dismay! I politely told him it was part of my job to promote business/commercial links, and that there was no question of personal benefit to be derived from carrying out my responsibility. I never heard from this "official" again.

The second incident took place on a Moscow street one evening when a traffic policeman stopped my car and requested me to show him my ID, driver's licence, and car registration papers. After a mere glance at them, he remarked that my rear signal light was not in good working order (it was working perfectly!) and that a "fine" to the tune of US$20 was normally levied for such offences. I naturally disputed his claim and casually reminded him that I was a diplomat to which he calmly returned my documents and waved me on. During the course of my first tour, my second, and final tour of duty in Moscow, I would discuss the issue of corruption with many contacts, foreign and local, and learnt much from them as well, including their own experience with it.

Traffic policemen in Russia, including Moscow, on the whole were not considered paragons of virtue and it was commonly assumed they were all corrupt. However, that was not fully consonant with reality as shown by an unfortunate incident. My car was rammed by another (thankfully, the other party was in the wrong), while I was driving to the office one morning. Traffic policemen arrived after a few minutes (on many of Moscow's main arteries and broad avenues, a few traffic policemen would always be on duty, keeping a keen eye on motorists). They were polite and helpful to me, and there was no hint at all from them that a bribe was necessary to expedite the matter by doing a quick incident report in my favour. I suppose my diplomatic status helped but to be fair, the other party, a young Muscovite was not "shaken down" as far as I could tell. In short, one bad apple can spoil the whole barrel.

Fledgling Market Economy

Money, or rather the lack of it, was a perennial issue in early post-Soviet Russia. Journalists were not spared this fact of life. I recall having met a few Russian journalists who would propose visiting Singapore to write about us, provided the Singapore Government paid for their airfare and accommodation as well as a *per diem*. They would openly state that they or their dailies/journals did not have the resources for such an undertaking. Since our economic interest in Russia in the

1990s was rather limited, we obviously did not react to such offers. That would change as our relations with Russia gained momentum in the early and later years of this century.

Another incident comes to mind — one of them wrote an article for a Singapore daily which sent him a cheque as payment. He requested my help to "cash" it since that cheque could not be cashed in any Russian bank. I gladly obliged, of course (the Singapore daily reimbursed me subsequently). That journalist would subsequently go on to very great heights in his career.

At the time, I knew of the existence of only one ATM, to be found in the lobby of a luxury hotel! There must have been a few others but neither I nor any of my expatriate contacts knew of them. I found it exasperating because I could not exercise a simple task like getting cash from any other ATM but this one. I was quite certain that Muscovites and foreigners were incommoded by the lack of ATMs.

Lack of money was a problem that also afflicted the government. The loans-for-shares scandal in 1995 became an example of the depths to which the Russian state's financial woes had fallen. Facing fiscal deficits, a number of the country's valuable entities were privatised in what later was revealed to have been under dubious and questionable circumstances. Essentially, the government secured loans from Russia's then leading tycoons (the oligarchs); in return, the tycoons acquired a number of valuable industrial and energy assets on-the-cheap. I could have been one of the few non-Western diplomats who was alerted to this plan just before it was announced. For Singapore, however, such information was not critical, given our very limited politico-economic engagement of Russia and vice versa.

Nuclear Weapons

In the 1990s, one of the West's main concerns was whether some of Russia's nuclear weapons could fall into the hands of terrorists, or countries considered hostile. Its fear was grounded in the assumption that the weak Russian state could lose control of its nuclear arsenal. It was a topic of conversation among diplomats and journalists, among others. Fortunately, none of the nightmare scenarios came to pass. I did not pay much attention to the issue. Realistically speaking, only the Western powers had the power and resources to deal with this challenge.

Reaching Out

An important part of a diplomat's job is to reach out to his host country's young people, including and especially its students, who would become its future leaders. Thankfully, Sergei Markov invited me to address his students in MGU in 1996 (he then taught Political Science and International Relations). I did so in an informal manner, no slides, no prepared texts, but just an interactive discussion on what they felt were challenges in Russia's then ongoing development and transition into a market economy from the Soviet command system. They were all, without exception, talented, well-spoken, thoughtful, and in a word, intelligent individuals who had a relatively strong command of the English language. Not surprisingly, most of them were quite critical of the sad state of their country's economy and socio-political health. I tried to comfort them by emphasising that for a large and complex country like Russia to achieve changes fast enough to satisfy its people's needs and wants, required more time than most had imagined. Since they knew little of Singapore, I gladly narrated as much as I could about our country.

Markov would become, with the start of the Putinite era, one of its leading academic and public faces in the West, presenting his country's standpoint on many issues in international events and conferences as well as in Russia. He would also become one of the most cited Russian experts in the Western media.

During my first, second, and final assignments in Moscow, Markov would provide me his insights into and assessments of domestic and international events, and they were invariably thought-provoking, sober and realistic, even if I myself did not always share his standpoint on any particular issue(s). His assessments and those of quite a few other Russians I became acquainted with, like a leading observer, Alexei Pushkov, were the *fons et origo* of my understanding of developments in Russia's domestic affairs and foreign policy.

Markov and his family became very good friends of mine and my family. I had the honour of being invited to his parents' wedding anniversary celebrations in Dubna, about 80 miles from Moscow; it has the status of a "town of science" (*naukograd*). Indeed, both his parents were trained engineers. It was a very close-knit party; my wife and I were the only foreign guests. I was given the honour of delivering an extempore speech in Russian which I only too happily obliged. From his parents and their elderly guests, I learnt how their lives had markedly changed. Under President Yeltsin, they complained of having lived with much difficulty while under Putin, for whom they had only admiration, their lives had become better. The Lucullan variety of food at the celebratory event highlighted again Russian hospitality at its best. Mind you, they were people of simple means.

He visited Singapore in 2006 to attend a Singapore MFA-sponsored event. Being a close friend, I personally attended to his visit here and hosted him as my guest in my flat after the official part of his visit was over. I showed him around Singapore, including exploring Pulau Ubin, a small island off the main island of Singapore and hiking in Bukit Timah Nature Reserve as well as having a feast of durians in Geylang.[4] He loved durians, unlike most white foreigners! All told, Markov came away impressed with Singapore's development, despite its small size.

Building Links with Russia

Being a novice in the ways of the market economy, Russia and especially Moscow in the mid- to late-1990s, was eager to learn as much from the outside world. The West naturally stood out as its model but Singapore's experience was also considered worthwhile learning. Moscow city authorities therefore requested and we, in return, organised a series of study visits to Singapore for them to tap our experience in urban and city planning and other aspects of socio-economic development.

These study visits would stretch from the 1990s till the 2000s, from the then administration of the powerful Mayor of Moscow, the late

---

[4] Geylang is a residential area in Singapore; durian is a popular fruit in Southeast Asia and is known for its pungent smell.

Yuri Luzhkov to his equally-powerful successor, Sergei Sobyanin. (Sobyanin is said to be close to Putin). I could not help but to be proud to have been part of this process. I felt that for Moscow, the capital of the world's largest country with a long and world-historical role, to have sought to learn from the developmental experience of a small and young city-state, was surely more than a compliment to us. My role in the whole process, however, was modest, being confined to making the necessary logistical and other related matters.

Russia's cultural talents and achievements are world-renowned. Our desire to build links with the country was not confined to the economic and political spheres of common interest. In that regard, in 1996, I helped arrange the visit of Russia's famed Alexandrov Ensemble (sometimes referred to as the Red Army Choir) to Singapore, working with our Ministry of Culture. Unfortunately, like most, if not all state-run and state-funded organisations at that difficult time in post-Soviet Russia, the Ensemble could not fully finance its trip to Singapore and hence, our side had to extend its help in that regard. It was money well-spent. I do not doubt that the Ensemble's performance in Singapore must have been the toast of the town. I attended a few of their musical and singing concerts prior to and after their visit to Singapore and was captivated by their performances, as were all the other members of the audience. I read with sadness that many members of the Ensemble lost their lives in a tragic plane crash in December 2016.

In the 1990s, post-Soviet Russia was no longer the Soviet Union, which had preached and supported world revolution. It no longer posed an ideological, political, or military threat to many states, including Singapore, not only because it had forsaken Communism but also due to the fact that its economy was in tatters. However, despite its many challenges and problems, the country's defence and military-related industries still produced top-quality weapons. Even so, state subsidies to the sector had been vastly reduced and revenues had declined, due to a shrunken military within Russia itself and falling demand in the former Soviet Republics, as well as former Soviet bloc or pro-Soviet states which themselves were going through trying economic times. Hence, exports for cold, hard cash, to countries outside the erstwhile Soviet Republics, former Soviet bloc or pro-Soviet states, were one answer to this challenge.

Under those circumstances, we began to develop a defence relationship with post-Soviet Russia. Singapore's Defence Ministry issued a news release on 15 October 1997, announcing the acquisition of the IGLA, a SAM (surface-to-air missile) system, in what was to be its first from post-Soviet Russia. The purchase even received attention from the Russian media; the Kommersant Daily, a business newspaper reported on this event, according to the 22 October 1997 edition of the *Aerospace Daily and Defence Report*.

The whole process — exploratory talks, negotiations, conclusion — began shortly before I assumed my post and ended some time in 1997. I was personally involved in it. Apart from my job as First Secretary dealing with political and economic affairs, I was, for all practical purposes, the Military Attache (as well as Trade and Cultural Attache). Naturally, I had to work with our Defence Ministry on the purchase of this weapon. The Defence Ministry sent many of its technical and other experts to Moscow to meet officials of Rosvoorouzhenie, the Russian state weapons agency in charge of exports/imports; it, in turn, sent its officials to Singapore as well for the same purposes. The intervals between their visits were also spent on dealing with many details related to the IGLA's purchase, such as terms and conditions as well as technical details of the system, all of which I had to handle.

It was an experience I treasured. Although it was challenging in terms of dealing with technical and other details (our Defence Ministry naturally provided me with all the necessary guidance), it provided me a valuable lesson in dealing with Russian officialdom in the persons of Rosvoorouzhenie officials. I must also say, in retrospect, that dealing with Russian officialdom was not as difficult as I had initially imagined. However, that did not mean everything was plain sailing. One had to meet them quite a few times to iron out what one would have thought were routine issues but this perception obviously was not necessarily shared by them. There were nevertheless occasions when I could not help thinking they were dilly-dallying on this-or-that-issue because they did not have the answers to our questions. In any case, both we and they were determined to conclude the whole process as it was in our mutual interest to do so — in ours, as we could secure a good weapon and in theirs, as we could pay in cold, hard cash, unlike many other countries which purchased Russian weapons but had to secure a loan or pay for them in some form of barter.

Our desire to build-up our links with Russia and vice versa included establishing links with its intelligence officials. The first encounter for me took place when I accompanied Ambassador Kausikan in 1994 to a lunch in a high-end but empty restaurant on the Sadovaya Koltso (Garden Ring, one of the main thoroughfares of Moscow) with a high-ranking FSK officer (FSK, or Federal Counterintelligence Service). The FSK was the successor organisation to the KGB; the FSK was later renamed the FSB, or Federal Security Service.

Indeed, we were the only guests in the restaurant, to our surprise! Ambassador Kausikan and I subsequently came to the conclusion that the restaurant must have either been owned by the FSK (or a sympathiser) or it must have been reserved just for us. A year or so later, I met the same officer with Ambassador Mark Hong, Ambassador Kausikan's successor. During our two meetings with this officer, he enlightened us with an overall picture of the major political developments surrounding Russia's foreign relations.

Subsequently, I personally met lower-ranking FSB officers perhaps twice or thrice over lunch during my second and third/final assignments to Moscow, in response to their suggestion to meet over a getting-to-know-you meal. A colleague of mine was also present during those lunch meetings. They were liaison officers who had served in Chechnya and hence had field and combat experience which they did not seek to hide, in response to my questions. However, they were not garrulous when it came to speaking about their experience in Chechnya — I realised it must have been either traumatic or top secret or both. Being the professional and intelligent individuals as intelligence operatives are supposed to be, they did not chat much overall but left it to us to pose questions which were met with monosyllabic answers most of the time. And yet they had suggested we ought to "get to know one another"!

During my second and final tours of duty, the FSB Director would hold New Year receptions for members of the diplomatic community. I attended a few of them; in the process, I had the opportunity to exchange a few words with two of Russia's most powerful men. At the receptions in 2007 and 2008, FSB Director Nikolai Patrushev took time to chat with all those present; with me, our short chat in Russian revolved around Singapore's development which he found impressive. He also expressed the hope he would be able to visit Singapore someday, which he did — details are found in a subsequent chapter.

Patrushev's successor, Alexander Bortnikov, continued this tradition and hence, I also had the opportunity to meet him and to exchange a few words with him. Although my encounters with them were rather fleeting, these men who were and remain part of Putin's inner circle, came across as forceful and committed personalities.

A former Russian intelligence official with whom I was personally acquainted was Mr. Yuri Kobaladze, a charming, affable, articulate, and confident individual whose six-foot four-inch frame only accentuated these traits.

I first met him at a reception in late-1994; he was then in the employ of the press service of one of the Russian intelligence services and receptive to meeting journalists as well as diplomats. He later joined the media world, before going into the private sector.

From the time I first made his acquaintance till around 2011/2012, I would occasionally meet him over a meal and discuss the then politico-economic situation as well as Russian foreign policy. His assessments of developments were always sharp and straightforward, expressed with an air of confidence in fluent English — a fitting testimony to his training and career in the intelligence service, which was and remains a premier institution.

Overall, my first assignment represented a learning curve for me — getting to know the host country as much as one can. One cannot hope to become an expert on any country in three short years, especially one with a long and tortured history, a country that had been until a few years before, the Soviet Union, a superpower whose writ extended across the largest country in the world (Russia remains the largest country), and a country which had been going through rapid structural changes in its political, economic, social as well as moral fabric. Yet, three months of intensive Russian language training and three years of working as a diplomat in Moscow were more than sufficient for me to have formed indelible impressions of the country and its people.

Chapter 5

Russia Becomes Less of an Enigma

General Observations

Russia is a fascinating land. In the 1990s, and at least up to 2013 when I left the country for good, one could make a number of observations about it. They boiled down to the following.

In contrast to the Soviet era, freedom of speech became part-and-parcel of the new Russia. Russian media would not hesitate to take the government or its officials to task if they believed they deserved it or if a cock-up had been made. And there were many a cock-up in those days. Nevertheless, the average Russian (not however the liberal-minded) I would chat with about the notion of freedom of speech or democracy, would, without fail, say that he did not need it as much as a decent life. Could we eat democracy, freedom of speech, he would ask rhetorically and in a derogatory tone of voice. I could not but agree with them.

With President Putin's ascent to power, the media came to be seen as a tool of his policies. Relative to the Yeltsin era, the Putin epoch would see less strident criticisms of the *vlast* (powers-that-be) but to be fair, one cannot argue that criticisms of the system by the media were totally prohibited or suppressed. State television channels which I used to regularly watch during the Putin era did give some, even if limited air-time to criticisms of the system and issues like corruption and bureaucratic caprice. Moreover, *Radio Echo Moscow*, a well-known and consistent critic of the government, has been operating all these years, although its majority shareholder is Gazprom, the state-run gas company which is controlled by Alexei Miller. Miller and Putin are Leningraders (the former St. Petersburg). He worked with Putin in the Leningrad Mayor's office.

Overall though, my impression was that the Russian media under Putin sought and still seek to play a balanced role between protecting (and promoting) their notions of press freedom and maintaining stability in the country, which is a cherished Putinite goal. Given post-Soviet Russia's difficult transition, one can hardly blame President Putin for placing a premium on maintaining stability.

Second, absorbing Western culture wholesale might not have been Yeltsin's or Putin's cup of tea in the 1990s, but my sense was that Russians wished to become like Westerners, and above all, live like Westerners. Western, specifically American television and films, were widely available and popular. Russian television programmes also adopted and copied much from their Western counterparts, not only in terms of content but also presentation. An example would suffice: many popular television programmes were modelled after American or British reality shows. This trend was seen in programmes on general knowledge quizzes, domestic or personal issues like sex and love, married life and the like. I was given to understand that such television programmes did not feature much on Soviet television channels.

Third, unlike their parents' generation, post-Soviet Russians began to enjoy the right to travel abroad. The West then and even today, was and remains the most-desired and favourite destination of those who could afford it. The majority of globe-trotting Russians remain hitherto predisposed to visiting the West, even after years of Western sanctions and the rather strained relationship between Russia and the West. Nevertheless, like many people in large countries, many Russians were quite content with holidaying in their own big country which is not devoid of fantastically beautiful places. However, the only issue in the 1990s and early years of this century, was the level and quality, not to mention availability of "normal"[1] tourist facilities in their own country.

---

[1] By "normal", Russians meant and still regard Western standards as the yardstick to measure their progress *vis-à-vis* the "civilised" world, viz. the West.

Fortunately, there were quite a number of Russians who ventured into Southeast Asia and Singapore, thanks to the efforts of a few enterprising Singapore travel firms. In 1994/1995, the Embassy was kept relatively busy issuing tourist visas, and as the years went by, the number grew by leaps and bounds. Singapore and Bali were popular destinations. Transaero, the first private company approved for scheduled passenger services in the Soviet Union, began services to Singapore in 1996/1997, if my memory serves me right. Together with members of some of the ASEAN embassies, I was given the honour of addressing its head, Aleksander Pleshakov, and Singapore travel firms at an event, to mark this occasion. I did so, in a speech in Russian, prepared by a Russian staff member of the Embassy, to the delight of the Russian members of the audience, welcoming Transaero and Russian tourists to Singapore and our part of the world.

Finally, the free market, a notion long alien to Russians, became a more familiar concept, albeit its workings were far from that of a Western developed society. In the 1990s, the free market became associated with criminality and lawlessness, thanks to shock therapy's disastrous consequences. Nevertheless, the concept of private property slowly, but surely began to take root in the 1990s, after seven decades of Communism. At the time, most people's experience with private property was linked with their flats which were privatised during the Gorbachev era. I detected a general suspicion and envy among the common folk about private property when it was linked with those of the nouveau riche or new rich (the new Russian or Novi Russki became a term associated with envy). The man-in-the-street could not fathom how a Novi Russki could acquire so much wealth in such a short period of time. Hence, the terms *zhulik* (swindler, con-man) and *vor* (thief) were casually used to describe the Novi Russki. I myself thought then that these perceptions of extremely wealthy people were not entirely off-the-mark for it appeared that the privatisation programme had benefitted the few at the expense of the many.

Indeed, negative perceptions of the wealthy, in particular, the provenance of their wealth, remain entrenched, if a study by the Carnegie Moscow Centre (CMC), a well-known think-tank, and the Levada Centre, Russia's leading independent polling agency, is anything to go by. According to the study based on polls conducted across the country in August 2018, "two-thirds of respondents believe that it's impossible to become rich while remaining honest, while only a quarter believe otherwise".[2]

My other observations revolve around the human and social traits of the Muscovites/Russians. I use this term interchangeably; of course, Moscow is not Russia. Many Russians, Muscovites, and non-Muscovites, whom I met would consistently impress upon me this fact. However, since I lived and worked in Moscow and did not travel across the large country as often as I would have liked for leisure or on official business, my observations of the "Russian" must be mainly based on my experience in Moscow. I have already touched upon the tremendous generosity and hospitality of the Russians in an earlier chapter.

Left as a strong imprint on my consciousness is that while they are so polite and friendly on an individual level towards one another and foreigners, they can be rather morose and even ill-mannered, as a mass. I encountered this Jekyll-and-Hyde personality, if I may describe it thus, on the streets of Moscow and on its metro (Underground or Mass Transit system). I attributed this split personality to the harsh life that many Muscovites/Russians faced at that time — it is really a challenge to be cheerful and friendly to strangers, let alone foreigners, when one must think constantly about how one can fulfil one's daily basic needs. Russians in this sense, are not different from other people.

However, impoliteness appeared to be the norm, at least on the metro. No one ever thanked me whenever I held the exit door open on the way out of any metro station. At first, I was under the impression that those impolite passengers were the exception. However, in a bid to convince myself, I once held the exit door open for my fellow passengers for a full five minutes in three different metro stations and no one even bothered to exchange a glance at me, let alone express a word of thanks!

---

[2] See article dated 18 January 2019 and entitled "Pragmatic Paternalism: the Russian Public and Private Sector" by Andrei Kolesnikov and Denis Volkov published by the CMC.

I thought to myself that their daily lives must be so ridden with stress that they did not (justifiably) have any reason to show joy in public or express thanks to a stranger or foreigner, for that matter, who held the exit door open for them.

The longer I lived in Moscow, the better I got to know the mores and customs of its people and, in time, I came to the conclusion that their difficult and stressful lives as a result of their tortured history between 1917 and 1991 had made Muscovites in particular and Russians as a whole both distrustful and suspicious of strangers and foreigners. Why would one smile at, be nice or polite to a stranger who might be one's competitor for scarce goods and services or even a potential enemy?

Their difficult lives were also expressed on their faces and that was plain for all to see. The stresses and strains on their society and country which had a direct impact on their own lives, were the main factor accounting for their "unfriendly" look. To have a stranger smile at one in those days was indeed rare. I was not, unfortunately, afforded this luxury.

On the other hand, Russians exhibit a very distinct liking for children, especially very young children. They would bestow unsolicited attention to them in the form of sincerely-expressed sentiments with respect to their health and well-being. This my wife and I would experience quite a few times on the streets, in the metro or on the bus with respect to our then little child.

Russian Superstitions

Unlike Westerners and Germans whom I met while in Bonn and in Moscow itself, Russians appeared to be more inclined towards superstition. I first came to learn of this through my interactions with my Russian staff members and subsequently with my professional and other contacts; independent of their social status, they were not embarrassed to say that they subscribed to this or that superstition. A few illustrations are in order.

One of the most interesting superstitions relates to travel. Before one undertakes a long journey, one ought to sit down for a short while.

Not to do so would only invite danger during one's journey. This ritual was first made known to me by my first private driver. I hired him to drive my daughter to her school in my personal car; like most Russians then, that was one of his many jobs he had held to make ends meet. His wife worked in a hair salon but would earn extra on the side by catering to "private customers." He brought this superstition to my attention one day while we were chatting in my car. Subsequently, other Russians I came into contact with, confirmed this ritual, in response to my question. I must admit that since then, my wife and I would get cold feet about embarking on any journey without first having observed this ritual as well. In this sense, we have long become Russian!

Another noteworthy superstition has to do with drinking — one must never leave an empty bottle (wine, beer, water, etc.) on the table. To do so risks financial loss. On more than a few occasions, I would notice my Russian guests placing empty bottles on the floor or removing them from the table and a number of them rather matter-of-factly would explain the reasons for their action, in reply to my question.

Surely, this third example is worth mentioning. One must never shake another's hand on the threshold of a flat/house, viz. by the door. This was made clear to me by the first Russian guests in my flat when I greeted them by the door and in my ignorance, immediately stretched out my hand to them. I was told that evil spirits wandered in the threshold of the door to a house/flat!

A fourth example concerns gifts — one is never to present knives or sharp objects for they are considered an omen of enmity. This superstition was related to me one evening over dinner by some Russian acquaintances.

Whistling indoors could lead to financial ruin, which was first made clear to me by Mr. P one morning when he heard me whistling on my way to his class.

Finally, if one wishes to present someone with flowers, one's bouquet must have an odd number of flowers. Bouquets in even numbers are brought to cemeteries or funerals only.

Habits and Attitudes

Quite a few Russians love sunflower seeds. I would see many a man or woman on a street corner, or in a park, nibbling on sunflower seeds. But seeing them nibbling on sunflower feeds while on their haunches, was a sight I can never forget. I would see many Russians in many of the other cities I visited over the years, enjoying their sunflower seeds that way. My observation is not meant, in any way, to insult Russians — until I had come to Russia, I had never seen any white person doing that. I have not since then come across such a sight anywhere else in Europe, North America or New Zealand.

I must address a widespread stereotype of Russians in the 1990s and into the 2000s, viz. that they could be bibulous and even topers. True, there were many Russians who could consume more alcohol, especially vodka, than foreigners. Ambassador Kausikan can testify to this fact, too. He and I, on a few occasions, had Russian guests in his Residence who had quaffed more spirits than I or he could or would. On the other hand, there were quite a number of Russians I had become acquainted with who either were teetotallers or did not drink alcohol excessively. This is not to say that excessive alcohol consumption did not represent a real health hazard in post-Soviet Russia. This unfortunate state of affairs can be attributed to the stresses and strains of having to live under the difficult conditions that Russian society was undergoing then. I was also told that their harsh climate had made those who drink hardier than people from mild climates.

In any case, the Russian threshold for alcohol, especially their traditional spirit, vodka, must never be underestimated. I have already related my experience in Vladivostok with respect to this in September 1994.

The rather nonchalant attitude towards wastage, be it of energy or water, was also very apparent. The flats and buildings in the country would always be overheated so much so that one could easily perspire in them even in the dead of winter! Most flats and buildings in the 1990s which were not "Western-renovated", the Russian term for renovation according to Western standards, would not be armed with dials for turning the heat up or down, which was common in the FRG.

Hence, one could not adjust the room temperature at all. My family and I would be dressed in T-shirts and shorts at home while outside, the temperature might hover well below freezing point.

With respect to water use, I would observe many a Russian literally letting water run from their taps as if there were no tomorrow. When I posed the question as to why water was being allowed to run from the tap to one of the Embassy's maids, her answer was that "Russia is a vast country with lots of water and natural wealth"! Moreover, the level of heating and water utilities tariffs did not correspond with the level of their use. Up to my departure from Moscow in mid-2013, tariffs were not, in my view, reflective of real market conditions; any move to do raise them would meet with popular disapproval.

Russians are also not embarrassed to talk about their personal issues with a foreigner, if they trust and value one's friendship; of course, this observation can apply to all and sundry. However, my experience showed that while Westerners and Singaporeans might not be so inclined to go into details about their personal problems, Russians are less inhibited. That combined with their noted hospitality make the Russian a friend who would bare his soul without much of a second thought. Of course, he would do that with all good, close friends or acquaintances, only after sizing them up.

Russians would also tell me that connections were important in their daily lives. One could resolve issues *po blatu* (securing favours or resolving problems through one's connections). In a sense, it cannot be said to have been or to be unique to Russia; the difference, I suppose, is that in the 1990s, this practice was probably stronger in Russia than many countries in Western Europe, given the more than trying circumstances Russia had found itself in at the time. I assume it remains an established practice; as it is steeped in centuries of history and traditions, to expect it to be eliminated, root-and-branch, in the relatively short historical time since the Soviet collapse, is unrealistic.

My regular trips on the Moscow metro, buses, and trams gave me the opportunity to observe Russian behaviour on public transport and in public as a whole. Unlike commuters in Singapore or Western cities like London, New York, San Francisco, Berlin, or Paris where I had the opportunity to use public transport, including their trains, Russian commuters were relatively quiet. Very, very seldom would I hear loud and unabashed conversation, let alone screaming children, playing on the train or bus. I put it all down to the Russian desire not to attract attention. Perhaps, it was the outcome of having had to live for so long in a controlled society that the Soviet Union had been. What was really an earache was the noise generated by many of Moscow's old trains, which nevertheless, I reiterate, would arrive every minute or two or even less. Moreover, in an obvious sign of the high rate of education in the country, I would observe that nine out of 10 commuters would be reading either a book or newspaper, even while standing, cheek-by-jowl with many other passengers.

Political Culture

One could not fail to notice during the 1990s, the Russian tendency to succumb to authority even while complaining privately about its excesses. For instance, many Russians then did not hesitate to denounce the voucher privatisation programme as it was apparently riddled with corruption. This process took place between 1992 and 1994: eager to speed-up the break-up of the command economy, Yeltsin's government undertook a widescale privatisation programme to sell state assets to members of the Russian public. Vouchers were distributed equally among the population and could be exchanged for shares in the state enterprises to be privatised. However, since most people were either not well-informed about the nature of the programme or were very poor, enterprising individuals or even criminal elements who were better-prepared for and well-informed about these massive changes, could and did purchase the vouchers from the ill-informed or poor at low prices. Insiders too acquired vouchers at low prices. The majority of the people felt cheated, and justifiably so, it would appear. Not one Russian with whom I would chat about this issue, even well-off individuals, had anything positive to say about this matter.

However, there were no mass protests against this perversion of the restructuring of the command economy into a market economy. My assessment was that the Russian people having only a few years before experienced the Soviet collapse and in its train, monumental changes to their lives, yearned for order, discipline and stability. No one was in the mood to participate in large demonstrations against the *vlast* (powers-that-be). People were simply too tired, physically, emotionally and mentally and resigned to their *sudba* (fate). That noun was used liberally by many Russians I got to know to describe their acceptance of their (invariably miserable) situation and helplessness and in not seeing any sense in trying to change things for the better. Naturally, in the two decades since then, the rise of a younger generation with little or no memory of the 1990s, the emergence of a growing and increasingly vocal middle class, and the impact of the internet and social media on Russia, have led to a new situation in which open demonstrations against any perceived abuse of power are no longer unthinkable. However, in Yeltsinite Russia, the majority of the people had neither the strength nor inclination to challenge the power of the state and its perceived excesses.

Russia's tortured and violent history also explains to a large extent the fear that turning against Yeltsin would lead to a settling of scores amid intense violence. The notion of *lex talionis* was alive and well in Russia, judging by the experiences of Russia's distant past (associated with figures like Ivan the Terrible) and recent past (the excesses of the 1917 Bolshevik Revolution, Stalin's purges and collectivisation which led to the deaths of millions in the 1930s).

People would more often than not tell me that summer would bring an end to Yeltsin's government (I would hear that many times between 1994 and the end of the century, up to the early years of the Putin era; thereafter, this refrain almost disappeared from conversations). Russians would link the summer to a period when the *narod* (people) would have had enough and react against the *vlast*. Many felt the warmth of summer would inject energy into people to take to the streets. Some of my sources even speculated that since Mikhail Gorbachev, the last Soviet leader was ousted in August 1991, any revolt was likely to take place in summer as well! Any Russian *bunt* (uprising or revolt) would be violent and unforgiving of those in power.

One must not rush to judgement about the excessive violence that accompanied politico-economic and social changes in Russian history. Unlike Western Europe, Russia had never had any real representative government, its Tsars ran the country by *droit divin* longer than in the West while its economy was not as developed as its European neighbours. Ill-educated and poverty-ridden serfs were beholden to their masters for a roof over their heads. Added to these facts is the enormous size of the country. It was not and is not easy to run such a immense country. The harsh climate and the brutality of World War II also made the *narod* tougher than ever. It is my firm belief that the Russians are made of sterner stuff than the rest of Europe and the US. They have endured and can endure material and other deprivations far longer with a stoicism that is lacking or even absent in many of their Western neighbours.

Patriotism

Russian patriotism and heroism in recent history made itself evident when the Soviets fought the Germans for three years before the Second Front was opened in June 1944 with Operation Overlord, the allied invasion of France. The Great Patriotic War (GPW) as WW II is described in the Soviet Union and post-Soviet Russia, was the most murderous and brutal conflict in history. The Soviet Union was said to have lost more than 20 million lives in the war and its aftermath while the American, British and other European countries' losses were incomparable. Only China could claim to have lost just as many lives in the 1937–1945 conflict with Japan. Whatever one's view of Stalin is, one must concede that his leadership was decisive in the war against Nazi Germany. He was shrewd enough to appeal more to Russian patriotism to rally the country against Nazism, not the questionable slogans of the proletariat.

Russians are very patriotic, and when it comes to celebrating the Soviet victory over Nazi Germany, are very solemn and dedicated to making the 9 May (Victory Day) a very special day for their country's surviving World War II veterans, and to honouring and celebrating with pride their fallen heroes as well.

I first observed the Russian fervour for the 9th of May when as CDA a.i., I was fortunate enough to have been invited to join the 50th anniversary of their victory over Nazi Germany on 9 May 1995. President Yeltsin presided over the event, marked by a grand military parade and marches by veterans and members of the Armed Forces. Fittingly, it was held in Victory Park where the Museum devoted to the GPW is situated. The event touched the nerves of those present. If one were to engage Russians in conversation about the GPW, most would tell you that they lost one or some members of their families or relatives in the GPW, and that would not be an exaggeration. Hence, it was not surprising for me to see many Russian attendees well-up with tears on that day.

The 9 May celebration, an annual event, began to assume grander proportions during the Putinite era, because there was not only more money to be spent but also because President Putin sought to imbue into his people an even stronger sense of patriotism. In that, he has succeeded far more than he had bargained for.

Apart from strong patriotic feelings, a vivid reminder of the Russian people's strong emotions in the wake of the Soviet collapse was their sympathetic attitude towards the millions of their fellow ethnic kinsmen who lived and still live in the "*blizhneye zarubezhye*" (the Near Abroad), as the former Soviet Republics were then referred to.

In the mid-1990s, an academic in one of Russia's leading think-tanks dealing with the Asia-Pacific wistfully related to me the fate of his relatives and friends in Ukraine and the Baltics. While he did not question their independence, he deplored widespread reports that ethnic Russians there had to live under "official pressure". Separately, the wife of a Russian airline official, both of whom had lived in Singapore, told me that life for her friends and relatives in the Baltics had become difficult. My Russian language part-time tutor, who was born in Georgia, also echoed this sentiment. She had relatives and friends in Georgia, and spoke of their not-so-pleasant lives there, being ethnic Russians. In fact, quite of number of Russians I had met, including some staff members of the Embassy claimed to have known people who had relatives and friends in the Near Abroad who were experiencing "difficulties".

At the time, I did not get a real sense of what those "difficulties" meant. Years later, I would read that they related to language issues and job opportunities for ethnic Russians in the Near Abroad. Most, if not all, expressed some level of regret that the Soviet Union had ceased to exist, and that as a consequence, their fellow kinsmen had been left to fend for themselves in the Near Abroad. Indeed, in his annual State-of-the-Nation speech in 2005, President Putin spoke to this very concern when he described the collapse of the Soviet Union as "the greatest geopolitical catastrophe" of the 20th century, adding that break-up of the Soviet Union in 1991 was "a real drama" which had left tens of millions of ethnic Russians outside the Russian Federation.

The following data throw some light onto this issue. An article dated 1 October 2002 published by the Migration Policy Institute,[3] and written by Timothy Heleniak, a Research Associate at the University of Maryland, International Development Consultant, and Editor of *Polar Geography*, is worth quoting extensively. He wrote that:

"just prior to the Soviet collapse, the share that the 25.3 million Russians made up of the non-Russian states varied considerably, from 37.8 percent of the population of Kazakhstan to just 1.6 percent of Armenia. Of the Russians living outside Russia, 11.4 million, or 45 percent, resided in Ukraine, whose inhabitants are ethnically close to Russians. Another quarter, or 6.5 million, lived in the more ethnically distant Kazakhstan, in Central Asia. Uzbekistan, Latvia, Belarus, and Kyrgyzstan all had sizeable Russian populations of between 1.6 million and 900,000 while the remaining states all had less than a half million Russians. Like migrants elsewhere in the world, Russians in the non-Russian states tended to live disproportionately in urban areas and even more so in the capitals of these states. While Russians constituted on average 16 percent of the population of the non-Russian states, they made up 24 percent of the urban populations and 30 percent of capital city residents. In the capitals of Kazakhstan, Kyrgyzstan, and Latvia, Russians actually

---

[3] The Migration Policy Institute is an independent, non-partisan think-tank based in Washington, D.C., dedicated to analysing the movement of people worldwide.

outnumbered the natives. Thus, the capitals and other large cities of the non-Russian states were Russian exclaves where Russians could enjoy their traditional cultural life, speak their language freely, and never have to learn the local language. Russians also enjoyed a privileged occupational status, making up disproportionate shares of industrial enterprise managers, scientists, professors, engineering-technical specialists, and other high-wage, high-prestige professions. The breakup of the Soviet Union amounted to an abrupt upheaval in the centuries-old history of Russian expansion, with huge consequences in terms of migration. When the Soviet Union ceased to exist and Russia became an independent state, established a liberal democracy, and started the transition towards a market economy, little thought was given to the impact of these policies on migration and other demographic trends. Insofar as they looked ahead, policy makers had simply expected a post-breakup reconcentration of ethnic groups into their homelands among the 15 post-Soviet states. While this diaspora migration has accounted for a large portion of the migration at both the national and sub-national levels, it has certainly not accounted for all movements in the post-Soviet period."

Racism

Open racism and ethnic profiling, if I may use these terms — an unfortunate but expected outcome of the Soviet collapse, and the brutal war in Chechnya, located in Russia's restive Caucausus, a mainly Muslim and non-Slavic region — were to be observed in the early days of post-Soviet Russia. Chechnya was then fighting for independence which even Yeltsin, a self-declared democrat, could not grant, for it could have led to a break-up of Russia itself and political suicide for the Russian President. That was the overall assessment of Russian and foreign observers whom I spoke to, which I fully shared. The Chechen attempt to gain independence could not be expected to win approval from any Russian leader.

I had read that open racism and ethnic profiling were unacceptable during the Soviet period when Soviet citizens were "brothers" and "comrades". One of my Embassy staff members related to me that during the Soviet period, Russians could not behave like "Russians" and always had to take into account the feelings of the non-Russians, in line with the CPSU's ideological stance of universal "proletarian brotherhood". He was glad that in post-Soviet Russia, Russians could be "Russian" again — by that, he meant, they could now assert and be openly proud of their ethnicity. He added that he had also resented the fact that Russia had to "feed" the non-Russian Soviet republics, the Warsaw Pact states and Third World allies, the outcome being that Russia had become "poorer".[4] Moreover, he did not approve of *smugli* (swarthy) Caucasian natives dating Russian women, citing how he had witnessed a carload of them harassing and then forcing a young ethnic Russian lady into their car on the street in broad daylight, near MGU.

Unfortunately, resentment found some expression in racist attitudes towards the non-Slavs and those from the former Soviet Republics who lived and worked in the country.

My private driver exemplified perhaps the attitude of many ethnic Russians towards non-Slavs in their midst when he pejoratively labelled Chechens, Georgians, Armenians, and other Caucausian "dark-skinned" natives as well as Central Asians as *natsmen* (*natsionalny menshentsvo* or national minorities, a term the Soviets used to refer to the non-Slavs of the Soviet Union). He was the first person to have brought my attention to this term. Many other Russians with whom I would casually chat about domestic terrorism or other social problems, would never directly criticise Chechens (or non-Slavs) but made it crystal clear there was no love lost between them, making polite remarks about the supposed ethnic characteristics of the Chechens or other Caucasian natives, as opposed to ethnic Russians.

There appeared to be a directly proportional relationship between the number of Russian casualties in the brutal war in Chechnya and the sentiments of the ethnic Russians towards natives of the Caucasus, especially Chechens. Without doubt, the socio-economic difficulties

---

[4] During the Soviet period, its allies overseas and in the Warsaw Pact as well as energy-poor Soviet republics received assistance from Moscow in the form of grants, loans and outright assistance, from energy supplies to weapons.

brought about by shock therapy added fuel to the fire. I came to the conclusion that perhaps only dyed-in-the-wool Russian Communists or liberals really believed at the time that inter-ethnic relations were beyond all reproach.

An academic study published in 2015, entitled *Ethnic Relations in Post-Soviet Russia: Russians and non-Russians in the North Caucasus* by Dr. Andrew Foxall, confirms my personal observations. According to Foxall, "ethnic relations turned increasingly violent from the mid-1990s onwards as the realities of post-Soviet transition wrought widespread economic and social hardship for the majority of the Russian population". Foxall adds that ethnic Russians began to turn against not only non-Slav migrants from Central Asia and the Caucasus, while North Caucasus natives, despite being Russian citizens, "became increasingly viewed as 'foreigners'".[5]

Many Russians shared the sentiments of my Embassy staff member and my private driver. It was not surprising, in any case. To put this matter in context, one must understand that the Soviet break-up affected Russia not only at the state level, but more important, the personal lives of millions. As related above, most Russians I became acquainted with had friends or relatives or family members who were now in "another country" as they put it. Quite a number left Central Asia for Russia after the Soviet collapse, which in varying degrees, led to the localisation of the civil service, the military, the education, social and other spheres of life. It was therefore to be expected, while not to be excused, that resentment and anger were sentiments that accompanied the departure of ethnic Russians from many of the ex-Soviet Republics.

A direct consequence of the above developments was overt intolerance and suspicion of non-Slavs, and in many cases, physical as well as verbal abuse. Unpleasant incidents were reported in the vernacular media and the *Moscow Times*, the city's premier English language daily. Let me cite some concrete cases from personal experience.

---

[5] See pp. 19 and 20 of Foxall's study for more details.

My acquaintanceship with a businessman, Mr. M from Dagestan, a Muslim region in the Caucasus, was instrumental in providing me with a picture of inter-ethnic relations, as seen through the eyes of a simple Caucasian individual. Mr. M was a businessman who had a flat in Moscow and another in Makhachkala, the capital of Dagestan. The people of Dagestan are mainly Muslims, like the Chechens. Located near Chechnya, it could not shield itself from the conflict there. Islamic insurgency also began to rise there in the 1990s. For these reasons, many Russians began to view all Caucasians with a measure of distrust.

Mr. M related how he and his family members would be glared at or eyed with suspicion by some of their fellow Russian neighbours in their flat block where they had lived for quite some time. Ditto in the metro. He attributed the uncomfortable atmosphere to the Chechen conflict. Like all Russian citizens, whether Slavic or non-Slavic, Mr. M was a very generous and hospitable host. An admirer of Singapore, he would relate to me how often he had visited Singapore with his family, not only for business reasons but also to enjoy the peace and stability here. He once went out of his way to slaughter a lamb, skin it, cook it, and transport it to our National Day reception — I was a witness to the whole process. That was the first and last time in my life that I had witnessed the slaughter of an animal and its subsequent skinning (not a pleasant experience) and then consumption by people, including me!

I too personally experienced racism in one form or another, a number of times.

The first incident took place in a fruit and vegetable store on Stary Arbat, literally a stone's throw from the Embassy (it did not have any name, but just a number, like all shops in the Soviet era and immediate post-Soviet era). I would spend many a lunch hour walking on Stary and/or Novi Arbat. One fine day, just weeks after I had started work in the Embassy, I stepped into this store. Looking over some apples, I instinctively picked up a few, seconds after which I heard a rude and imperious female voice say that one must not touch any fruit. That in itself was not racism of course, but her tone of voice to me smacked of such a sentiment.

Naturally, I was incensed, and stressed, *expressis verbis*, that I had more than enough to pay for the apples. To drive home the point, I waved a wad of US$100 notes at her surprised face. In retrospect, I regret doing this, for I perhaps could have displayed my displeasure with her insult in another manner. But at the time, I felt I must make it plain to her that even a non-Russian had the means to purchase an apple and much more in her store.

Incidentally, when I was working in Bonn a decade earlier, I also encountered a milder, but no less insidious form of racism. While waiting in a queue in my bank to deposit some cash, I stood behind an old German lady. A few seconds after I took my place behind her, she just happened to turn around and glanced at me, and in that second, clutched her handbag as if she had been afraid I would grab it. In doing so, she muttered to herself that of all people to stand behind her, it had to be a foreigner. Being already fluent in the German language by then, I forcefully responded that I was in the queue to deposit quite a large sum of cash, and would not need to steal her hard-earned pension money and that one did not have to be a German to be an individual of impeccable standing. Her facial expression was one of bewilderment; I was certain she did not expect a foreigner to have been able to reply to her injudicious comments in fluent German and in a forceful tone to boot. Needless to say, she did not respond to my remarks.

The second incident was more a case of ethnic profiling, in this instance, a hugely mistaken case. One fine evening, in the summer of 1996, while I was driving back to my flat after work, I was flagged down by a traffic policeman on Kosygina Street close to MGU (the street was named after the late Soviet Prime Minister, Alexei Kosygin; my flat was located relatively close to it). Very politely, he requested me to open my car boot. I could have invoked diplomatic immunity but chose not to, for I must admit, I was very curious about the reasons for his action. I casually asked him why he had stopped me and requested me to show him what was in my car boot: his reply was delivered in a very matter-of-fact manner. Chechen terrorists could have hijacked my car with the purpose of transporting weapons; a vehicle with diplomatic plates would provide a "good cover", he emphasised.

Upon hearing this, I burst out in laughter, and asked him whether I resembled a Chechen in any way, to which he too burst out in laughter, saying "*Konechno nyet*" (of course not)! Accepting my offer of a cigarette with good grace, he and I chatted a few minutes before I took my leave. I comforted myself that not all traffic policemen were out to impose "fines" on motorists. There was no ill-will on his or my part but it was a manifestation of the fact that law enforcement officers in the city and country were on the *qui vive*, thanks to the Chechen conflict.

The third incident occurred in the summer of 1997. While walking along one of the city's many broad avenues, on a summer evening (darkness descends about 2300 hours in the summer), I was suddenly and without any provocation, set upon by two young thugs, screaming at me to "go back to your f.... country, *churka*".[6] Fortunately for me, I had a plastic bag filled with a can of beer and some groceries which I had bought earlier — the bag was used successively by me not only to ward-off their blows to my head and upper torso but to strike back at them as well. Everything was over within a few minutes, for the thugs were "persuaded" to leave in haste by a small gathering of onlookers, many of whom threatened to ring the police. I naturally expressed my gratitude to them. Had it not been for them, those thugs who were manifestly drunk, and well over six feet tall, would have overwhelmed me and put Yours Truly into hospital! Naturally, the onlookers played a key role in ensuring that I did not come further into harm's way. I felt relieved in the thought that racist sentiments were confined to the very few.

The fourth incident took place just a few weeks later, before I was to leave Moscow on the conclusion of my first tour of duty, on a weekend in late July 1997. While having dinner at the bar counter of a family-oriented restaurant situated on one of Moscow's major thoroughfares, three burly men in their early 30s "joined" me. One of them started an uninvited "conversation" with me, heaping verbal abuse on me as a

---

[6] *Churka* is a derogatory term for Central Asians and Caucasians; my thick beard probably fit their perception of a Central Asian.

"filthy Asian". He also made unfounded and insulting comments about Asian women being whores. At that moment, I could not help thinking that he must have been living in an alternate universe.

It was definitely well-known in the 1990s, that unfortunately, quite a number of women from Russia and the former Soviet Republics were in the very dire straits and earning their living in the very way he had referred to. They were to be seen on some of the streets, in nightclubs and bars, etc. Obviously, I did not even think of conveying these thoughts of mine, in no uncertain terms, to him. Although I was hot under the collar, I did not fly off the handle, since they were burly and much younger. Hence, I reluctantly chose to remain silent.

Obviously, my silence must have unnerved the chap seated right next to me, who all of a sudden, punched me below my right eye, whereupon my spectacles flew over the bar counter. He then proceeded to impose a chokehold over me with his huge arm, from which I freed myself by applying my still-burning, half-smoked cigarette on his arm. It was a godsent that during that second or two surprise and unprovoked assault on my person, I still had the presence of mind to hang onto my cigarette and that saved the day for me! For much less than a minute, he and I just glared at each other. I thanked the Almighty that his friends chose to simply watch and not join in the fray against me.

To my great relief, a policeman appeared a few seconds later (one of the restaurant staff members must have rung the police). The matter ended there and then. Thanks to the restaurant staff members and policeman, all I suffered was literally a black-eye. At the "suggestion" of the policeman, the trio trooped to me, full of perfunctory apologies, which I accepted and we ended our "conflict" with cigarettes supplied by Yours Truly to them. It was amazing how over a cigarette or two, they and I were immediately able to forget the hostility and tensions that had existed just a few minutes before. These chaps were certainly not representative of the warm and friendly Russian people, many of whom I had come to know.

Unfortunately for me, I was to experience another physical assault by two self-proclaimed followers of the Fuehrer, in 2012. One fine autumn evening, while out on a walk in a neighbourhood not far from the centre of town, I was accosted by two teenagers, who demanded fare for the metro. Seeing my obvious refusal in my facial expression of disapproval, they proceeded to threaten me, using vulgar street argot to emphasise the point that they were skinheads, and raising their hands in the Hitler salute, in an obvious effort to intimidate me.

When I reminded them that the Nazis had been inordinately cruel to their people and then immediately proceeded on my way, their reaction was to rain blows on my arms and head. While I did not expect violence from them, my first reaction was naturally to defend myself as best I could; I was literally saved from further attack by a chap with a bat, who appeared all of a sudden. On seeing him, these two "storm-troopers" fled without hesitation. My "saviour" told me he had observed us from his window and decided to take action; he advised me to leave immediately which I obviously did. Thankfully, I was not really hurt in the incident; my arms were slightly bruised though.

I had come across right-wing types when I was in Bonn. In summer 1985, I observed purported German nationalists in the woods while out on a hike; this group of young men was very disciplined in their demeanour and well-dressed, singing songs of praise for their country. In any case, thankfully, they did not even look at me, the only non-white foreigner in their presence. I also came across tough-looking skinheads at a petrol station a few months later — again thankfully, they did not even glance at me. The fact that they did not assault me appeared to have given the lie to many reports that they were inherently and instinctively aggressive towards non-whites. Perhaps I was plain lucky not to have come into their sights!

In all my time in Moscow, I never ceased to be more than surprised to learn that skinheads openly adored Hitler and Nazism in the very country that had played a crucial role in Nazism's defeat. But what intrigued me about Russian skinheads was the fact that they would openly give the Hitler salute, have tattoos on their arms stating in German "*Meine Ehre heist Treue*" (My honour is loyalty) — a motto of the SS! (I had watched documentaries on Russian TV which focused on Russian neo-Nazis who openly showed all these signs). That Russian neo-Nazis and skinheads worshipped Hitler and the SS, is of course quite perplexing. Only they themselves can explain the reasons for their idol worship of the Fuehrer and the SS who regarded Russians as *"slavische Untermenschen"* (Slavic sub-humans) and treated them with much bestiality.

I relate these personal experiences not to exaggerate the level of racism and ethnic profiling in Moscow and Russia at that time or to paint the Russian people in a negative light, but to graphically illustrate the rising tensions in Russian society as a consequence of the rapid changes in its economy, political, and social life, and the impact of the conflict in Chechnya on the country's social fabric. I also want to point out that many decent people had gone out of their way to help me out of these unpleasant situations. They vastly outnumber the minority of racists or skinheads who chose to make me one of their victims.

Living Conditions

A word or two about my living conditions in Moscow would be in order. It would give the reader a sense of how expatriates and other foreigners lived at a turbulent time in Russia's modern history.

Our flat was situated about half an hour's drive from the Embassy, not too far from MGU, in a compound reserved for foreigners only and run by the GlavUPDK.[7] All the residents in this gated community were either diplomats, journalists, businessmen or company executives.

All my predecessors had lived in the flat as well. It was decently furnished by the Embassy, was comfortable and cosy. However, its walls were so thin that one could hear our immediate neighbours, without having to place one's ears to the walls, quarrelling or engaging in other "activities"! Secondly, its windows were not double-glazed and windproof like those I had in my house in Unkel-am-Rhein, by Bonn, during my previous assignment. We would stuff the little cracks in-between the window panes and the window frames with cotton

---

[7] Its website states that it is "a commercial organisation subordinate to the Ministry of Foreign Affairs. The Government of the Russian Federation, the Federal Agency for State Property Management and the Ministry of Foreign Affairs of Russia act as the company's founders".

wool to keep out the cold, winter air! Third, the ceiling was unusually low, which I found strange, considering the fact that Russians are, on average, taller than Singaporeans (flats in Singapore have not too high ceilings either). Finally, the lifts in all the three high-rise buildings of this compound were too slow for my comfort; they had black floor buttons which would pop-out when one reached one's floor, a rather primitive contraption. All-in-all though, I cannot say my living conditions were bad.

Apart from skiing in the winter, and riding my bike in the summer, I would stair-climb in my block as well in the neighbouring blocks of flats. That was one of the advantages of living in a high-rise building.

On the whole, the neighbourhood was safe and convenient with respect to facilities like grocery stores. Within walking distance was the Cheryomushkinskiy Rynok, a large wet market where we would buy fresh vegetables and fruits.

My wife and I were therefore quite sad on being told that my assignment would end in August 1997. I had cherished the hope that my assignment could be extended a year or more. We had grown very fond of the city and its people, of all our acquaintances and friends, Russians and foreigners. We also had a whale of a time in Moscow. However, little did we know then that within two-and-half-years, we would be back.

Chapter 6

Life and Work in the Putinite Era

I neither expected nor planned to be in Moscow a second time. However, favourable circumstances presented themselves to me. After a younger colleague had turned down his assignment to Moscow, it was offered to me. Unlike my first assignment, I looked forward to working and living in Moscow for the second time.

We arrived in Moscow on a cold and snowy day in December 1999 — a sight my family and I loved and which we had looked forward to. The first thing we did after arriving in our flat (the same one we had lived in between 1994 and 1997), was to head out to get ice cream sold by vendors on a street not far from us; it was a real treat to have ice cream amidst heavy snowfall and a cold wind.

Better Living Conditions

After a year or so, we moved, with the permission of my HQ, into a larger flat in the city centre. By then, the real estate sector in Moscow had developed fast and one had quite a large and varied choice of flats to choose from. It was situated in an old building within walking distance of the Embassy, had a high ceiling and a large dining room which was perfect for the many dinner parties my wife and I would organise during the next five years. It was also well-furnished. The only issues I had with this flat were firstly, the lift was slow, old, and had the same black-coloured pop-out buttons, and secondly, the consistently late-night renovation carried out by stay-in construction workers in the flat above ours; they would work till 2 am or 3 am even on weekends, for months on end. My complaints to the security guard and building managers came to naught. There were naturally laws and regulations with respect to renovation work and noise pollution. I had even written letters of complaint to the city district, to no avail. After a while, I realised that law and regulations would not necessarily be obeyed, let alone, enforced. Finally, living in the city centre had its hazards, especially in winter. Frozen snow and ice on the roofs of many buildings represented a danger to life and limb if they were not regularly removed.

One cold winter morning, I was awoken by the security guard and told that a large block of ice had fallen onto my car and broken its sun-roof. Indeed, the damage was irreparable but I was thankful it had not fallen onto me, for if it had, I would have met the Creator there-and-then. In fact, quite a few unfortunate people had been killed by fallen ice blocks or heavy snow on the streets of Moscow or other cities. Unfortunately, this was one of the hazards of living in a country with a very cold and harsh climate. Nevertheless, we were very happy to be staying in our new flat since it was situated not far from the office and all the facilities one would require — supermarkets, cinemas, bookstores, theatres, etc.

Yeltsin's Resignation

My second tour coincided with one of post-Soviet Russia's momentous political events — the unexpected resignation of President Yeltsin six months before his term ended, and the appointment of then Prime Minister, Vladimir Putin in his place, as Acting President. Yeltsin's popularity then was falling due to the "lost" war in Chechnya, the continuing economic and social instability as a consequence of the 1998 default, and his own displays of behaviour perceived as unbecoming of the President. He was said to have been sozzled during a number of official events, at home and abroad. Moreover, Yeltsin regularly fell ill and had a heart condition. Yet, his resignation came as a surprise to observers.

I recall watching his resignation on Russian television on 31 December 1999; he came across as a very tired, discouraged, and beaten man, apologising to his people for having failed to accomplish his declared goals for the country. It was really moving to have watched him giving up power in such a poignant way. His appointment of Putin was meant to clear the way for his election to the office in the following year. Putin was then becoming popular for his tough stance and talk on the war in Chechnya, emphasis on the need to re-establish law and order, and promises to bring stability and prosperity to the country and to reduce social inequality as well as to regain Russia's place in the sun.

Putin Takes the Helm — his Achievements and Challenges

There was another crucial and decisive but underrated reason for Yeltsin's resignation: Putin was not only younger but also physically fit (reportedly, he neither drinks nor smokes, and is keen on physical fitness). He conveyed the impression of being a martinet and also represented what most Russians desired, viz. a former KGB officer who was seen and indeed acted like the strongman Russia needed to bring it out of its second Smutnoye Vremya (or the Time of Troubles).[1] Moreover, far from being a mere adlatus of Yeltsin, Putin became his own man sooner than expected.

In my position as First Secretary, or the number two man in the Embassy, I did not have the opportunity to observe, let alone meet Russia's new leader up-close-and-personal. (An Ambassador would always have that opportunity when he or she presents his or her credentials to the President). However, Lady Luck smiled on me when I attended, in the absence of the Ambassador, an important event in the Kremlin on 12 June 2002 on the occasion of Day of Russia.[2] Amid the

---

[1] *Smutnoye Vremya*, or the Time of Troubles was the period in Russian history between 1598 and 1613 when instability brought famine, and wars with the Poles and Lithuanians, resulting in the loss of many lives. It ended with the establishment of the Romanov Dynasty which lasted three centuries, until it fell in the Bolshevik Revolution.

[2] The Day of Russia is an event that commemorates the adoption of the Declaration of State Sovereignty of the Russian Soviet Federative Socialist Republic, or RSFSR, on 12 June 1990.

pomp and within the majestic premises of the Kremlin, I was treated to the honour of watching President Putin address his guests. While I was seated quite a distance from the lectern from whence he spoke, he was still within sight, and his voice and demeanour conveyed an air of confidence and enthusiasm which could not have been matched by his aged predecessor. Watching him on television was obviously not the same as observing him in the flesh. The next opportunity I had to attend this same event was in June 2010 when Medvedev was the President.

Having observed first-hand the difficult years of Yeltsinite Russia, I could totally understand the Russian yearning for order, discipline, stability, and prosperity. Perhaps Putin would be able to achieve what Yeltsin wanted but could not accomplish. It was therefore not surprising that Putin won the Presidency at the polls in March 2000, beating Communist leader Gennady Zyuganov, and Grigory Yavlinsky of the liberal party, Yabloko. With that election, the spectre of a return to Communism was dealt a *coup de grace* (Zyuganov won a little over 29% of the vote, against Putin's 53%; Yavlinsky received just under 6%).

Putin's assumption to power as President coincided with the worldwide rise in energy prices. Being a major energy producer, this development added much-needed resources to the Russian Treasury. According to a leading foreign expert on the Russian economy who runs Macro-Advisory Eurasia Strategic Consulting (MAESC), a business consultancy, Chris Weafer, the oil/gas-driven growth model helped to create the boom that increased Russia's GDP from US$199 billion in 2000 to US$2.2 trillion in 2013. During this period, Russia earned US$3 trillion from oil and gas exports. On the other hand, Russian individuals and enterprises have exported an estimated US$1 trillion over the last 25 years, which constitutes 60% of the country's current GDP. Most observers would term this outflow capital flight.[3]

However, at the start of Putin's Presidency, the situation was dire. Indeed, Russia's foreign reserves stood at US$8.5 billion in January

---

[3] Source: *Russia — A Basic Guide*, July 2019 issue. Weafer has been resident in Russia since 1998.

2000 when Putin was Acting President and the government's external debt totalled US$133 billion, according to two American experts on Russia, Fiona Hill and Clifford G. Gaddy of the Brookings Institution. They pointed out that by the end of 2007, government foreign debt stood at US$37 billion while foreign reserves rose to over US$600 billion by mid-2008 — the third largest in the world.[4]

Well into the Putin era, Ben Aris,[5] an authoritative Russia-hand who reports on economic issues, wrote in an article dated 13 April 2018 in *Intellinews.com*, that Russia today is a "normal" country, compared to the "basket case" it had been in the 1990s. He correctly pointed out that "at the time of the 1998 crisis, Russia had a total of US$8 billion in reserves. That is lunch money today compared to the US$450 billion sitting in state coffers. All the macro indicators are also nearly normal: inflation has fallen from over 2,000% to 2.4% now; unemployment from 50% to 5%; and after a decade of contraction in the Yeltsin era, GDP growth is positive albeit lacklustre".

It would not be fair, however, to ascribe Russia's new-found prosperity to high energy prices alone. Putin also had the benefit of sound advice from Herman Gref who now runs Sberbank, the country's largest bank and Elvira Nabiullina, currently head of Russia's Central Bank, with respect to the need to introduce structural economic reforms. At the beginning of the century, Gref, an economic liberal, was Minister for Economic Development and Trade while Nabiullina was his deputy. Moreover, in the person of Alexei Kudrin, surely one of post-Soviet Russia's foremost minds, Putin had a very capable Finance Minister. Kudrin implemented much-needed tax reforms, including a flat income tax rate of 13%, which helped to raise much-needed tax revenue.

---

[4] See p. 86 of their book, *Mr Putin, Operative in the Kremlin*.

[5] Aris is a keen and perceptive observer of Russia; the third longest serving foreign correspondent in Russia, he lived and worked in Moscow between 1993 and 2003, where he was bureau chief for the *Daily Telegraph* as well as a contributing editor at *The Banker*, *Euromoney* and *The Business*). He is also a regular contributor to many of the best-known international business titles such as *The Wall Street Journal*, *The Financial Times*, *Institutional Investor* and many others.

Not having had to pay taxes on many items during the Soviet period, Russians had yet to get used to the need, the obligation, and indeed the responsibility of citizens to pay taxes. To an extent, tax evasion was considered not only like a "badge of honour" but also a "right". This was the standpoint of many a Russian, regardless of his or her background whom I had become acquainted with during those turbulent times. The major question they would rhetorically pose to me, with respect to taxes, would be: what do I receive in return from the state were I to pay my taxes in full or at all? Their answer: Nothing much. Roads are bad, the police force is corrupt, crime is rampant, people are not paid their wages on time or at all, the health and educational sectors are in dire need of financing, housing is inadequate, etc. If anyone should be paying taxes at all, that burden should fall on the oligarchs and the wealthy, would be their parting comment.

This negative attitude towards taxes would change with the passage of time, as the Russian economy grew and prosperity filtered down. Indeed, Aris pointed out in his article that apart from the low-tax rate, Putin "also totally made over the labour code, set up a federal treasury system that took tax collecting responsibilities away from the regions and launched a raft of other business-friendly reforms that laid the foundation for the subsequent decade-long economic boom".

Thanks to the tax and fiscal reforms established by Kudrin, as well as rising energy prices, Russia began to enjoy surplus revenue. Under his direction, and the economic liberals, the Stabilisation Fund (SF) was established in 2004, (to which federal budget surpluses from oil proceeds were directed, with a view to using them on a rainy day). Most of Russia's Soviet-era debt was paid off a few years later, using the SF's resources. Between 1999 and 2007, the economy grew around 7% annually. Due to Kudrin's insistence on fiscal discipline, with support from President Putin and the IMF, Russia's reserves were not spent on more social programmes and infrastructure, which his critics advocated.

Indeed, Kudrin was consistently castigated by conservatives like the then powerful Moscow Mayor, Yuri Luzhkov, as well as members of the left, who called on the government to spend those resources on schools, roads, pensions, etc. Fortunately for the country, Kudrin's refusal with President Putin's backing, and Kudrin's steady and capable hands, guided the country in the early years of the Putin era and prepared it for the global financial crisis of 2008.

Prosperity and the Rise of Conspicuous Consumption

Between the time I assumed duty in the Embassy in December 1999 and March 2004, when my tour ended, the socio-economic consequences of the 1998 default were slowly but surely becoming a thing of the past. One could discern signs of prosperity on the streets of Moscow in the early years of the Putinite era.

I was not only pleasantly surprised but also felt more comfortable about living and working in Moscow, compared to the difficult 1990s. More well-stocked and beautifully-decorated shops and expensive restaurants were opened. My regular lunch-time walks on Stary Arbat and Novi Arbat became a real joy and much more interesting, with more choices in terms of food, drink, and shopping. Not only the facades but also the interiors of office buildings, commercial outlets, and retail malls were renovated to look like their Western-inspired counterparts. The world famous Soviet-era GUM (State Department Store) on Red Square turned from a gloomy and drab place during my first tour of duty in Moscow into an attractive mall with clean toilets (a rarity in the 1990s), always thronged with Russians and foreigners.

Everywhere on the streets of Moscow, I observed happier people, evident from the expressions on the faces. There were no more poorly-fed soldiers to be seen on the streets, begging for money or cigarettes, and no prostitutes loitering on street corners of the centre of town. If I may repeat myself, not far from the Embassy on a street corner, unescorted "ladies" with heavily-painted faces would be seen after dark in the early- and mid-1990s; they too would disappear in the early years of this century, with rising prosperity and the restoration of law and order on the streets.

A tangible sign of the new prosperity was apparent in the fact that the man-in-the-street was much better dressed. In the 1990s, most people one encountered on the streets of Moscow and other cities, not to mention the outlying villages where poverty was and remains more entrenched and widespread, were very poorly dressed and more often than not, would have drab-coloured clothes. The reasons were obvious and understandable. By the early-2000s, one would literally see a wide variety of colours reflected in the clothes of the pedestrian, metro passenger, or shop assistants, and just about everyone.

The beauty of the generally good-looking Russian female was enhanced and matched by better-designed and better-quality clothes, footwear, and headwear. The Russian was and remains very conscious of his or her appearance; it was not their fault that in the 1990s, they could not afford to look and feel good about themselves. Many men I met in the 1990s would have shabby and/or ill-fitting suits or jackets or shirts with frayed collars and unpolished, worn-out shoes. While the women, like everywhere else, would pay more attention to their appearance, one still could not help but notice that their clothes were not of good quality. Of course, I am generalising here — there were quite a few individuals I got to know who were always dressed-to-kill. However, they were more the exception than the rule.

Just a few years into the new century, one would immediately notice the better-quality clothes, shoes, gloves, scarfs, and other items of attire of many an individual on the streets. Many of those individuals whom I met in the 1990s and whose acquaintance I renewed during my second and final assignments, would be dressed in very good quality suits and shoes. The term *brosayet dengi na veter* ("to throw money to the wind, to waste money") was appropriate in the 2000s to refer to the "wild" spending habits of Russians; their Marginal Propensity to Consume (MPC) was certainly higher than their Marginal Propensity to Save (MPS), of that I was convinced. The wide gap between their MPC and MPS was principally due to the years of "*defizit*" during the Soviet era when mass consumerism was but a dream for most Russians. It was pent-up demand after decades of having to live with scarce goods and services; this pent-up demand would not really ease-up for many years to come in the Putinite era.

My impression was that the Russian did not have much faith in the future of his country and by extension, in his own future, given the tremendous and fast-paced changes of the 1990s. One therefore could not blame the Russian for spending like there was no tomorrow; anyone else in that position would have done likewise. Even today, I dare to argue that the Russian is more than willing to spend on luxury items than most people elsewhere. His country's tortured history ensures that he just cannot jettison his deep-seated fears about the future.

The term "*defizit*" was used by a number of my Russian contacts and acquaintances when talking about the Soviet era.

The most prominent Russian to have used the term was Mikhail Margelov, the then Chairman of the Foreign Affairs Committee of the Federation Council (the Upper House), during a meeting with Ambassador Simon de Cruz, who met him some time in 2009. I was also present at their meeting. Fluent in the English language, he explained to Ambassador de Cruz that during the Soviet era, consumer goods and services were few and far between, unlike in the Putinite epoch. He rightly argued that the prosperity of the Putin era had made Russians "forget", to some extent, the "*defizit*" years of the Soviet era. Margelov is now Vice-President of Transneft, a state-owned oil pipeline company. Like many Russian leaders, he has been to Singapore and met his counterparts.

A tangible indicator of the growing prosperity was the rise in the number of vehicles — in other words, heavier and more traffic jams on the boulevards and main arteries of Moscow. When I first arrived in Moscow in 1994, that was one the first things which struck me. I had half-expected to see more pedestrians than vehicles on the streets; I was wrong. Traffic jams were already becoming a fixture of Moscow; granted, one could discern many Soviet-era vehicles in the traffic jams of the 1990s; the 2000s would see many of them replaced by Japanese, Korean, and Western cars, jeeps, and even lorries, in greater numbers.

Wage increases

The rising prosperity of the Putinite epoch inevitably led to rising expectations of the people, in terms of wages. That was clearly seen in the first instance by the growing number of requests of the Embassy's

Russian staff members for wage increases. We naturally had to balance them with our own budgetary considerations but in the main, we granted their requests within what we felt were reasonable limits. And like most of their fellow countrymen, they insisted on being paid in US dollars as had been the case in the mid-1990s when I started on my first tour of duty in the Embassy.

For me personally, the beginning of the Putinite era meant I too had to raise the salary of my personal driver who drove my daughter to school (from US$100 to US$150). My driver then was a middle-aged lady who claimed to be a physician, specifically a paediatrician in a state hospital. Singaporean and foreign businesses too had to adapt to the new situation. A Singaporean businessman who was engaged in trading in food and beverages even remarked to me that staff turnover was becoming an issue — workers would leave one firm for another just to secure a wage raise, without taking into consideration other factors like job stability and career prospects.

The issue of low or unpaid wages was on the mend but not totally eliminated. One could not expect this challenge to be overcome overnight, despite the fact that President Putin had more resources at his disposal than his predecessor. Some employers would engage in cunctatory tactics to avoid paying their staff members, faced with issues like cash flow, back tax payments, or the need to set aside cash for their "*krysha*".

If I may repeat myself, people with education, especially those who were middle-aged or older, remained poor or could not secure jobs which matched their qualifications and experience. The personal aspect of this story was seen in some of the Embassy's employees' profiles which have been described earlier. The Embassy was not the only place of employment for such trained people. Quite of number of foreign entities also had them on the payrolls, if my conversations with expatriates were anything to go by.

Growing prosperity in the country could not raise overnight the low standard of living. The lion's share of the average Russian's salary was spent on food and rent, as well as conspicuous consumption, leaving little, if any, to set aside as savings.

An unintended consequence of low wages and wage arrears is brain-drain. This issue took shape during my first tour of duty. There were occasional media reports of Russia's loss of talented people and various estimates were put forward from the thousands, hundreds of thousands, to even millions. I was not and am not in a position to comment on the accuracy or inaccuracy of these figures. What I can say is that I came across some examples of the brain-drain. It concerned scientists and professionals like engineers and physicians. I would hear accounts from my contacts and acquaintances, foreign and locals about their friends, family members, or contacts who had chosen to leave Russia for the West or elsewhere to find jobs that matched their qualifications and expectations.

I was to deal with a few cases myself — some scientists from another city applied for visas to visit Singapore for interviews. Out of curiosity, I interviewed them and they revealed, without hesitation, that they had to leave Russia for there appeared to be little career prospects (apart from the fact that salaries were low and not regularly paid). I did not have any idea whether they landed any jobs in Singapore. The fact that they applied for them in Singapore and not in the West, reflected the extent of their desperation to get out of the country to work.

I make this point as I was and still am of the view that Russians as a whole, feel more at home in the West than in Asia or any non-Western country. Despite a chequered history and the past as well as the current tense political relationship with the West, ethnic Slav Russians are ultimately white Europeans whose language, ethnicity, culture, traditions, and religion are related to the wider Western world. No surprise therefore that they are still European- and Western-centred in their social orientation and foreign policy, despite their all protestations to the contrary.

Rise of Confidence

Confidence in the country found some expression in the views of a leading Russian economist whom I was acquainted with. According to him, Russia did not need foreign direct investments (FDI) as much as other countries since it was rich in mineral resources. Moreover, the massive amounts of capital flight, were they to return to Russia, would be higher than any FDI that could be attracted to the country. What was required was to enact policies to manage the country's natural resources well without structural inefficiencies and challenges like deep-seated corruption. To attract capital flight back, one had to create an environment in which these large amounts of money could be invested in worthwhile projects. He conceded however doing all this was Russia's greatest challenge.

That did not mean Russia was not interested in trying to attract more FDI than it already had and to learn from the experience of other countries, including Singapore. I was approached by a Russian contact to present a picture of our success in attracting FDI, despite our small size and the absence of any raw materials, as well as to arrange possible meetings with our Economic Development Board (EDB), a government body which is charged with attracting foreign investments into Singapore. This contact claimed to have had the blessings of top government officials. A seminar was held in which I, representatives of some Western companies present in Russia, and government officials were invited to discuss the challenges of attracting FDI to Russia. Nothing concrete, unfortunately, resulted from this seminar; the initial expressed interest in learning from our EDB petered out as well. I concluded that my Russian economist acquaintance's views on FDI must have been the prevailing standpoint. No surprise, since Russia is rich in natural wealth.

Another example of this confidence in Russia's future was also evident in the comments of a top Russian tax official during a meeting with Minister Mentor (MM) Lee Kuan Yew about his plans to overhaul the Russian tax system and his vision of developing the tourism sector in Siberia, including the world-famous Lake Baikal.

He had a difficult and challenging job with respect to the former, given the then still strong aversion to paying taxes and other structural challenges. However, he was confident that proper reforms would resolve this. Indeed, his reputation was greatly enhanced some years later when he successfully introduced an efficient tax service with the use of IT.

On the latter, he outlined how Siberia, with its natural beauty, could become a tourist paradise for the country, citing Lake Baikal as an instance. He agreed with MM Lee's view that tourist infrastructure like proper hotels and enough air connections to the outside world and rest of the country would be crucial to ensure success in any development plan for the region. (Not surprisingly, his career would take off years later, landing him into one of the highest offices in the country).

It was however President Putin who epitomised his country's newfound confidence and assertiveness on the global stage; it was symbolised by his relative youth and energy, in contrast to his predecessor's declining age and illness. He himself emphasised in his many public appearances, the glories of Tsarist Russia and its great power status (*derzhava*), signalling the country's return to the world arena after the chaotic decade in the 1990s which was marked by its relative retreat from the international stage. His people were naturally attracted to their youthful and energetic President and his strong rhetoric with respect to his uncompromising stance towards Chechen terrorist acts, his consistent pledge to return Russia to its rightful place in the world, as well as criticism of the still-powerful but very unpopular oligarchs and above all, their better living conditions under his Presidency.

Dealing with the Oligarchs

President Putin's strong language about the need to deal harshly with Chechen terrorism captured world attention in late-1999 when he was the Prime Minister. He was quoted as saying that terrorists would be eliminated everywhere, including in the loo. Such straight talk resonated with his people who were tired and fearful of the Chechen war since it had cost so many lives, and terrorism had been brought into a number of Russian cities, including Moscow. However, I would argue the crucial source of his popularity at that time was his no-holds-barred handling of the detested oligarchs.

As I had pointed out earlier in this book, shock therapy had led to the impoverishment of the majority of the people and the enrichment of a small group of extremely wealthy men, many of whom were seen to have been closely associated with President Yeltsin. They had come to be regarded as the epitome of Russian-style capitalism and the market economy — as vulgar and heartless. The term, Novi Russki, which had become *en vogue* in the 1990s, acquired an even more sinister meaning when it came to the oligarchs, for their huge wealth was believed to have been illegally acquired at the expense of the state. President Putin cleverly exploited their unpopularity by making it crystal clear that they could retain their wealth but had to refrain from engaging in politics. During Yeltsin's Presidency, they were seen as the power-behind-the-throne.

Two well-known oligarchs — Mikhail Khodorkovsky and Boris Berezovski, who was close to Yeltsin and his family and had held a government post — became a thorn in Putin's side and chose to openly challenge him on the way he ran the country. The outcome was predictable — the former was arrested and charged with fraud in October 2003, jailed and pardoned, and finally released in December 2013. The latter fled to the UK where he died in 2013.

A popular topic during events and cocktails as well as dinner parties with Russians and foreigners was not if but *when* Khodorkovsky and Berezovsky would be dealt with. Everyone I chatted with believed the tycoons' fate was already sealed. If they themselves had not seen the writing on the wall when Putin assumed the Presidency, then they must have either been politically blind or must have underestimated him. The rest of the oligarchs thereupon chose not to indulge in anything to provoke or upset the President.

Almost without exception, the Russians I chatted with about the tycoons felt that they got their just desserts. My impression was that the oligarchs' handling by President Putin met with the silent approval of the majority. This confirmed my own conviction that almost a decade after the Soviet break-up, the socio-economic transformation of the command economy into the market economy and capitalism (Russian-style) had yet to be accepted as legitimate by the masses. The main reason for this was the fact that the gap between the haves and haves-not had more than anything, only widened. One would hear every so often that the wealthy were "criminals, crooks and mafia members". I would hear the same refrain even in 2013, the year I left the country, albeit on a lower scale.

While I never had the opportunity to meet these tycoons in person, I did have the occasion to observe both men at close quarters at diplomatic events. I recall seeing Berezovsky at an event in 1997 — he was chatting animatedly with his interlocutors and conveyed the impression that he was an extrovert, and an excitable one at that.

Khodorkovsky, in contrast, came across to me as a person who chose to deliberately pose as an unassuming personality. He walked past me on his way to the US Ambassador's Residence (situated a stone's throw from our Embassy) for the 4 July event (US Independence Day) in 2003 — there was a long queue of vehicles on the one-way street leading to the Residence and it made sense to walk there. He was not accompanied by the usual large number of burly and tall bodyguards but by only one chap, which I thought did not tally with the popular perception that men of such wealth would be surrounded by a retinue of bodyguards. During the reception, he was surrounded by a number of people, all of whom appeared eager to exchange a word or two with him.

Law-and-order

President Putin in the West at that time was seen in quite a negative light. The general impression of him that one would read in the foreign media and liberal Russian press was that of an authoritarian, who sought to replace the hard-won democratic freedom that Yeltsin had introduced into Russia, with a highly centralised federal state, with him at the core. The killing of prominent journalist, Anna Politkovskaya, a critic of Putin, which took place in October 2006, just before I assumed my third and final assignment in Moscow, tarnished somewhat the image of Russia and its leader in the West. The murders of other journalists in the earlier years and subsequent periods of Putin's Presidency only added to Russia's negative image. Yet, considerations of Realpolitik as well as plain economics, ensured that Western relations with Russia were not unduly harmed by their tragic deaths.

That aside, his critics did not seem to pay much attention to the fact that his challenges were quite monumental — having to run the world's largest country, armed to the teeth with nuclear weapons (which was a source of concern to the West, as there was a fear that some of them could fall into the hands of terrorists or states hostile to the West), but with a weak economy and relatively unstable society, divided by the growing gap between the small number of rich and larger number of poor people, with powerful organised crime groups seemingly having their way.

From Yeltsin, Putin had inherited a country which had yet to recover from the ravages of the 1990s; the Russian Federation was beset by independence-seeking power centres located in its volatile Caucasus region, and even some of its distant Siberian and Far East regions. Moscow's writ did not appear to effectively extend all over the country. President Putin did not have much of choice but to restore law and order (he termed it "dictatorship of the law") by resorting to actions which did not meet Western standards of political governance, in the eyes of his critics. However, he was not a dictator in the classical sense of the term.

In the first two years of Putin's Presidency, after many meetings and many intensive discussions with diplomats, Russian academics, Russian journalists, businessmen and research with open material, I reached the conclusion that Putin's "dictatorship of the law" had yet to be implemented fully and effectively across his vast country. That is not to say he was a weak leader. However, securing his grip on a country the size of Russia with its myriad of challenges at the beginning of this century required time and patience as well as an iron will, coupled with willing and able subordinates to implement the President's policies. Hence, much of his first term as President was spent consolidating his power and introducing a semblance of much-needed order to his vast country.

Russia's challenges in the 1990s could not be overcome within a short time-frame. Lining one's pocket, a perennial challenge from the Tsarist and Soviet eras, and which worsened during the freewheeling days in the 1990s, was and remains a serious issue. The organised crime groups of the 1990s were said to have "merged" with corrupt elements of law enforcement organs and became a scourge of businessmen.

My business contacts would repeat the same points from the 1990s viz. encounters with corrupt officials in the law enforcement and other sections of the bureaucracy; Russian media also reported widely on corruption. Businessmen, especially small- and medium-sized enterprises, would be subject to "inspections" by officials who would levy heavy fines or threaten to shut down a business; one could of course deal with this problem by "employing" them as one's *krysha*.

A pot-calling-the-kettle-black story about corruption is in order at this point. During the Putinite era, I met quite a number of individuals chatting about the very issue. From most of them, I would hear expressions of outrage over the extent of corruption in Russia; the irony was that these individuals' countries were then, and even to this day, are known to be suffering from high levels of corruption!

My long-standing belief that a negative and enduring aspect of human nature is epicaricacy, was only reinforced by encounters with these individuals.

Terrorism

Terrorism in Russia, a consequence of the Chechen war of the 1990s, remained a serious challenge to Putin's law-and-order agenda, as well as to Russia's stability.

This came home to me personally in the seizure of the Dubrovka Theatre in Moscow in October 2002 by Chechen militants. It was reported live on cable television, causing concern on the part of some officials in my HQ. These officials were wondering whether I was a member of the audience. Since no one could get in touch with me on the phone, the Ambassador's secretary came to my flat to inform me about HQ's concern. (I was then CDA a.i.). I had neither listened to the radio nor watched television the night before. I was more shocked than anything else on being told of the incident, but was relieved to hear subsequently that no Singaporean was among the unfortunate members of the audience who had been taken hostage.

The Beslan attack in September 2004 took place a few months after my departure from Moscow but I remained very much interested in following developments there. Beslan is a small city in the North Caucasus and the takeover of a school there by Chechen militants only served to harden President Putin's resolve to rid Russia of them, using all means possible and to strengthen his hold on the country. The former had been his goal since the end of the last century and was not about to change; the attack provided him with the opportunity to stamp his authority on the vast country's regions and autonomous republics by abolishing elections to the governorships and assuming the power to appoint the country's 89 regional leaders who had then to be confirmed by the regional legislatures. He justified the move as necessary to hold the country together.

Earlier in 2000, the country's federal structure was re-organised on the basis of its seven military districts with the President having the power to appoint Presidential Envoys to oversee each district. These moves were made in response to the perceived chaos and weakness of the 1990s when Russia's regions were seen to be drifting out of Moscow's control and to be ignoring its decrees and regulations. President Putin made it his business to rein in regional leaders and bring them back into line. It was apparent that trying to run Russia like a Western democracy was simply a case of trying to build castles in the air.

Ethnic Relations

Ethnic relations during the first term of Putin's Presidency remained tense (for all the reasons mentioned earlier), at least from my observation post in Moscow. However, racist attacks on non-Slavs, regardless of whether they were Central Asian, Caucasian, Southeast Asian, East Asian, or African were not reported frequently. Nevertheless, there were enough cases published in the local media and the English language daily, *The Moscow Times*, to become a source of concern to the non-white residents of Moscow.

I recall reading about Malaysians and Thais falling victim to the skinheads and racist thugs on the streets of Moscow and other Russian cities where they were students, tourists, or long-time residents. My fellow colleagues in the other ASEAN embassies would also report incidents of this sort. The situation reached such a stage that the ASEAN embassies and those of many other countries were forced to send the then Russian Foreign Minister, Igor Ivanov, a *demarche* calling on the Russian Government to increase its measures to protect the citizens of other countries from such outrageous acts. Thankfully, Ivanov promised action and I can say that thereafter, attacks on citizens of ASEAN countries at least, appeared to have decreased.

Putin has never, during his long Presidency, openly supported, let alone called for any policy which would favour ethnic Slav Russians over the many large minorities in the country. Indeed, he has always believed that for Russia to remain strong, its diverse peoples must be united. Indeed, with a large Muslim community and other non-Slav minorities, no Russian leader can afford to conduct an ethnically-based policy. According to an expert on Islam, Alexei Malashenko of the Moscow Carnegie Centre, there are about 16 million Muslims in Russia who are citizens of the country.[6]

I would say that Putin was, and remains a bulwark against the xenophobic, extreme nationalist, and openly racist forces in the country which have been calling for the establishment of a "pure" ethnic Slav Russian state. Running a large country with so many different ethnic and racial as well as religious groups is a very tall order for any Russian leader.

The largest ethnic riots in post-Soviet Russia took place in December 2010 in the very centre of Moscow. (I was not a witness to it, having been on holiday at the time). The spark was the shooting of an ethnic Slav Russian football fan, allegedly by Caucasians. According to an article dated 19 December 2010 in *The Guardian*, to Yevgeny Valyaev, the cause was clear. This newspaper cited him as the leader of Russky Obraz, an ultra-nationalist group that helped gather some of the 5,000 men who descended upon the Kremlin on 11 December, launching the unrest.

---

[6] See his article titled "The Dynamics of Russian Islam", dated February 2013.

"It's not one death. It's a pressure that's been building for several years," *The Guardian* quoted him as saying. "There was no way we could not gather — because he was a football fan and because he was Russian," he said, referring to Yegor Sviridov (the football fan who had been shot). "It was a protest against ethnic banditry."

That term was a clear reference to Caucasians who were a focus of hate and discrimination.

Our Embassy's Singaporean staff members were advised to be alert and watchful for thugs out for "revenge" on the streets of Moscow; thankfully, they did not fall victim to any physical or verbal assault in the weeks and months after these riots. I have already related my own experience with racism and thugs earlier.

Hence, domestic stability and the return of law and order were significant items on President Putin's agenda. One can only appreciate how much of a challenge this was for him, or any Russian leader, given the country's many problems and immense size.

Running a Vast Country

Managing the largest country in the world is no mean feat, even for Putin, a strong and determined leader. I have already related the challenges of doing this. Allow me to cite personal experience to bring home the point of the problems associated with the country's immense size.

I found another opportunity to experience its vastness in the summer of 2000 when I accompanied the Singapore delegation to the Second Children of Asia International Sports Games which were held in Yakutsk, the capital of the Sakha Republic. This is Russia's premier diamond-producing region which also has large gold, tin, antimony and other mineral resources. It is located far from Moscow, in the Russian Far East, and is a very large but sparsely populated region. The Games, a popular event there, were held in conjunction with the summer Olympics, under the patronage of the International Olympic Committee.

Being a diplomat and the official representative of Singapore, I had the privilege of being accorded a minder. While his name escapes me, I recall that he was an ethnic Yakut (a Turkic people). It was he who opened my eyes to life in his capital city. He spoke fluent English but we preferred to converse in Russian. Without my prompting, he invited me to his home for lunch on the second day of my visit; his home was a small flat in a typical Soviet-style building. What caught my eye was that the building, like many in its surroundings, stood at a distinct tilt and appeared to have been sunk or to be sinking into the ground!

Responding to my question, he nonchalantly said that the buildings had been constructed decades before, and little consideration and thought had been given to the harsh climate in Yakutia. Yakutsk is the coldest city in the world; permafrost is a perennial challenge of nature when it comes to constructing a building; heat from a building subsequently sinks into the ground, causing the permafrost to melt and the building to sink; hence, most structures must be built on concrete pillars.

His tiny flat was very modestly furnished but bore the marks of relative poverty, which were clearly seen in the peeling paint on the walls and torn floor carpet. The whole building in which his flat was situated needed massive renovation; the lifts were old and I distinctly recall feelings of despair as soon as he and I stepped into the lift. I was worried it would get stuck between floors and we would not be able to get out in time for me to attend the events of the Games scheduled later that afternoon!

In the great Russian tradition of hospitality, he served me a full meal of meat and potatoes as well as compote. He told me he had prepared the meal in advance of my visit, and was hoping I would accept his lunch invitation. We had a good chat about life in his home town; he was very candid, saying his salary was only US$20, like most of the people of his city!

Apologising to him if I was speaking out of turn, I expressed doubts about how anyone could live on such a meagre amount. He did not take any offence and smiling, said, "*Eta Rossiya*" ("This is Russia"). He added that he and his fellow citizens in Yakutsk did not have a choice but to find ways to supplement their low income, without going into details. To eke out a living was not uncommon for the man in-the-street across the whole country, and hence, I was not surprised and chose not to pursue the matter.

My first thought after listening to him was: how could the people of this region, this city, live on such low salaries when there was so much wealth in the ground? I answered my own question in my head: corruption, inefficiency, the absence of a strong and committed local government, lack of incentives, inertia, and the ongoing consequences of the politico-economic and social chaos following the Soviet collapse. I could only wonder whether President Putin could achieve the unenviable and monumental task of trying to bring order and stability back into his vast country; to me, it was like trying to put Humpty Dumpty back together again. Good luck to him, I thought.

The vastness of Russia as well as Sakha Republic's immense size was again brought home to me when our hosts organised what they termed a "short" boat-cruise for the diplomatic representatives of the Games' participating countries along the Lena, the 11th longest river in the world. The "short" cruise lasted the better part of a whole afternoon and evening (summer nights are long in the Far North of Russia), and we did not even reach any large settlement along the way. Our hosts had told us that the cruise would cover a very minute section of the river. Their concept of "minute" obviously did not correspond to mine, or the rest of their guests. Again, Russian/Yakut hospitality knew no bounds for we had more than enough to eat and drink to kill time on the cruise.

One did not expect to meet any foreigner from a warm clime to be living and working in Yakutsk, but at a reception held for the Games' participating countries' officials and diplomats, I met an enterprising foreign gentleman, whom I shall address as Mr. S. He gave me to understand that the profits to be made outweighed the difficulties of living and working in one of the world's coldest cities. He would later move to the Russian Far East. Mr. S would relate the difficulties of doing business in Russia — the usual points were raised — corruption, *krysha*, contradictory and fast-changing regulations, and the like.

I was to meet quite a number of foreigners during the subsequent years of my second tour of duty and during my third and last tour; all the foreigners would share their similar experiences and assessments of the business climate. Nevertheless, Mr. S could not complain for business was good, despite or in spite of all the difficulties he had encountered. Indeed, the profit motive is *ueber alles*!

Russia and the West

Russia's relations with the West began their downward spiral with the US invasion of Iraq in 2003 which Russia opposed. It believed it was not only a violation of Iraqi sovereignty but would also lead to instability in the country and the region. It was furthermore reported that Russia was concerned about the future of its oil interests in an Iraq without Saddam Hussein. As events turned out, Russia's reservations and objections were vindicated — but this unfortunately is the benefit of hindsight.

Nevertheless, Russian concern about developments in the Middle East would be reiterated when the Arab Spring in 2011 became world news. Russian experts on the Middle East whom I met, correctly predicted that Syria would not be Libya and that any conflict there would be protracted and bloody.

I was a witness to Russian public anger over the US invasion of Iraq on the streets of Moscow. There were quite a number of demonstrations by large crowds in front of the US Embassy, over the course of a few days. I decided to observe one of them just a few days after the US invasion even though there were reports that skinhead thugs were among the demonstrators. However, what is life if one does not take any chances? In this case, I was confident that the skinheads would be more focussed on the source of their anger, viz. the US Embassy, than with one lone non-white foreigner. In the event, I was right.

There were quite a few skinheads at the demonstration in front of the US Embassy. I happened to be standing not far from them (reluctantly). I could not pick and choose my spot for the mass of moving demonstrators meant one, too, had to move with them or be pushed aside. None of the skinheads glanced at me for they appeared to revel in throwing all manner of objects at the Embassy! Ditto for the non-skinhead demonstrators as well. Many screamed at the top of their voices "USA, out of Iraq" and carried banners with the same message.

I derived a measure of professional satisfaction from being in the crowd, not because I agreed with their actions, but because I could almost feel their energy and emotions, which I believed then, were sincere. In any large assembly or group of people, fired-up by anger or frustration over a controversial issue, the possibility of violence breaking out is always present. Hence, I chose not to attend further demonstrations in front of the US Embassy; I did not think Lady Luck would smile on me again.

The EU's and US' growing criticism of Putin's political system fuelled his suspicion of Western motives (he believed they were planning to weaken his government with a view to eventually unseating him). This perception contributed to the deterioration in relations with the West. However, just a few years earlier, it was not apparent that this state of affairs would become entrenched. If anything, there were some indications of President Putin's interest in joining the West.

For instance, he stressed that Russia might join NATO, in an interview on 5 March 2000, on BBC Breakfast with Frost. In reply to David Frost's question about whether it was "possible Russia could join NATO?", Putin replied:

"I don't see why not. I would not rule out such a possibility — but I repeat — if and when Russia's views are taken into account as those of an equal partner. I want to stress this again and again. The situation that was laid down in the founding principles of the United Nations — that was the situation that obtained in the world at the end of World War Two. All right, the situation may have changed. Let's assume there is a desire on the part of those who perceive the change to install new mechanisms of ensuring international security.

But pretending — or proceeding from the assumption — that Russia has nothing to do with it and trying to exclude it from this process is hardly feasible. And when we talk about our opposition to NATO's expansion — mind you, we have never ever declared any region of the world a zone of our special interests, I prefer to talk about strategic partnership. Its attempts to exclude us from the process is what causes opposition and concern on our part. But that does not mean we are going to shut ourselves off from the rest of the world. Isolationism is not an option."

Putin also emphasised that:

"Russia is part of the European culture. And I cannot imagine my own country in isolation from Europe and what we often call the civilised world. So it is hard for me to visualise NATO as an enemy. I think even posing the question this way will not do any good to Russia or the world. The very question is capable of causing damage. Russia strives for equitable and candid relations with its partners. The main problem here lies in attempts to discard previously agreed common instruments — mainly in resolving issues of international security. We are open to equitable co-operation, to partnership. We believe we can talk about more profound integration with NATO but only if Russia is regarded an equal partner. You are aware we have been constantly voicing our opposition to NATO's eastward expansion."

President Putin's words from the interview have been cited verbatim for it is worth noting his actual remarks about NATO and Russia's European heritage. Since then, of course, the situation has changed but his outlook on Russia's European traditions and culture has not. And that has coloured and will colour his perception of and actions towards the West.

He was the first foreign leader to have given President Bush a ring after the events of 11 September 2001. And he did this reportedly against the advice of his military and security officials. In an article in

The Telegraph dated 18 November 2001, Anne Applebaum, an American journalist wrote that "Putin went over their heads when he rang George Bush on September 11 to tell him that 'we are with you'."

She cited the open letter of protest against the direction of Russian foreign policy signed by 18 top brass members a week before her article was written. She added that "Putin himself has led the policy of strategic rapprochement with the United States, dragging his generals kicking and screaming behind him. Putin made them hand over intelligence about Afghanistan, and open up bases in Tajikistan and Uzbekistan to American troops. Unprompted, he also ordered them to close Russian intelligence-gathering bases in Cuba and Vietnam, provoking howls about 'one-sided sacrifices' in the Russian press."

However, the US' decision in December 2001 to withdraw from the Anti-Ballistic Treaty (ABM) of 1972 was a strong factor in President Putin's reassessment of his earlier attitude towards the West, especially the US.

The New York Times reported in an article dated 13 December 2001 that "Putin, while saying that the decision was not unexpected, repeated in a nationwide television address Russia's oft-stated position that the treaty is a cornerstone of world security. He said the decision to withdraw was 'an erroneous one'". The article went on to quote President Putin as stressing that the US' decision "does not pose a threat to the national security of the Russian Federation". However, it also quoted the head of Russia's Armed Forces, General Anatoly Kvashnin, as saying that the decision "will alter the nature of the international strategic balance in freeing the hands of a series of countries to restart an arms buildup".

President Putin's actual feeling about the US decision was made crystal clear years later in his 1 March 2018 annual State-of-the-Nation speech in which he stressed that Russia "was categorically against this" (the US decision). He added that even after the US' withdrawal from the Treaty,[7] "we tried working together in this area to ease concerns and

---

[7] According to a fact-sheet by the Arms Control Association updated in August 2012, "the Treaty was signed on the 26 May 1972 and entered into force on the 3 October 1972. The

maintain the atmosphere of trust", noting that "all our proposals, absolutely all of them, were rejected".

To the Russians, the US' withdrawal from the ABM Treaty opened the way to an arms race and threatened Russia's security and nuclear deterrent, a point President Putin stressed in his 1 March 2018 speech. More details on Russo-Western relations in the Putinite era are found in subsequent chapters.

---

treaty, from which the United States withdrew on the 13 June 2002, barred Washington and Moscow from deploying nationwide defences against strategic ballistic missiles. In the treaty preamble, the two sides asserted that effective limits on anti-missile systems would be a "substantial factor in curbing the race in strategic offensive arms".

Members of the Singapore trade delegation wait on the tarmac of Vladivostok Airport in 1994; the aircraft was functional but not terribly comfortable. I spied a few loose panels on the plane, to my discomfort which, in the event, proved groundless.

View of Vladivostok harbour in 1994. It was a closed city till 1992, presumably because of its strategic location and it being the home base of the Soviet Pacific Fleet.

Members of the trade delegation at a meeting with regional officials in the Russian Far East (RFE) in 1994. Note the portrait of Lenin on the wall. Regrettably, while I did not take any photos in the RFE, one of the things which struck me about the region was the almost ubiquitous presence of Japanese and South Korean makes of almost all vehicles, testimony to the region's close links with the Asia-Pacific region.

Moscow State University (MGU), the country's best institution of higher learning, in winter. I learnt the Russian language in MGU. Note the broad avenues leading to and from the structure. It is one of seven skyscrapers in Moscow, popularly known as the "Seven Sisters". They were built during the Stalinist period. One of the seven is the Soviet, later Russian, Ministry of Foreign Affairs building.

MGU, early in the autumn. On its huge grounds, my family and I would cross-country ski in winter; in summer and autumn, we would also enjoy many a stroll. I would also cycle on its miles of paved and broad streets in summer.

The Aurora, a museum ship moored in St Petersburg. The warship served in the 1904–1905 war against Japan. The photo was taken in 1995 during my private visit to the city.

My family members with an American expat's family enjoying a barbecue by a small town in the Moscow region; note the small kremlin (citadel) and a church within. An engineer in a US telecommunications company, he was one of quite a few foreigners who worked in Moscow in the 1990s and 2000s.

Outside the monastery grounds of Sergiev Posad, Russia's spiritual centre. It attracted many Orthodox faithful as well as tourists, domestic and foreign. All first-time visitors to Moscow must visit it.

Assumption Cathedral of the Trinity Lavra of St. Sergius in Sergiev Posad. Inside are wonders to be seen.

Professor S. Jayakumar, then Singapore's Foreign Minister, on his first visit to Russia in September 2002. Here he is seen with me (in the middle) and Bilahari Kausikan, Second Permanent Secretary (of the Foreign Affairs Ministry), to my right, descending the steps of the Cathedral of Christ the Saviour. It served as a swimming pool during the Soviet period; it was rebuilt and restored after the Soviet era.

Professor Jayakumar laying a wreath at the Tomb of the Unknown Soldier, a war memorial dedicated to the Soviet/Russian troops who fell in World War II.

The world-famous Red Square with the GUM (State Department Store) on the left, St. Basil's Cathedral in the centre, and Lenin's Mausoleum on the right.

Here I am by a restaurant in the city centre of Krasnodar. Its clean, ordered, and tree-lined streets were full of life — restaurants, bars, and cafes — where one could eat and drink at very low prices, compared to Moscow. Krasnodar lies in Russia's south, not far from the Black Sea. It's a city to be visited, if one finds oneself in the region.

Waterfront scene in Gelendzhik, a resort town on the Black Sea. Its warm weather with a host of activities attracted many tourists, mainly Russians.

A typical Russian house in the countryside outside Moscow. It could be sparse, like the one in this photo, or luxurious. Most were quite modest.

Another modest dwelling in the countryside. The contrast between the luxury and prosperity in Moscow and the relative poverty outside the city and in the surrounding countryside was very visible.

Sparrow Hills was a favourite spot for my family and me for easy downhill skiing. My daughter is seen here skiing down the gentle slope. Note Luzhniki Stadium in the background, one of Moscow's iconic structures; it served as the main stadium for the 1980 Olympic Games. It is the largest football stadium in Russia and the ninth largest in Europe.

My daughter and wife take a much-needed break from our usual weekend 15- to 20-mile cross-country ski runs on the frozen Moscow River, and in Serebryany Bor, an enormous forest park, on the left. Note the Orthodox Church's spire in the background (right).

My tired expression and icicles on my moustache and beard, thanks to my sweat frozen over by sub-zero temperatures and wind chill after hours of non-stop cross-country skiing, did not dampen my ardour for the sport. My family and I spent almost every winter weekend cross-country or downhill skiing during my three assignments in Moscow.

Here I am, skiing down the slopes of Ylas, northern Finland. The pristine air and cleanliness of the ski resort provided a welcome escape from the hustle and bustle of Moscow, as well as its not-too-clean air. It became a favourite winter haunt for my family and me.

A large hotel in Dombay ski resort in Russia's south. Note the rather monotonous Soviet-style façade. I did not stay there during my visit; instead, I stayed in a small, nondescript hotel which had all the creature comforts at a very modest rate.

The cracks in the gondola lift's panels are plain to see in this photo, taken on the way up the mountain in Dombay. This was a sign of the sad state of the economy in that region, whose standard of living was below that of prosperous Moscow.

The view from one of the ridges. Dombay was a great place to ski, despite the obvious lack of standard amenities at the time.

The makeshift loo on the mountain, surely not a place one should visit, unless one must!

Good quality food and drinks to be had in these cafes were very inexpensive. They provided the weary skier a welcome relief after hours on the slopes.

Queueing was not on the minds of any skier there! One had to gently push and shove one's way to get onto the ski-lifts!

A street scene in Irkutsk. Note the Soviet-era slogans on the building.

A bus on the streets of Irkutsk. I took the opportunity to ride in one of them; it was not comfortable.

The state of many houses in Irkutsk was found wanting. Here in these photos, one sees that clearly.

On the road from Irkutsk to Ulan-Ude, I came across quite a few picturesque villages by the shores of Lake Baikal. Their poverty was a poignant reminder of the sad state of the country's economy, but that did not distract me from enjoying the clean air and quiet environment surrounding these villages.

If one was hungry or thirsty, one need only turn to the many vendors by the road. Pictured here is a lone lady selling fruits in her buckets and a customer.

In this photo, taken at one of the pit stops on the road to Ulan-Ude, villagers sell omul, a fish found only in Lake Baikal. I tried some of it, although fish is not my cup of tea.

On the outskirts of Ulan-Ude, the capital of Buryatia, one of the many constituent republics of the Russian Federation, one can see the Buddhist structure of a building. The Buryats are Mongolian people; the majority's religion is Buddhism, but shamanism is also reportedly practised.

Cities and towns visited by the author

SIBERIAN
Yakutsk
Yuzhno-Sakhalinsk
Vanino
Khabarovsk
yarsk
Lake
Baikal
Irkutsk
Ulan-Ude
Vladivostok
Nakhodka

The most visible object that greets one in Ulan-Ude's centre is this large bust of Lenin.

The late Minister Mentor, Mr. Lee Kuan Yew, poses with members of the Singapore Embassy's diplomatic and Russian staff members during one of his frequent visits in the first decade of the century.

In the newly-renovated Embassy, I stand proud and happy to have contributed my part to the renovation process. Renovation was completed after a year or so, during which all staff members had to work in makeshift Nissen-like huts placed in the Embassy's car park at the rear of the building. Prior to renovation, the Embassy's interior had walls, ceilings, windows, as well as floors from the Soviet era, all of which were colourless and not pleasing to the eye. The Embassy acquired a modern look after renovation.

Chapter 7

Travels Across A Vast Land

While I was privileged enough to have lived and worked in Moscow for quite some time, I was not able to fully grasp and understand the country as much as I would have liked. Also, coming from one of the world's smallest countries, it was overwhelming for me to live and work in such a huge city as Moscow where the streets and buildings are proportionally much, much larger than those in Singapore. Knowing that Russia is the world's largest country cannot equate to experiencing it. In 1994, I had occasion to fly from Moscow to Yuzhno-Sakhalinsk in the Russian Far East and was amazed that the flight took almost nine hours in Russian airspace! I could not help but be mesmerised by Russia's sheer vastness.

Therefore, during my second and final tour of duty in Moscow, I deliberately made a choice to spend my holidays in Russia.

My travel experiences also gave me an opportunity to see first-hand and assess the state of the country beyond the relative prosperity and stability of Moscow, the centre of the country's economy and political life. This was obviously not the reason behind my decision to become a tourist in Russia; but being a consummate diplomat, I could not help but observe my surroundings with a professional eye.

Dombay

Being an avid Alpine, as well as cross-country skier, I naturally gravitated to Russia's ski slopes and discovered the joys of Dombay in 2003. It is situated in the Karachay-Cherkessia republic in the Northern Caucasus, within sight of Mount Elbrus.

My journey to the ski resort began when I flew to a town called Mineralnye Vodi, a two- to three-hour flight from Moscow as far as I can recall. Upon landing, I was astonished to find that there was no air-bridge — one had to disembark on a gangway, like in the days of old. I was dismayed to see taxi drivers on the runway itself, offering their services! (I wondered why there was no airport security).

The taxi trip to Dombay, a four-hour drive, was quite unforgettable. After bargaining over the fare to the ski resort with at least five taxi drivers, I decided to take the trip with an ethnic Slav Russian whose fare offer was the most reasonable and whose vehicle, an old German make, seemed to be the most comfortable, compared to the Ladas of the other taxi drivers. I admit, I had more faith in it than the Ladas.

He calmly remarked that he had been a member of the *spetsnaz* (special forces) and had fought in Chechnya. I thought to myself that he volunteered that "information" not only to impress but also to assure me that I would be in good hands during the long drive.

Just outside the airport, we had to stop at a police checkpoint. Upon inspecting my diplomatic passport, the officer declared I was an "illegal immigrant" as there was no proper residence visa in my passport! He turned a deaf ear to my point that I had a diplomatic visa. I was told to accompany him to his small office, during which he would "ring Moscow for advice". That turned out to be quite a long call for I had to cool my heels on a rickety chair; he subsequently handed me my passport, without apologising or offering any explanation for all the fuss. It was obvious that by keeping me waiting, he was hoping for some "compensation" but of course, I neither offered any nor even considered making one.

On the way to Dombay, my taxi had to stop at perhaps four checkpoints where I was posed the same question about my visa and was unnecessarily delayed for a few minutes. My taxi driver stated the obvious to me: the officers at the checkpoints simply wanted a bribe. Moreover, I must have been the only (non-Western) foreigner in their zone of responsibility and that must have piqued their interest in me.

Candidly speaking, I was not in the least surprised by the actions of the chaps manning the checkpoints but I must admit, I was taken aback by their brazen attitude in trying to "shake-down" a diplomat from a small and friendly country. It then dawned on me that these chaps were provincials and most probably had never even heard of Singapore.

On my return trip to the airport after my stay in Dombay, I was stopped at the same checkpoints and posed the very same questions! Only this time, they did not take their own sweet time to let me pass. It was obvious they were doing it just to raise my blood pressure. The ubiquitous checkpoints were also a sign of the gravity of the situation in nearby Chechnya and the commitment of the local authorities to ensure that the Chechen conflict did not spill over into their region.

On my return to Moscow, I casually mentioned this incident to some Russian contacts and friends; none of them were surprised by it, and their common refrain was: *Eta Rossiya* ("This is Russia"). One of them even quipped that the writ of Moscow did not run far beyond the Ring Road, a highway which represents the boundaries of Moscow and separates it from the immediate region and the rest of the vast country.

Most would use the term *bespredel* (which means no limits to indicate a state of chaos) to describe not only my experience but the situation in the country as a whole. *Bespredel* can be used to refer to any situation in which one can seemingly do what one wants without fear of consequences. Hence, it was used to explain my situation in which members of a regional law enforcement body were trying to secure a bribe from me or simply to kill time. It was used by a number of contacts to describe the perceived high levels of corruption among officials and their perceived untouchability. It was a word I would come across being used by Russians even in 2013, before my departure from Russia, and at a time when the country was far more prosperous and more stable than in the 1990s and early years of this century. It was meant to convey their sense of helplessness in the face of the *vlast* (the powers-that-be).

My trip to Dombay was well worth it, all things considered.

It was one of the best places I had skied hitherto and since; it had beautiful views but its ski runs were unfortunately unmarked — more on that later. However, its facilities left much to be desired. For instance, at that time, the nearest toilet facilities on the mountain, as far as I could discern, were simple unheated huts with a deep pit (with no toilet throne) in the frozen ground! Naturally, one could not take comfort from having to use them, especially with heavy and large ski boots on; I myself had to take the ski lift down to my hotel just to answer the call of nature!

The ski lifts and hotels were also in various stages of disrepair. Subsequently, I had a conversation on these matters with some locals, being the nosy parker that I am. Not surprisingly, they told me that the local and regional authorities lacked the funds to undertake the required major renovations to the infrastructure. Official corruption and geographical proximity to strife-torn Chechnya were other factors which had inhibited the resort's development, I was given to understand.

Another disadvantage was the fact that the ski runs were not marked (if they had been, I for one did not see any). While I love Alpine skiing, I was and am not an accomplished Alpine skier but can hold my own on steep slopes, if I know when and where to expect them. However, the steep slope I encountered one late afternoon was unexpected, for there was no sign marking it as one (subsequently, I would be told that it was a "black diamond" slope, meaning the steepest). The outcome: in the few seconds when I realised that the slope was too steep for me, it was too late to stop in my tracks and I simply skied down the ungroomed slope.

Losing control with every inch downward, I tumbled down the slope, one of my skis having been unfastened from my foot, and my spectacles simply having flown from my face. I came to an abrupt halt perhaps about 250 yards or so from where one of my skis had lain by the side, upslope. Fortunately, no bones were broken; dazed, I thanked

Providence for that and the fact I had brought an extra pair of spectacles in a strong spectacle case. I must have been sitting on the steep slope for at least 15 minutes, cursing and swearing at myself for being overconfident. When I finally sat up and looked around, I realised I had another three or more miles to ski downhill before I could reach the nearest ski-lifts (they were visible from my position); from there, one could take the ski lift down to the hotel.

However, I could not move without the other ski which lay on the slope, way above me. I tried to walk up the slope to get to the other ski but could not make much progress for the snow was deep and soft. Moreover, walking up a steep slope with one ski and a 20-pound backpack (with lots of water and food) added to the burden. And I was tired after five hours or so of non-stop skiing. I had overestimated the level of my stamina. It was getting dark fast while the wind became stronger. The situation was made worse by the fact that the sky was heavily overcast. I was worried about whether I could get to my other ski in time to get down to the ski-lifts before dark. I therefore struggled to move faster up the steep slope and deep, soft snow. At one point, I sat down and screamed at the top of my voice for help, although I knew none of the skiers I could see on the slopes below could hear me and even if they could, would not be able to ascertain what I was trying to say. There was no ski rescue patrol in sight either.

Panic set in quickly but, just at that point, I looked up and saw a Russian skier grabbing my ski; in a minute, he was beside me, helping me to put it on. I of course thanked him but before I could ascertain his name, he was off, down the slope. Regretfully, I never saw him again. I made it to the ski-lifts in time before complete darkness fell. If the Russian skier had not turned up and not brought me my ski, I might not have made it to the ski-lifts before dark.

In short, I could have been injured skiing downslope in the dark, on my way to the ski-lifts, if I had to retrieve my other ski myself. If I had had to spend the night on that slope, I might have succumbed to the cold at worst. At best, I certainly would have suffered from hypothermia had I had to spend a night on the slope. I felt I had cheated death by a hair's breadth, thanks to this kind Russian; I shall never forget my possible brush with death on the slope and this unknown guardian angel.

One more note to make on my trip to Dombay. I passed some small towns and villages on the way there and back, and while I cannot remember their names, I vividly recall my impression of them. Unfortunately, they were run-down places where poverty was very visible. To me, one of the tell-tale signs of poverty of any place is the state of its public toilets; one must avail oneself of this facility wherever one finds oneself. I could not however avail myself of any public loo in any of these small towns for they were filthy beyond belief. I therefore had to make use of the "facilities" in nature! That was my taxi driver's well-considered advice as well.

Apart from the public loos, the homes, public buildings, shops, etc., that one would see, were in obvious need of repair. The poverty of the people on the streets was evident in their shabby clothes. Compared to Muscovites, they were not as fortunate. Indeed, the Caucasus was and remains one of the underdeveloped regions of Russia. It will take a long time before that region reaches the level of prosperity in Moscow or Western Europe. Years later, I met officials of the region and federal government in Moscow, and was told that domestic and foreign investment was being sought to develop that region. I was not surprised for it is really a beautiful place to ski and enjoy winter.

Today, life there is much better, judging by what I have read and seen on Russian television. Coincidentally, on 2 January 2020, there was a documentary on *Rossia 24*, Russian state television, on Russian ski resorts which I happen to have watched. Dombay was featured in it. Judging by what I saw onscreen, the resort's facilities have definitely improved. I wish I could revisit Dombay someday.

Sochi

This city is certainly a wonderful place to visit. Even in 2007 when I was there, it was a city not to be missed, surrounded by the beauty of nature and the friendliness of its people. At that time, its ski facilities in Krasnaya Polyanna (KP) were not as developed as they would later become in preparation for the Winter Olympics in 2014. Sochi then appeared to be preparing itself for this honour, judging by the many banners I had seen in the city, confidently proclaiming that this honour would fall to it (which it did, hosting this event in 2014). Its winter sports facilities were adequate and better than Dombay's. Its ski runs were marked, its ski-lifts and toilets were what one expected in a modern winter tourist attraction, and new facilities were being built then-and-there.

I did not ski much for I had arrived in late spring when most of the snow had already melted. But what little time I could spend on some of the slopes which had just enough snow on a few ski runs, was certainly a joy for me. KP's immediate surroundings, however, like the city of Sochi itself at the time, did not reflect any visible long-term prosperity. Many buildings were either in a state of disrepair or required massive renovation. However, manifest poverty like that I had observed in Dombay and its surrounding environs was not to be seen in either Sochi or KP.

What struck me was the fact that Sochi's airport did not do justice to its tourist attractions and potential. It was small, old, inefficient, and was more suited to serve a provincial backwater than one of the Soviet Union's and post-Soviet Russia's major tourist resorts! (Little did I know then that a few years later, a Singapore company would help modernise the airport.) Fortunately, the situation has changed dramatically since then, thanks to the Winter Olympics of 2014. Unfortunately, I did not have any opportunity to revisit the city and KP since my first and only stay.

The one incident which remains embedded in my memory of my stay there was my encounter with border guards during a hiking trip. Upon the advice of my hotel receptionist, I undertook a hike into the surrounding area. Not armed with any map (none was to be found in my small hotel in KP), I simply followed the advice of the receptionist to visit a spring on the trail. I was neither told nor bothered to ascertain beforehand (in hindsight, I should have done so) where the border lies between KP and Abkhazia. After hiking for an hour or two in a picturesque landscape with no other hiker in sight, I chanced upon a group of armed border guards sitting by a stream. Upon seeing me, they all stood-up and motioned me towards them, pointing their AK-47s at me! Alarmed, I did as they instructed; fortunately, after checking my passport and after I calmly told them I was a mere tourist and a diplomat from Singapore, a friendly country, they allowed me to proceed to my destination, a spring, a few miles up the trail.

Their commander, whose rank I could not discern as his badge patch was unrecognisable, told me, in a rather threatening tone with a strong non-Russian accent,[1] not to "cross the border near the spring" for I did not have a visa to enter Abkhazia. He added that the border area was "sensitive", while I repeated myself a few times that I was a tourist and diplomat from a country friendly to Russia. The whole encounter lasted no more than five minutes, and even while the commander and I exchanged words, his men's weapons remained trained on me. I must admit, for a second or two, I was in fear of my life during those few minutes when they pointed their weapons at me (that was the first time I had been in such a situation). The fact that their faces were covered with thick stubble, and they had dirty and scruffy uniforms, gave them a certain "menacing" look.

That was reason enough for me to entertain the rather morbid thought that in a worst-case scenario, they could have shot me there and then as a "spy" and no one would have been the wiser. There were no other hikers on the trail at all during my trip to and from the spring.

Upon my return to the hotel, I narrated my experience to the receptionist who apologised for not having warned me about the presence of border guards and the proximity of the trail to Abkhazia. To be fair, it was not her fault but mine — I should have done my "homework" before hiking to the spring. Had I known that I would be hiking close to Abkhazia, I certainly would not have undertaken the hike. However, having done so, I have never regretted my decision; it was certainly an experience to have AK-47s pointed at me by men who

---

[1] The border guards and their commander were not ethnic Slav Russian — but had the physical features of a Meditteranean-type people.

most certainly had never heard of Singapore and even had they known something about us, would not have given a hoot.[2]

Anapa, Gelendzhik, and Krasnodar

These three towns are situated not far from Sochi and Dombay. The climate is Mediterranean and so are most of its local inhabitants. (I would imagine that to many Singaporeans, Russians are believed to be white people with blonde hair and blue eyes. The fact is Russia has one of the most diverse populations in the world, racially, ethnically, and religiously, and is much more diverse than Singapore and many other countries in the world. In the region where the above three cities are located, the population is composed mainly of Russians/Cossacks, and Mediterranean-type Tatars, Armenians, and the local Adyghe people as well as a host of other ethnic groups.)

Anapa and Gelendzhik lie on the Black Sea, and are attractive resort towns. Krasnodar is a larger city and capital of Krasnodar region and is located inland. Unlike Anapa, Gelendzhik, Sochi, and Dombay, Krasnodar was a more attractive place to visit. Its broad, clean main street was lined with good restaurants and cafes, and staffed by friendly waiters and waitresses. Prices were more than reasonable, when compared to Moscow's outrageous prices. Krasnodar's architecture, restored churches, and modestly-priced accommodation, made my visit not only pleasant but light on my pocket.

I do not have any "incidents" or stories to relate about my visits to Krasnodar, Anapa, and Gelendzhik in 2007, for they were relatively short (about a week in these three cities). Nothing untoward or unforgettable happened to me during that short period of time.

Suffice it to say that while my trip there was uneventful, it opened my eyes to Russia's ethnic, religious, and cultural diversity in that

---

[2] According to Wikipedia, Abkhazia, a separatist polity, formally the Republic of Abkhazia, is recognised only by Russia and a small number of countries. While Georgia lacks control over Abkhazia, the Georgian government and the UN, and the majority of the world's governments consider Abkhazia part of Georgia.

region. Moreover, it was crystal clear to me that the tourist potential there was not being fully exploited — accommodation, transport, and other facilities for the tourist (especially non-Russian foreigners) were not up to standard. For instance, to travel to Anapa and Gelendzhik, I hired a "taxi" (like in many Russian cities then, one could simply flag down any vehicle on the road). Bus or train services, to my recollection, were not worth the time and trouble to avail oneself of. My taxi driver, an ethnic Armenian who claimed to have been a "businessman", was not only loquacious but also a nosy parker who posed me too many questions of a personal nature and even had the cheek to suggest that he and I go into business in Krasnodar! Like Sochi, a Singapore company would invest in the modernisation of the airports of these three cities, years after my visit.

Irkutsk

Irkutsk is situated not far from Lake Baikal in Siberia. According to Wikipedia, Lake Baikal is the largest freshwater lake by volume in the world, containing 22%–23% of the world's fresh surface water, more than the North American Great Lakes combined. With a maximum depth of 5,387 feet, Lake Baikal is the world's deepest lake. It is considered among the world's cleanest lakes and is considered the world's oldest lake — at 25 million years. It is also the seventh largest lake in the world by surface area.

For these very reasons, I chose to make a visit to this part of Russia, about six hours flight time from Moscow in 2008. To see the natural beauty and experience the vastness of Russia, a visit to Irkutsk and Lake Baikal is a must and one would definitely not regret it.

At the time, its airport was found wanting. It reminded me of the airports in Russia's south which I had visited the year before. Fortunately, it was a very pleasant city. For one thing, I did not observe any traffic jams on the scale to be found in many large cities in Russia. (Traffic jams were a sign of growing prosperity in Russia. I was told and had read that during the Soviet era, private vehicles were a rare sight and their number could not be compared to that of the post-Soviet period.)

This did not mean Irkutsk was not prosperous; I felt the city was probably better prepared and organised to deal with this challenge of urbanism. Moreover, it was smaller than Moscow where traffic jams were the order of the day. Unlike cities and towns in European Russia, many vehicles were either Japanese or South Korean make. That was and I think still is the case in Siberia and the Russian Far East, a testimony of that region's close links with the Asia-Pacific region.

But what was truly breath-taking for me was a trip to the mighty Angara River and a long ride skirting Lake Baikal to Ulan-Ude, the capital of the nearby Buryatia republic.

Lake Baikal was a sight to behold. Russia indeed is blessed to have it. Its waters were clear, clean but cold, as I ascertained when I decided to take a dip into it during one of the many pit stops on the long drive to Ulan-Ude. I thought to myself that Lake Baikal could surely attract many tourists but would then lose its "innocence", not to mention the very real possibility that its environment would be negatively affected in some way. At the time of my visit, there were not many facilities that catered to tourists. I believe the situation has changed since then, with more hotels and other tourist facilities, but thankfully, Lake Baikal has yet to lose its "innocence".

From Irkutsk, I found a willing chap who agreed to drive me the 280-mile, six-hour journey in his old Lada to Ulan-Ude for US$100 (the actual trip took about 10 hours for I had stopped at many points to take photos and chat with food vendors by the road). An ethnic Slav Russian, I literally picked him from a group of "taxi drivers" loitering outside my hotel. As I wrote earlier, in those days, any Tom, Dick, or Harry could become a taxi driver. An unregulated, technology-less "Uber" started and flourished in Russia way before the tech company took root.

The road to Ulan-Ude is full of beautiful and interesting sights of Lake Baikal, marked by a number of villages. Unfortunately, all the villages I passed by were markedly poor as were its inhabitants, many of whom appeared to be making their living hawking fruits, vegetables and a local fish they called Omul.[3]

On the advice of my taxi driver, I tried Omul which many villagers along the road sold cooked, or should I say, fried. I must admit, I did not take to it though, for fish and seafood are not my cup of tea.

At one of my pit stops, a villager I came across tried a pig-in-a-poke sale to me — he was politely insistent that I purchase a sealed carton of fruits, trying to convince me it was full of fresh bananas! The sceptic in me politely refused his offer. This was an example of Russian entrepreneurial skills at their worst, I thought.

Apart from food, one would encounter villagers who appeared to have had one too many, and would stagger and stumble on the road! I wondered to myself how fast any individual could become inebriated on a hot summer day. It then occurred to me that I had witnessed such scenes in the Polish countryside when I first drove through it from Bonn in 1984. I would see quite a number of men literally drunk on the country roads. I was told that many were jobless and if they had any work, it was most certainly low-paid. Poland then was under the cosh, politically and economically. Post-Soviet Russia was undergoing a similar situation and therefore, to have seen drunk villagers in a region far from the relative wealth of Moscow, was surely not unusual. I felt nothing but pity for the poor fellows.

In Ulan-Ude, a rather drab city, a large bust of Lenin greeted me when I stepped foot into the city centre. It was clear that Soviet Russia's history remained embedded in the people's consciousness, even in a city so far from Moscow, the former centre of Soviet power. The city is the capital of the Buryat Republic,[4] but ethnic Slav Russians and other ethnic groups from the former Soviet Republics were also to be seen.

---

[3] According to Wikipedia, it is a whitefish species of the salmon family native to Lake Baikal. It's considered a delicacy and is the object of one of the largest commercial fisheries on Lake Baikal. In 2004, it was listed in Russia as an endangered species.

[4] According to Wikipedia, the Buryat people are descended from various Siberian and Mongol peoples that inhabited the Lake Baikal Region including Kurykans, who are also the ancestors of the Siberian Turkic-speaking Yakuts.

While having a smoke on the street the day of my arrival, I was approached by an elderly Buryat who spoke to me in his language; he had taken me to be a Buryat. Of course, I had to disabuse him of this notion, whereupon he remarked that he did not know where Singapore is situated! During our short chat, he expressed surprise to have encountered a fellow Asian in Ulan-Ude who was not a "Soviet". He must have been about 50 although his face betrayed an age at least 10 years older. (As I wrote earlier, I met many ethnic Russians and non-Slav Russian citizens who looked older than they actually were).

He spoke nostalgically about the Soviet period during which his life was better. Indeed, this was the refrain I would hear from most older Russians or older non-ethnic Russian citizens whom I had met on the street or in the market and with whom I had chatted, irrespective of the city, town or village I would find myself in, from my first to my last tour of duty in Russia.

This chap spoke fluent Russian, and I observed that the Buryats spoke Russian to each other as well. I was told by a Buryat staff member of my hotel that only older members of the Buryat community were able to speak their own language to some extent. Russification of the non-Slavs in Tsarist and Soviet Russia was the order of the day, and naturally, I was not surprised to learn that the Buryats spoke better Russian than their own language. (Every non-Slav I met in the whole country could speak fluent Russian, a testimony to the effectiveness of the Russification of the country.) Unlike the Slavs however, the Buryats are not Orthodox Christians, illustrating the limits of Russification in Tsarist and Soviet Russia. I had noticed a few Buddhist temples in Ulan-Ude and on the main highway/road to the city, I spied many a Buddhist flag fluttering in the strong wind.

For a change, I decided to take the train back to Irkutsk from Ulan-Ude. The more than seven-hour train ride proved to be a prized experience for me. I sat in a cabin meant for six adults but had another two in it! In all my time in Russia, I would get the impression that simple rules and regulations would very rarely be taken seriously, let alone be respected or obeyed.

The ethnic Slav Russian and Buryat passengers in my cabin brought their own food and drinks and shared them with me, without a second thought (Russian hospitality at its best, again). Foolishly, I did not think of getting food and drinks, believing I could buy anything on the train. While it had a service wagon, there was not much by way of choice or quality. My fellow passengers' home-cooked food tasted better; of that I was convinced. During the long trip, they regaled me with stories of their personal lives, responding to my questions without any hesitation and inhibitions. The common thread in their stories was the challenge of living and working in their region, the fact that they had to live on meagre salaries, that the local and regional authorities were not carrying out their responsibilities towards the inhabitants. Yet, despite their trying circumstances, there was no talk at all about launching a revolution, about changing the *status quo* either in their region or in the whole country. They seemed to have become resigned to their unfortunate circumstances.

I must have heard umpteen complaints about how difficult life was in the country, from one end of the country to the other, from my first tour in 1994 and just before my departure in 2013, during my casual chats with people from all walks of life. However, no one would talk much about bringing change to the country. This was the *vox populi*, I concluded. It was plain to see that Muscovites, perceived by many non-Muscovites as spoilt and pampered, had a different perspective on developments in the country. They would be more amenable than the rest of the fellow countrymen to think about and advocate politico-social changes; but that was then. Today, judging from media and other reports, many people in cities and towns far from Moscow have apparently become more interested in effecting change in the country. Moscow and its immediate region were and remain the most prosperous city and region in the country. Many outsiders desire(d) to live and work there, for more and higher-paying jobs were/are to be had there.

St. Petersburg is Russia's most attractive city that must also be visited. I shall not dwell on any detail of its beauty for there is so much information online to be had. What I can say though it should be visited at the height of summer when the days are long, during the

"White Nights". I have already described in an earlier chapter my first trip to this city in 1994; I visited it again a few more times, on official business and privately. With time, the city became more attractive in terms of cleanliness and organisation as well as facilities for tourists. Any visitor to the city must visit The Hermitage, certainly one of the best museums in the world.

Apart from these cities, I also visited a number of other small towns within the Moscow region but I shall spare the reader the details of these trips for they were not as interesting as the above visits. Suffice it to say that rural Russia is more beautiful than its large cities. I say this for I love and prefer the wide and open spaces in the countryside and small towns to the crowds and larger built-up areas in urban Russia.

Chapter 8

The Curtain Falls: My Final Assignment (2006–2013)

The last seven years of my life in Moscow were anything but boring. My relationships with a number of Russian individuals were strengthened while developments in Russia continued to merit my attention and consume my time.

Russia had become stronger in more ways than one and began to assert itself accordingly on the world stage.

Russia and the West

Into his second term as President (till 2008), Putin had consolidated his power and the economy was not only on the mend but on the rise, thanks to rising energy prices and his economic and fiscal policies. All this brought about even more visible prosperity to Moscow and the country. However, what I really noticed among the Russians I knew, particularly the officials, businessmen, journalists, and others with a high education and a good job, was that with more material wealth came a renewed sense of purpose and above all, more confidence in themselves and their country and a heightened resolve to regain what they felt was their rightful place in the world, after the domestic chaos and Russia's international retreat of the 1990s.

That self-confidence and resolve were clearly demonstrated by President Putin in February 2007 at the Munich Conference on Security Policy; his speech marked a turning point in Russia's relationship with the West. He strongly criticised the US, stressing that "We are seeing a greater and greater disdain for the basic principles of international law. And independent legal norms are, as a matter of fact, coming increasingly closer to one state's legal system. One state and, of course, first and foremost the United States, has overstepped its national borders in every way. This is visible in the economic, political, cultural and educational policies it imposes on other nations. Well, who likes this? Who is happy about this?"

From then on, ties with the West, in particular the US, visibly deteriorated. The factors which led to this state of affairs were varied.

NATO Expansion

The roots of Russian distrust of, disappointment and frustration with the West which persist today, go back to the West's decision in the 1990s to expand NATO eastwards to include former Warsaw Pact countries and the former Soviet Baltic states (whose incorporation into the Soviet Union was never recognised by the West).

No less a prominent figure than George Kennan argued strongly against NATO expansion in an article dated 5 February 1997 in the *New York Times*. He was prescient enough to have seen that Russia would not react positively. He argued strongly that "…expanding NATO would be the most fateful error of American policy in the entire post-Cold War era. Such a decision may be expected to inflame the nationalistic, anti-Western and militaristic tendencies in Russian opinion; to have an adverse effect on the development of Russian democracy; to restore the atmosphere of the Cold War to East–West relations, and to impel Russian foreign policy in directions decidedly not to our liking".

He hit the nail on the head when he predicted that "Russians are little impressed with American assurances that it reflects no hostile intentions. They would see their prestige (always uppermost in the Russian mind) and their security interests as adversely affected." Kennan is associated with the term "containment" of the Soviet Union.[1]

NATO's eastward expansion predictably was not met with any enthusiasm by Russia. Russian media and commentators, academics, and even the man-in-the-street (for instance, even the gypsy taxi drivers I would chat with), and all of my acquaintances and friends would not hide their anger, frustration, and distrust of this development which, by and large, was considered a threat to Russian security. Russia was and remains loathe to the US acting, in its view, as the *arbiter mundi* of world affairs.

Underlying this sentiment was also the anger and disbelief that post-Soviet Russia which had itself removed Communism from power, could still be seen as a threat to the West.

Russians were then and remain convinced even today that NATO expansion was and is directed against their country. Their misgivings about NATO's eastward expansion have been given some basis, if one gives credence to revelations by two researchers, Svetlana Savranskaya, Director of Russia programmes at the National Security Archive (NSA), George Washington University, and Tom Blanton, Director of the NSA, also at George Washington University. In their Briefing Book #621, dated 16 March 2018, published by the NSA, they maintain that:

"declassified documents from US and Russian archives show that US officials led Russian President Boris Yeltsin to believe in 1993 that the Partnership for Peace (PFP) was the alternative to NATO expansion, rather than a precursor to it, while simultaneously planning for expansion after Yeltsin's re-election bid in 1996 and telling the Russians repeatedly that the future European security system would include, not exclude, Russia. The declassified US account of one key conversation on October 22, 1993 shows Secretary of State Warren Christopher

---

[1] In 1999, Poland, Hungary, and the Czech Republic joined NATO, followed by Bulgaria, Estonia, Latvia, Lithuania, Romania, Slovakia, and Slovenia in 2004. Albania and Croatia joined in 2009, followed by Montenegro in 2017. North Macedonia is its newest member, having joined the Atlantic Alliance in 2020.

assuring Yeltsin in Moscow that the Partnership for Peace was about including Russia together with all European countries, not creating a new membership list of just some European countries for NATO; and Yeltsin responding, 'This is genius!' Christopher later claimed in his memoir that Yeltsin misunderstood — perhaps from being drunk — the real message that the Partnership for Peace would in fact 'lead to gradual expansion of NATO'; but the actual American-written cable reporting the conversation supports subsequent Russian complaints about being misled."

For background information, NATO's Media Backgrounder dated April 2018 provides its version of the PFP. It states that "in June 1994, Russia became the first country to join NATO's Partnership for Peace, a programme of practical bilateral cooperation between NATO and partner countries. The Brussels Summit Declaration defined the goals of PFP as expanding and intensifying political and military cooperation in Europe, increasing stability, diminishing threats to peace, and building strengthened security relationship."

The reader should read the Briefing Book in its entirety and come to his own final conclusion about NATO's eastward expansion. Suffice it to say that this issue remains a major cause of the current state of Russo-Western relations.

The US Invasion of Iraq

The US invasion of Iraq in 2003 which took place without UNSC sanction and Russia's open opposition, added another wedge into Russo-US/Western relations. Russia was concerned about future stability in the Middle East, not to mention, reservations about the use of US military power without UNSC sanction. It was also said that Russia was concerned about its oil interests which had been concluded with Saddam Hussein. The issue remained an ongoing matter which coloured Russian perceptions of the US, even years after the US invasion of Iraq.

Instability in the Former Soviet republics

The Rose Revolution in Georgia in late-2003 which brought the pro-Western Mikhail Saakashvili to power as President, was another source of concern of Russia. The Orange Revolution in 2004 in Ukraine which saw the rise of Viktor Yushschenko, also regarded as a pro-Western politician, was seen in a similar light but with even deeper concern, given Ukraine's close historical, cultural, and ethnic links with Russia, not to mention its strategic position in Europe. Georgia's and Ukraine's declared objectives to join NATO and move closer to the West, alarmed Russia, which then and still considers both countries as part of the Russian sphere of interest. In both the Rose and Orange Revolutions, Russia saw the hand of the West behind their fomenting and success.

Ukraine was to feel the wrath of Russia in the energy field. Not too long after Yushchenko's inauguration in January 2005, a dispute arose between the two countries over gas prices. The Russo-Ukrainian conflict/dispute over gas prices between 2009 and 2013, and the Maidan revolution of 2014 during which President Viktor Yanukovich was swept from power, the hostilities in eastern Ukraine and Russia's annexation of the Crimea in 2014, exacerbated relations with the EU and the US, as well as Russo-Ukrainian ties till this day.

Russia perceived Western attempts to strengthen relations with the former Soviet republics as a zero-sum game. Moreover, Western NGOs' activities in Russia itself and Western governments' criticism of the Russian government's perceived human rights violations and democracy standards only raised the level of Russian distrust.

Russia's reaction against perceived Western attempts to increase its influence in the post-Soviet space at Moscow's expense was evident in the Russo-Georgian war of August 2008. The short and limited conflict effectively put paid to Georgia's objective of joining NATO. Russia's victory in the war had apparently ended what must have been seen hitherto (in Moscow's eyes) as Georgia's cock-a-snook policy towards its erstwhile Soviet "comrade".

The short Russo-Georgian war was supported by every Russian I spoke to, regardless of their social status, including those who did not consider themselves followers of President Putin. The short conflict was seen as Russia's justified reaction to firstly, Georgia's perceived aggression against South Ossetia and Abkhazia, which are Georgian breakaway territories, backed by Russia and secondly, to Georgia's open aspirations to join NATO and the EU.

The conflict took the West by surprise but relations with Russia did not suffer much damage. It was clear that raw power politics was at play here. The interests of the West in maintaining good and stable ties with Russia, outweighed any possible interest in supporting Georgia, a small country, to the hilt, and risk an open conflict with Moscow. Georgia did not secure any Western military assistance in its short war with Russia.

The conflict also had consequences on commercial as well as social levels. A Russian acquaintance who worked in a Russian company importing Georgian wine and mineral water related to me how the company began to experience difficulties in securing supplies during and after the conflict, as a consequence of the deteriorating political relationship between the two countries. This company eventually had to close down. Socially, some Georgians resident in Russia, became objects of verbal and even physical abuse, in extreme cases.

Georgian friends of my part-time Russian language tutor, an ethnic Slav Russian who was resident in Georgia almost all her life but later moved to Moscow, recounted their experiences to me over dinner in her flat one evening, not long after the conflict's end. While Georgians and other swarthy non-Russians had become inured to discriminatory actions on the part of policemen, the conflict appeared to have led to even more hostile behaviour, according to my Georgian interlocutors. They were convinced however that many policemen had not become more anti-Georgian *per se* but were merely exploiting the prevailing anti-Georgian political mood to demand higher bribes.

The Arab Spring

The Arab Spring of 2011 — Libyan leader Muammar Gaddafi's fall and Western intervention there, as well as developments in Syria which led to the ongoing civil war and Western/US support for Syrian President Assad's opponents — also explain tensions in Russia's relations with the West.

In that regard, Yevgeny Satanovski, a leading expert on the Middle East, was prescient when he told me in 2011 that Assad was not Gaddafi and Syria was not Libya — in other words, Assad and Syria would not go the way of Gaddafi. Syria's Armed Forces were disciplined, well-trained, well-armed, and had combat experience from conflicts in the Lebanese civil war (1975–1990) and against Israel (1967, 1973, and intermittent clashes over the Golan Heights). Professor Vitaly Naumkin, another prominent expert on the Middle East, also conveyed the same standpoint.[2]

In 2011, both experts were convinced (and proven right) that any Western attempt to weaken or unseat Assad would lead to higher levels of violence and more instability in the Middle East. Russia's military intervention in 2015 on the side of Assad which was crucial in his regaining control of Syria, has been another factor accounting for the downward trend in relations with the West.

Kosovo

Another major cause of Russian anger with the West concerned Kosovo — unrest there led to NATO's bombardment of Serbia in 1999, until Serbian leaders agreed to allow peacekeepers there and to withdraw its security forces to enable the transfer governance to the United Nations. Kosovo's unilateral declaration of independence in 2008, while having been recognised by 113 UN member states, did not

---

[2] He subsequently assumed a position as a consultant to Staffan de Mistura, who was the United Nations Special Envoy on Syria from 2014 to 2019.

meet with Russia's support. Traditionally a supporter of Serbia, a fellow Orthodox Church country, Russia has never hidden its displeasure with Western support of Kosovo against Serbia.

Magnitsky and Snowden

Apart from these developments, two events — the Magnitsky Act and Edward Snowden's flight and stay in Russia — further strained relations with the US. The former, Sergei Magnitsky Rule of Law Accountability Act of 2012, is a bipartisan bill passed by the US Congress and signed by President Obama in December 2012; its purpose is to punish Russian officials the US holds responsible for the death of Russian tax accountant, Sergei Magnitsky in a Moscow prison in 2009. Magnitsky died in a Moscow prison after investigating a US$230 million fraud allegedly involving Russian tax officials.

In response, the State Duma adopted the Dima Yakovlev Act, which imposed a ban on adoptions of Russian orphans by Americans, a prohibition of any political activities by NGOs receiving funding from the US if such activities may prove detrimental to Russian interests, as well as a series of sanctions levied against US officials thought to have violated human rights. The Russian bill is named after Dima Yakovlev, a two-year-old boy who died in the US state of Virginia after his foster father left him in a locked car in the sun. The case was widely publicised in the Russian print and electronic media.

Snowden was a former CIA employee and former contractor for the US government who copied and leaked classified information from the National Security Agency (NSA) in 2013 without authorisation. Fleeing the US, he arrived in Moscow in June 2013, and spent five weeks in the airport before he was eventually given the right to remain in Russia temporarily. He was granted a three-year residence permit in August 2014. According to an article by Shaun Walker of *The Guardian* dated 18 January 2017, Snowden's leave to remain in Russia was extended for three years. The article quoted his lawyer, Anatoly Kucherena, as telling the *RIA Novosti* news agency that the permit had been extended until 2020. A *CNN* report dated 17 April 2020 cited a *TASS* news agency article as saying that Snowden had filed a request to extend his residency permit in Russia for three more years, quoting Kucherena.

Domestic Developments

Between 2006 and 2013, Russia experienced not only economic growth but also recession, following the financial crisis in 2008. Crude oil prices, the mainstay of its economy, fell from US$144 per barrel to below US$55, and federal budget revenue fell 4.8% along with it. Its economy contracted by 7.9%. However, Russia recovered fast, returning to growth in 2010, thanks to the efforts of Finance Minister Kudrin and Minister of Economic Development Elvira Nabiullina (today, she heads the country's Central Bank).

Medvedev as President

Putin returned to the Presidency in 2012 after four years as PM while his trusted colleague, Dmitry Medvedev held the country's highest office in what was known as the "tandem" (the term used to describe the political arrangement between the two men to run the country). Putin was constitutionally barred from seeking a third consecutive term during the 2008 presidential elections. During the 2008–2012 of Putin's Prime Ministership, it was widely felt that he was running the show, behind the scenes.

He was considered the *primus inter pares* in the country. No one really knew, except both men and those closest to them. I can testify that having often watched both men on Russian television almost daily when they appeared at cabinet meetings or other public events, I could not help but notice Putin's rather standoffish and even bored attitude, which he did not seem to hide. That to me was a clear indication of the unequal relationship between the two men. Medvedev himself was smart enough and politically savvy not to try to steal a march on his mentor.

Nevertheless, Medvedev's Presidency (2008–2012) was marked by purported aspects of modernisation and liberalisation of the economy, political system and in foreign policy. Some examples suffice to illustrate this. In April 2011, top government officials were instructed to step down from their posts in state corporations. In April 2012, Medvedev signed into law a bill that made it easier to register political parties. According to this bill, a party only needed 500 members to register rather than 40,000. In May 2012, Medvedev signed into law a bill that made it easier for political parties to participate in elections. Political parties would not have to gather signatures in order to participate in elections to the Duma or local parliaments. However, parties not currently represented in the Duma or local bodies must secure the signatures of 100,000 voters. These two pieces of legislation were clearly meant to calm the political waters after the mass demonstrations of late 2011 and early 2012 in Moscow and some other cities (see below for details).

In foreign affairs, Medvedev apparently supported Russia's abstention in the UNSC resolution of March 2011 establishing a no-fly zone over Libya, a course of action which Putin severely criticised, labelling the resolution "defective and erroneous", reminding him of "a medieval call for crusades". Medvedev reacted by describing Putin's language "unacceptable". Observers then (erroneously) speculated that the "tandem" was in political trouble.

Putin's critics and political opponents, domestic and foreign must have been hoping that Medvedev would challenge Putin's control of the country and even seek re-election. As President, Medvedev's open admiration for Western music, as well as use of language loaded with references to "democracy", "innovation", and the like, had fuelled rumours and hopes among Putin's domestic and foreign critics that he would run for re-election.

Medvedev never sought to hide his preference for Western music groups, principally Deep Purple. In February 2008, Gazprom, the Russian natural gas company, organised a concert to celebrate its 15th anniversary which featured the rock group and Tina Turner. I was present, having been invited by a Gazprom contact. From my vantage point in the Kremlin Palace, a huge venue which seats up to 6,000 people, making it the largest concert hall in Russia, I observed how leading members of Gazprom and the government were clearly enjoying themselves, in particular, then DPM Medvedev (by then, it was crystal clear that Putin would nominate him for the Presidency). The concert which lasted more than four hours, was opened by Putin himself. He however left during the intermission.

It was a forlorn hope. I myself believed that while both men might and did have differences of views of domestic and international issues, they would not allow them to lead to any struggle over political power in the country, let alone, the collapse of the tandem. I also believed that given their long and close personal and political relationship, publicly-uttered differences over issues like the one cited above, would not be allowed to upset the political balance. There was also the very real possibility that both men could have been deliberately playing up their differences for public consumption, to show their foreign and domestic critics that Russia was not an authoritarian state and that differences at the top with respect to various issues, could and did exist.

It was more realistic to assume that Putin would not choose political oblivion or retirement over his own oft-declared mission to revive, preserve, strengthen and maintain Russia's place in the world as well as to raise the living standards of his people. And that was my feeling then.

President Medvedev nevertheless had a worthy, even if it had seemed at the time, a very ambitious proposal, viz. to establish Moscow as a global financial centre. Announced in 2008, he spoke about it quite a few times during his Presidency and held meetings with top Russian officials and businessmen, including foreign businessmen, urging them to take the necessary measures to realise this goal, including at the annual St. Petersburg International Economic Forum (SPIEF).

A Russian judicial official whom I once met some time in 2012, posed me the question of what was needed for Moscow to become like Singapore, a global financial centre. My straightforward answer was that obviously the physical infrastructure in the then relatively newly-built Moscow City district with many impressive modern high-rise buildings, were not enough. Apart from that, Moscow had to deal with issues like the perceived lack of the rule of law, perceived corruption in the judiciary, in the bureaucracy, and in the law enforcement bodies, unattractive environment for foreign investors, lack of qualified talent in the financial sector, and overall negative image of Russia. While he had listened intently to my reply, it did not elicit any response from him.

My answer had not been based purely on my own assessment. Weeks before our meeting, I myself had spent quite some time speaking to as many reliable and qualified contacts as I could, on the matter. I had also done my own online research on this issue. No one seriously believed then that Medvedev's objective could be met in the foreseeable future while not totally ruling out its feasibility in the future.

Demonstrations Against the Establishment

A major development before Putin's return to the Presidency was the mass demonstrations in December 2011 in Moscow and some major cities over perceived legislative electoral fraud, which carried on into the 2012 Presidential election.

I was present at the first few mass demonstrations in Moscow and while I was impressed by their relatively large size, I did not think they were a real threat to President Putin's legitimacy. He still enjoyed the support of the masses who lived outside Moscow (and other large urban centres in which one could find the core of the anti-Putin movement).

Attending one of the first mass demonstrations which took place on a weekend on Novi Arbat, not far from my flat and the Embassy, I was taken aback by the rather casual atmosphere of the whole event. I half-expected that demonstrators would be in an aggressive mood. There were the usual speeches by anti-Putin figures from the cultural/arts scene as well as known opposition figures. However, I did not observe any open manifestations of anti-Putin behaviour.

At that time, tensions in the US–Russia relationship were becoming evident. The *cui bono* question was predictably raised by President Putin who alleged that the demonstrations had the support of the US, including that of then Secretary of State Hilary Clinton. In the event, the demonstrations eventually petered out; they also contributed to Putin's already heightened suspicions about Western and US involvement and backing for the anti-government demonstrations. That was an important factor which led to the deterioration of relations.

One interesting non-political personality I met at an event during this period of time was Mr. A, one of Russia's premier novelists. Mr. A was critical of the Russian government, but unlike some other personalities who were not fans of the powers-that-be, (a favourite term used by Russians), his criticism was measured and policy-centred, and not personality-based viz. not directed at Putin personally. Personalities like Mr. A, who were not enamoured of their government's policies and who did not seek to hide their sentiments, would find expressions in the public domain, in some form or another. The image that some had of Russia that no publicly expressed dissent would be tolerated was obviously not consonant with reality.

Terrorism

The 2000s would see a spate of terrorist acts. They began in September 1999 with the bombing of some blocks of flats in Moscow, Volgodonsk and Buinaksk by Chechen militants, according to the Russian government. These terrorist acts strengthened Putin's position to hand a *coup de grace* to Chechen attempts to gain independence from Moscow. They also acted as grist to his political mill as they strengthened his popularity and helped him to secure victory at the presidential polls in March 2000.

In 2002 and 2004, the hostage crisis in Dubrovka Theatre in Moscow and the school siege in Beslan (in the North Caucasus) were also defining moments in Russia's struggle against Chechen militancy. There were quite a few other terrorist acts in Russian cities, including in Moscow. I shall not list all of them for such information is freely available in the public domain. The following three examples suffice to make the point that the country had become a target of terrorism:

- February 2004 — a bomb in a crowded metro train in Moscow killed at least 39 and wounded more than 130 people;
- August 2004 — two passenger aircraft which took off from Domodedovo airport in Moscow were blown-up mid-air by female suicide bombers; 81 people perished; and
- January 2011 — a bomb went off in the arrival lobby of the same airport, apparently detonated by a suicide bomber, killing 35 and injuring more than 100 people. It was personally alarming to me and the rest of the Embassy staff members, for they and I had been in the very lobby many a time to receive and welcome friends and/or guests, both personal and official, on their arrival in Moscow.

Thankfully, the Embassy experienced a bomb scare only once, in the early years of the Putinite era. One morning, the militiaman/police guard for the Embassy (they were on duty round-the-clock, 365 days a year) reported to our Russian staff members that a car had been parked on the opposite end of the street in front of the Embassy for days on end. It was suspicious as only residents were allowed to park there for any length of time. The militiaman rang the police and a bomb-disposal unit was sent to inspect the car; everyone in the Embassy had to be evacuated. All of us waited, on the cordoned-off street, over 100 yards away, for the unit to carry out its job. Fortunately, the car did not contain any explosives and was towed away. The incident made the news, with even CNN sending its Moscow Bureau Chief, Jill Dougherty, to cover it.

During all that time, I personally took a number of steps to avoid becoming a victim of such acts.

First, I did not take my earlier regular lunch-time walks as often as I would have liked. Whenever I did indulge in this pastime, I would avoid crowds and walk along smaller side-streets and alleys. If I saw someone I believed was acting suspiciously, I would simply walk as fast and as far away from him/her. There would be no room for political correctness, if my life could be at stake.

Second, whenever I had to use the metro or bus, I would sit right at the back and/or as far away from anyone with a backpack or any bag I believed was large enough to hold a bomb or weapons. I must also admit that I would size-up any individual and if I believed that he/she fit the profile of a possible or potential terrorist, I would move away from him/her as far was physically possible. I was not born to become a hero. There were quite a number of individuals I had observed on the train or on the metro's platforms who could have been terrorists, judging by their appearance, but were not. While one must not judge a book by its cover, when my life and limb could be at stake, I was not and would not be bothered by considerations of political correctness.

Third, I reduced the frequency of my visits to cafes, restaurants, or pubs.

Finally, I would avoid being in the presence of crowds whenever and wherever that was possible, irrespective whether I would find myself in the airport lobby, a shopping mall, on the street, in a bus or in a metro station or on a train. It is always worthwhile to become a wee bit paranoid and take simple steps in order to live another day.

Chapter 9

Perspectives of Contemporaries in Moscow

My book would not be complete without including the perceptions of other individuals who lived and worked in post-Soviet Russia.

I have devoted an entire chapter to their views, as it is important to let the reader acquaint himself/herself with the entirety of their opinions and assessments. I also do not want to secure for myself the lion's share of providing the reader a picture of Russia. The viewpoints of my contemporaries will not only balance mine but also help the reader to come to his or her own conclusions about Russia.

These individuals generously donated their time by letting me have their perspectives on e-mail or chatted with me in person. Their standpoints are reproduced below, some of which, for the purpose of brevity, have been abridged.

Westerners' Standpoints

The views of a Western businessman with long-standing experience in Soviet and post-Soviet Russia are worth reading. He first lived in Moscow in the mid-1960s, stayed a few years, left the country, and returned in the late 1990s to live and work there until some years ago. He has chosen to remain anonymous. The following is his story; it has been edited only for structure but not content. I have done the same for all the other sources.

In his view, there was a huge difference between the experiences in the 1960s, 1970s, the 1990s, and then again, the gradual changes since Putin's rise to power. In the 1960s, Soviet society was closely watched by authorities, which made spontaneous contact with the people somewhat strained. On the one hand, one had close contact with one's embassy employees (all selected by the GlavUPDK), who were clearly briefed on how to behave. On the other hand, contact with the locals was very much influenced by one's lack of Russian language skills and some fear of running into trouble with the authorities, on the part of the locals themselves. In general, however, this businessman had good and positive memories of that time.

In his view, during the "mad" 1990s, things had changed dramatically; everything "Western" seemed to have become the "norm", strongly influenced by the invasion by Western media. As an example, he cited the fact that "we had girls coming to the office, dressed as if they had just walked out of a French fashion magazine; at one point, we had to ask them to go back home and get dressed!"

Reflecting on the chaos in Russian society, he noted that the 1990s "was also the time of the 'Wild West' type shoot-outs; we had one just outside the office and another one just down the road from our flat. This aspect of society also influenced our business contacts; you had to keep it in mind all the time when dealing with Russian business people. Some of my colleagues and friends were forced to leave the country for some time because of a real threat. Invitations to discuss 'business' further at *dacha*[1] weekends were usually declined politely!"

He laments the changes in attitudes in Russia towards Westerners with what he describes as "the Second Cold War, which, so far, has been successful in destroying the positive feeling towards the West of the Russian people. This has also killed the 'joy' we used to feel about living in Russia! In my mind, any politician that blows the nationalistic trumpet to bolster his power is a threat to humankind! Unfortunately, this seems to have become the norm!"

---

[1] *Dacha* is the Russian term for a country home.

With respect to the state of the economy, he asks rhetorically: "What does Russia produce, that people want to buy? (extracting or cutting down don't count!)"

He thinks that "the Russian economy depends entirely on the price of oil and gas. Any attempt so far at diversification has ended up costing a lot of money (mostly ending up in the wrong pockets, as well) and having no impact. Space and arms developments could be counted as an exception, but are mainly politically-influenced (as opposed to economically). Because of sanctions (import bans on Western food products), companies in this market (local, as well as international) have been forced to bring production on-shore for a lot of the banned products. They are all very happy that sanctions don't affect imports of equipment, by the way! Most of the Russian copies of equipment that I have worked with are a waste of time and effort. If most of the wealth, resulting from the boom period in the oil industry, had been used to support the development of local production of value goods instead of ending up in the pockets of the 'happy few' that support the government, things could have looked a lot different."

He is not optimistic about Russia's future, arguing that "unfortunately, with the present (international) power structure, further isolation must be the result. Foreign investment will be strongly discouraged, and I don't believe that repatriation of Russian wealth will happen at any significant level. The 'tit-for-tat' policy on sanctions looks like continuing for some time. How long will the 'nationalistic trumpet' enchant the Russian people? Who will convince them that a healthy economic policy is more important than trying to impose political clout on the international level through costly military expenditure?"

He also believes that "as long as the present power structure stays in place, I don't see much chance for improvement. Is it not unbelievable that the biggest country, with the vast natural riches it possesses, keeps stagnating in today's world of chances? The only positive thing I hear about Putin's influence on Russia is that he brought stability. Well... so did Brezhnev! No further comment! The only chance I see for improvement for Russia is in its young people; they seem to be the only ones that have the guts to stand up and speak out. Surely, still a minority, but with the communication possibilities of today, they will become a real power in the future."

A former US diplomat who lived and worked in Moscow from 1994–1997 and 2004–2005, and had personal experience with the Soviet Union and Russia between 1980 and 2011 (as a student in the summer of 1980, the fall of 1983, and the spring of 1985) has this perspective of post-Soviet Russia and the current situation:

"My longest stay, 1994–1997, made the most vivid impression on me, especially since I had a basis of comparison with my Soviet-era sojourns. It was a time of stark contrasts. On the one hand, it was a period of unprecedented freedom and openness. The tiresome, stilted propaganda slogans had vanished from the billboards, newspapers, and TV broadcasts. There was a blossoming of critical thinking about policy and the direction Russia should take. Unlike in Soviet times, it was fascinating to read the press, and the profession of investigative journalism — unknown in the Soviet Union — appeared with great vigour. There was more openness toward foreigners. The persecution of religion — still very evident during the 1980s — had ended, and the churches were being reopened and renovated. I recall my delighted surprise in 1992 seeing a Russian Orthodox monk for the first time on the streets of Moscow — an inconceivable sight even just a few years before. There was an unprecedented availability of consumer goods, especially quality foreign products. At the same time, there were many depressing aspects to Russian life in the mid-1990s. Poverty was everywhere apparent. It was common to see beggars on the sidewalk, or little groups of *babushki* (old ladies) trying to sell one or two articles of clothing to make ends meet. Veterans were reduced to selling their war medals. I was once approached by a young soldier asking for money or food. Even educated people, who had a decent living by Soviet standards, were often scrounging to make a living. Yes, there were far more goods available to buy than there had been in Soviet times, but they were beyond the reach of many pauperized Russians."

This former diplomat also found that the 1990s were also a very disorienting period for the Russian people. Decades of Soviet propaganda that "had assured them that they represented the very cutting edge of progressive humanity, that they were the envy of other peoples and a beacon for the rest of the world. Moreover, they were a superpower that was feared and respected by all. Triumphalist Soviet propaganda in the 1980s had crowed that the balance of forces (*sootnoshenie sil*) in the world had swung irrevocably in favour of the Soviet camp, and that the final victory of Socialism was not far off."

The Soviet collapse had taken most people by surprise and hence, "they were prone to explain the breakup of the Soviet Union with conspiracy theories about the role of the eternal Western enemy and the treason of Gorbachev, Shevardnadze, and Yeltsin. The sharp, sudden diminution of Russia's influence in the world came as a huge shock. Russians, accustomed to leading one of the two big blocs in global affairs, suddenly found themselves without a bloc and largely even without allies. Instead, they were supplicants and pupils to the West — a situation that was psychologically grating and ultimately unsustainable. Russia, accustomed to being an independent great power and the leader of its own bloc, was never going to play second fiddle in someone else's alliance."

The Soviet collapse was also an additional source of trauma for the Russians. Ostensibly, a multinational entity in which various peoples freely participated as equals, "for most Russians, it turns out that the Soviet Union really *was* Russia, and the constituent republics were simply an extension of Russia. This attitude was reflected in Putin's speech where he claimed that 'Russia' had lost $x\%$ of its territory, population, economy, etc., when the Soviet Union broke up. Russians had also been taught for generations that — unlike the nasty European empires — Russia had always expanded peacefully and largely with the consent and even enthusiastic participation of the non-Russian 'little brothers.' While European imperialists had ruthlessly plundered their colonies, Russia had selflessly poured resources into the territories it had annexed. Russians therefore assumed feelings of grateful tenderness on the part of the non-Russian peoples of the Soviet Union, so the national-separatist movements of the late 1980s and the ultimate breakup of the Soviet Union came as a huge shock. Once again, rather than question their earlier misconceptions, most Russians were inclined to assume that a combination of Western intrigue and shocking ingratitude on the part of the 'little brothers' had ruined everything."

Gilles Breton, a Canadian diplomat who worked in Moscow from 1983 to 1986, initially as Third Secretary and then, after two years, Second Secretary, from 1989 to 1991 as First Secretary, and 2008–2012 as Minister-Counsellor and Deputy Head of Mission, also has an interesting perspective, covering both Soviet and post-Soviet Russia.

In his view, "it is normal for a foreigner to have to learn to work in accordance with local practices. Yet, in Russia there prevailed an aura of mystery around the workings of the local bureaucracy. In my own experience, there was nothing so special that knowledge of the Russian language, an open mind, and the willingness to make the effort to understand, could not overcome. There were nevertheless some frustrating moments. Quite often, the emphasis was more on knowledge than on action. With the capacity to approve an action resting with the higher authority, it could be difficult and time-consuming to get things done in the context of a joint undertaking. During the Soviet period, the living conditions of a foreign diplomat had very little to do with the life of regular citizens. The secret was to learn how to plan your purchases from foreign sources so as to avoid the shortages engendered by the planned economy. On occasion, as a foreigner you were treated with such deference as to make you feel rather uneasy. Informal unauthorised contact with locals was complicated as any person entering in contact with a foreigner could be held to explain such an occurrence. Surveillance was par for the course, but could be more or less intrusive, depending on the interest the local authorities had in any one individual. In any event, as a foreigner, you so stood out that going unnoticed was virtually out of the question. Challenges varied — during the transition period (1989–1991) everything was difficult; the old communist era ways were no longer working, the new capitalist ways were only beginning."

Breton rightly notes that "the Soviet years were a time of constant shortages of consumer goods. The first 10 post-Soviet years were chaotic. It should not come as a surprise that the Russian people are generally happy to live in a 'consumer society'. That was the dream. There is no appetite to create a different kind of society."

He also observes that Russia's "stable 'managed democracy' system works for the time being. Two questions arise. First, how do you replace the strong leader when he has to go? Second, in the longer term, do you maintain the system as it is or do you make it more open and less managed to accommodate the wishes of the new voters born after the end of the Soviet Union?"

On the economic side of the coin, Breton believes that "the transition of the Russian economy into capitalism has not been accompanied by the empowerment of a great number of economic actors — a large part of the economy is under the control either of oligarchs or of state-owned enterprises. The economy functions under market rules, but it is controlled by a relatively small group of people who wield a lot of authority. This is not conducive to rapid growth. More specifically, it is not likely to lead to the emergence of SMEs that are considered the most dynamic elements in many modern economies. The problem is compounded by the lack of domestic capital that would be available to invest in new enterprises. The diversification of the economy and the promotion of innovation have rightly been identified as priorities. In addressing these priorities there is, however, still too much dependence on government initiatives, rather than on a dynamic and agile private sector."

Yet, Breton is cautiously confident about the future as he argues that "Russia has demonstrated a lot of resilience throughout the years, as well as more recently. There is no reason to believe that the resilience is at risk. There should be continuing political stability, with a new leader, but not necessarily with a rapprochement to the type of democracy that is practised in Western Europe. Change will happen. The pace of change, however, is the most difficult to predict."

Finally, the former Canadian diplomat's assessment on the negative side relates to the fact that "Russia suffers more acutely than Western countries from the shortage of skilled labour. With an education system that is geared to produce highly-qualified scientists and, nowadays, jurists, there is going to be a difficulty satisfying the demand for technical workers and engineers. On the positive side, one of the legacies of the Soviet system is that Russia has a very literate population. As a result, it also has a highly computer-literate population. It also has a strong software capacity. This should facilitate the digitalisation of the economy. There are enough non-US suppliers so that access to computer hardware, including processors, will not be a problem. The digitalisation process has been identified by the World Bank as one that could substantially accelerate economic growth in Russia. In a way, one could see Russia moving more quickly into the digital world than more advanced economies. Efficiency gains could be considerable."

A former Australian diplomat who had visited Moscow many times between 1974 and 2003, and worked there from 2003 to 2006, had this to say:

> "An extraordinarily stimulating and challenging environment; for an Australian, Moscow, a world capital, quickly proves to be neither a European nor an Asian city — architecturally and institutionally, it shares many features with European capitals but the mentality and shape of human organisation in the city is distinctly un-European. But neither is Moscow an Asian city; it lacks the subtlety and unassertiveness of a Bangkok, the discipline and orderliness of a Singapore, or the chaotic joyfulness of a Jakarta."

The former diplomat assessed that his experience had shown that "it was seldom the default position of Russian officials to seek for a 'win–win' solution to any issue I brought to them. More common was the view that if our side achieved what we had come to request, this must inevitably mean that the Russian side had to forfeit something, even if that something could not be readily identified. Suspicion of the foreigner seemed to be the default setting. There were exceptions, of course, and happily some of these arose in the area of Australian–Russian cooperation in Asia-Pacific matters, for example to do with the ARF (ASEAN Regional Forum) or APEC (Asia-Pacific Economic Cooperation). Intriguingly, another area where I found Russian officials very forthcoming was in military-to-military relations."

Like most observers, he found "economic conditions in Moscow during the decade 2000–2009 had greatly improved on the previous decade, although the disparity in wealth between the rich and the poor was already immense and growing rapidly. Of course, the disparity in wealth and economic outlook between Moscow, even central Moscow, and the rest of the country, with some few exceptions, was even more vast. One did not have to drive far from the centre of Moscow to encounter a level of economic development far removed from the glamour of Tverskaya or Gogolevsky Boulevard or the Arbatskaya Ploshchad. And once out of the city confines, roads were likely to deteriorate rapidly and the stock of housing to acquire a most dilapidated appearance."

With respect to reform efforts, the former diplomat is of the view that "the most serious weakness in Russian economic reform efforts is the absence of an independent judiciary and transparent body of law. In a system where judges and magistrates, and law enforcement officials are subject to political direction, however subtle (or not), the positive aspects of a well-regulated market economy will struggle to prevail. Where there is perceived corruption at the top of the ladder — and how can such inconceivable disparities in wealth and power exist between the oligarchs and the ordinary workers without such perceptions? Good economic policy decision-making will be difficult. Russia, like Australia, is a huge and largely underdeveloped country, rich in human and natural resources, but in need of foreign capital and an open and mutually beneficial set of international trading relationships. Fair, transparent and enforceable laws are a prerequisite for these conditions. And a major consideration is that President Putin seems to have no interest in real economic reform as this would only become a threat to his untrammelled authority."

The former diplomat is not optimistic about the future of Russia's relations with the West and Russia's democratic development, arguing that "with his (Putin) recent re-election for a further six-year term to 2024, we have to expect more of the same from the Kremlin as we have seen in recent years. This means a continuing combative stance towards the West, including Australia, ever tighter control on any domestic political opposition and, unfortunately, continued economic and demographic decline. Whether President Putin will engineer a change in the Russian constitution to allow him to serve beyond his current two-term limit or do another double-shuffle with Prime Minister Medvedev remains to be seen."

On Russia's geopolitical relationship with the West, the former diplomat believes that "Russia is not in a strong position to withstand concerted economic pressure from world developments and Vladimir Putin might be presiding over the country's last gasp as a putative Great Power. It is also possible that the increasing decrepitude of the Russian economy and societal fabric will lead to growing internal discontent which Putin, seeing it as an affront to his leadership, will be wont to put down violently, thereby only increasing dissatisfaction. I'm always mindful of the old Russian saying that all they want is a normal life and good roads. Neither looks likely for the foreseeable future."

Andrew Nagorski, *Newsweek's* Moscow Bureau Chief from 1981 to 1982, and from late-1994 to mid-1996, was very well-acquainted with the Soviet and post-Soviet Russia. He travelled in the country frequently from 1989 until his second tour there. After he left in 1996, he was still visiting Russia frequently until 2008. His impressions of post-Soviet Russia are invaluable. In his words:

> "As a foreign correspondent, I found the work environment dramatically changed in the 1990s, as compared to the Soviet period that I was familiar with (1981–1982). It was much easier to report since people were not afraid to speak to foreigners anymore, the tight Soviet rules about domestic travel for foreign correspondents were largely abandoned, and we were not automatically seen as representing an enemy power.

This did not mean it was always easy to work there. In the Soviet period, if something happened to you as a foreign correspondent — you were mugged, threatened, or anything else — you were quite sure that the authorities were behind this action. In the chaotic 1990s, this was not always the case. Something like the attempt to extort protection money from the *Newsweek* bureau appeared to have originated from a criminal gang and probably was not authorised by the government.

Yet despite the corruption, crime, and violence, this was a period when there was still hope that one day, Russia would become a more normal country, with functioning institutions that would protect the rights of its citizens, however imperfectly. It would also be a country that would be capable of taking a more honest view of its own tortured history. When I wrote then that this might happen in twenty years, I was clearly too optimistic.

By anointing Putin as his successor, Yeltsin set the stage for the huge step backwards that Russia had taken in political terms in recent years. While the economy improved considerably, particularly due to high oil prices in the early part of the 2000s, it has continued to suffer from a lack of accountability that allows large-scale corruption to continue to flourish, although it's not as random as it once was. There's no rule of law to speak of, since everyone knows that there's one set of rules for Putin's circle of oligarchs and one for everyone else. And the re-centralisation of power — with the Kremlin appointing governors, the clampdown on what had been an increasingly vibrant media scene, and the elimination of any potential serious political opponents — only encourages more corruption and abuse of power.

With Putin now in power as long as Brezhnev was, popular frustrations are likely to grow, even if it's difficult and dangerous for people to act politically. As the Kemerovo tragedy[2] demonstrates, it can erupt quickly, however, especially when ordinary people pay with their lives for the corruption of the system. And despite all the efforts by the regime to control information, this is an era where enterprising Russians know more and understand more about the outside world than ever before. They still have access to the internet, and they still travel extensively outside their country.

---

[2] The Kemerovo tragedy refers to a fire in March 2018 that engulfed a shopping mall and entertainment complex in Kemerovo, a city in Siberia. It killed at least 60 people (more than half of which children) according to official statements. The day of the tragedy was declared a national day of mourning in Russia. A rally was held in Kemerovo demanding the resignation of Kemerovo Mayor Ilya Seredyuk and the long-time regional governor, Aman Tuleyev. Tuleyev resigned in April 2018, citing "a heavy burden" of the Kemerovo fire; President Putin accepted his resignation.

This could produce surprises. Putin is likely to look all-powerful —
until that moment when he suddenly disappears from the scene as
dictators tend to do. But unless the Putin era gives way to genuine
reforms and the building of healthy political and economic
institutions, Russia will continue to fail to live up to its vast
potential."

Singaporeans' Views

A Singaporean, David Chew, worked in Moscow from the mid-1990s
to the end of the century, and had this to say about it:

"I was stationed in Moscow from 1997 to 2000 for a Singapore
company trading in electronics. From 2000 to 2007, I still travelled
between five and seven months each year to Russia while other
colleagues were stationed in Moscow. In 2007, the company I
worked for sold their business to a local customer; I stayed on for a
year as a consultant. In 2008, I started an edible oil company,
helping it set up the operation in Russia, and travelled four to six
months a year till 2013.

First touch of Russia

I first arrived in Moscow in April 1997. I told myself to spend the
next one to two years to get experience, but never did I expect Russia
to become a big part of my life for more than a decade. Boarding the
flight to Moscow was how my Russian experience started. Walking
down the aisle of the plane, I saw that most passengers on the flight
were white men. However, there was a distinct difference between
them. There were groups of white men who were cheerful and
chatting away while there were other groups which had quite a
serious look. That was how I saw the differences between the Russian
and the Western European.

Sheremetyevo is surely no Changi or Schiphol Airport. The
lighting was gloomy, the ceiling full of dust and each immigration
counter looked like a polling box. My colleague ushered me to the
line where the officer was a female, saying that female officers were
friendlier. However, it took us two hours to pass the immigration and

another one hour through the customs! When I stepped out of the airport, it was gloomy and cold. Met by a Malaysian friend, Bryan, in his Lada, we were stopped just outside the airport by the police. They opened the boot of his car, searched it, and asked for the ruble equivalent of about US$3. Bryan paid and we drove off. This happened four times till we reached the apartment. Not surprisingly, in my mind, I asked myself what had I got myself into!

First taste of business

After a day of settling down, my colleague got down to business and brought me to the electronics wholesale market. It was in the exhibition centre VDNKh, a giant park combined with beautiful pavilions that had been used for exhibitions during the Soviet era. Many of the pavilions were converted to wholesale centres selling assorted imported products like textiles, medical equipment, and kitchenware; most of the pavilions were selling consumer electronics. (It is like having 15 times of Sim Lim Square[3] in one location.) This is one of the main places where traders from all over the country would visit to buy products, especially imported products. Visiting the wholesale centre and exploring the market made me understand the need to set-up an operation in the Russian market.

Almost everything imported was new to the Russian. Consumer electronics were in high demand as it usually looked slicker than the Russian equivalent; advanced foreign technology and owning it became a symbol of having something from the outside world. To many Russians, the ownership of foreign consumer electronics was more valuable than having cash on hand. Products were being sold two to even three times the actual value. The market absorbed any incoming cargoes at a speed that I could not even describe. In summer, they would rush to buy video cameras, in winter, television sets, and mini Hifi. I actually had a Russian employee whose first pay check was used to buy a video camera.

---

[3] Sim Lim Square is a mall in Singapore that offers a wide variety of electronic goods and services ranging from DVDs, cameras, phones, video cameras, and computer parts and servicing.

Life in Russia

My life in Russia had been full of incidents, both good and bad. Particularly between 1997 to 2004, these were the challenging times. There were robberies, attacks by skinheads, pickpockets, harassment by different authorities, and harassment by different organised syndicates. The country also went through drastic events, currency devaluation, political turmoil, the Chechen war, and terrorist attacks which affected life in Russia. However, not all was bad. It was also during that time that I met some of my closest friends today, Singaporean, Russian, and other nationalities.

I am very grateful to the Singapore Embassy staff members. Without them, life in Russia would have been so much tougher. They really put in the effort to get the small group of Singaporeans together, we had regular gatherings, sometimes private social events and sometimes official events. Through the gatherings, we exchanged information about for instance, where to buy the best food as well as about the major events in the country. The Embassy staff members made the extra effort to help Singaporeans both on personal and official issues. And for a person like me who frequently got into trouble, I really appreciated the guardian angels from the Embassy who did not hesitate to step forward when I was in need.

My number one guardian angel was a Singapore Embassy officer. During my stay in Russia, I was detained and brought to a police station for three times for the most absurd reasons. I should emphasise 'detain' but I was never put into a prison cell because it seemed that each time, I was able to charm the police since this officer came to my rescue. The most serious incident was a gunpoint situation on New Year's Eve by a drunken police officer. I was driving back to my apartment after a night out with this officer and a few of our friends when we were stopped by a police officer. I made the mistake of trying to reason with the police officer not realising that he was already intoxicated and his focus was only getting some extra pocket money. I ended up agitating him and got him into an intimidation mode. Even when the police officer drew his weapon on me, this officer was calm but persisted trying to reason with the police officer. I cannot imagine the outcome if this officer had not been there.

My good friend, Chris Cheang, the author of this book, is also one of those guardian angels; he helped me out when my passport was stolen and even escorted me all the way to the airport, making sure I boarded my flight to reach Singapore safely. I have seen him switch to a sudden serious mode and take immediate action whenever he received news of Singaporeans in trouble. Knowing that there were people like them around, made us feel slightly more comfortable about staying in Russia.

The Russians

I have a strong feeling about Russians; we need to understand what they have been through to really comprehend how they react to situations. In 1997, when I first set foot into the country, the Russians were still in an adjustment period. Many of them had a trust issue due to what happened to the Soviet Union; they were suspicious of everyone and everything. They would rather make decisions that would benefit themselves today than have faith in the possibility of the future. To them, the future may just change overnight. The business environment was not focused on the long-term. A Russian trader would rather take the opportunity to make US$100 immediately than have the prospect of making US$30 each day for the next 10 days. The returns may be three times more but they would rather take an early profit. Initially, I took it that they just did not have long-term vision; however, after some understanding, it turned out that they just did not have faith in the future.

It took me a while but I soon learnt how to handle the Russians. The approach had to be to the bigger person and to gain their trust. Once you get into their trust circle, most Russians are actually good-hearted and approachable.

Between 1994 and 1999, the selling part of the business was swift and simple. Everyone wanted goods. Our risk in business mainly came from the authorities like the customs department, tax department, economics department, and even the local police station. Occasionally, there was also the organised crime syndicate that would knock on the door. No matter what the excuse they gave to visit, the result was that they wanted pocket money. I cannot remember how many times but the process usually involved a few hours of drinking sessions and then an envelope of cash. The payment would be collected with pride as if it was an entitlement. It was part of doing business in Russia at that time. The problem was the unstable government at that time. The structure kept changing and a new face from the same department may come along just weeks after an acquaintance was made with the predecessor and the process would have to start again.

After 1999, the system became more organised as the government became more stable. Lesser changes in the government department hierarchy meant problem-solving decisions became more organised. Crime syndicates also moved away from proper businesses. With more stability, Russians also became more confident, feeling better security. Many started having more long-term plans. We started to see Russian companies outgrow their foreign counterparts, investing into more assets as they realised that it was their home ground after all. Within years, the Russians changed the business playing field and took over many of the businesses that was earlier dominated by foreign players.

On 10 September 2001, the day before 9/11 attack, I was on a flight back to Singapore from Dubai. Sitting around me was a group of Russians going to Singapore for a holiday. They got excited as soon as they found out I am Singaporean and we chatted on the whole flight to Singapore. They even apologised for not letting me rest on the flight and gave me a box of Russian chocolates. This really reflected to me how fast the Russian character had changed and how well they had adapted to changes just within five years."

Mr. L, a Singaporean manager working for a Singapore company in St. Petersburg from 1993 to 1995, witnessed what he called the collapse of an "empire". Running a joint venture there, he found it "painful to see a factory that used to churn out 400,000 television sets a month grind to a halt because its supply network was cut off. The sudden switch to a free economy caused enormous hardship but the Russians were stoic. They learnt to survive. There was rampant corruption and we had to deal with it but we made a lot of money in that chaotic period. Crime was prevalent and it was not a joy to live in Moscow. After 18 months, I was exhausted and left Moscow."

He recounted that "during this turbulent period, the government was ineffective and paralyzed. They could not cope with the sudden switch from communism to the free market. So many adventurers and unscrupulous people went to Russia to make a killing. It was sad to witness a proud people being humbled. The laws were unclear and business was done with the mafia and protection of ex-KGB and FSB personnel. But there was honour amongst the crooks and most followed the rules unless one was prepared for the consequences."

The biggest challenge then was the lack of knowledge, talent and capital. However, Mr. L believed that "the Russians are a resilient lot and the smarter ones rose up and prospered. The other problem was their economy was totally not prepared for the sudden change. There was almost a total collapse of their manufacturing and everything had to be imported."

Mr. L felt that the West was happy to see Russia collapse and exploited the country, and does not think the Western attitude has changed. On Russia's future, he rightly credits the Russians "as an intelligent people with a long and proud history. They are strong in science and technology, and have vast resources. Their drawback is the elite. My sense is the political and business elite are either incapable or unwilling to lift the ordinary Russians out of their disadvantaged position. I have no feel how these two balances out for the future of Russia."

Another Singaporean who lived and worked in Moscow from 1990 till recently, and who wishes anonymity, had this to say about the 1990s and later:

"In 1990, all one saw were empty shelves, few restaurants; by 1995, there were big changes, with new supermarkets, more products and western goods were readily available. However, salaries were low, retail was still nascent, while rentals for offices, warehouses and flats were low. New bars, nightclubs, casinos proliferated and foreigners from all over the world were present, starting businesses and making money, together with foreign multinationals. Traffic jams became the norm. Crime rates also rose.

The market remained nascent and opportunities were mixed. It was good for businesses which imported goods, telecoms, food items but insignificant for warehouse automation. Hyperstores like METRO, Ikea, and Auchan started entering the market. Marketing was just getting started — advertisements were just beginning. 1995–2000 was a period of social and political upheavals, the 1998 crisis, privatisation issues, many bank closures. However, it became much easier to find qualified staff, in a friendlier environment and with more business opportunities. From 2000 onwards, steadily, stability crept in with growing income, accompanied by rising housing and inflation as well as increasing rents for flats. At times, it was also scary to read about bombs going off in Metro stations, and Asians being attacked by skinheads. On the other hand, the visa regime for foreigners to live and work in Russia became easier. E-commerce and social media started gathering pace while a wider variety of restaurants became available.

From 2014, oil prices fell and the ruble was devalued, due to the Ukrainian and Crimean issues. Sanctions meant no more imports of wine, salmon, cheese, etc. Locals and foreigners alike have had to forego imported food items, fruits, etc. Despite lower quality local substitutes, the local production of chicken, meat, fruits, milk, fish, wine, etc, rose. From 2017, oil prices stabilised as did the ruble. Russia today is even more plugged into the world economy. Russians travel in big numbers today. Education levels are going up. Businesses are becoming more sophisticated."

Yet another Singaporean (who also desires anonymity) first went to the Soviet Union in the 1980s, and stayed on in post-Soviet Russia till the Putin era, shared his impressions about working in the country. Citing a project he undertook for his company, this Singaporean encountered issues which I can only term as "business-unfriendly". In 1995, his company had negotiated to take over an old concert hall in the centre of Moscow and signed a long-term lease agreement with a Russian Government agency. Under the Agreement, it was required to renovate the whole lobby area which was in a dilapidated state[4] and to pay a monthly rental to the management committee of the building.

This Singaporean who ran the whole project for his company related that the company then had to undergo technical and other related obstacles, which added to the project's costs and delayed its planned completion. He cited the following obstacles and issues:

"We were then told that to get approval to use the building even after renovation; we had to renovate the whole building façade even though we were just using the ground and basement level of the equivalent five-storey building. As the building was considered historical, expensive preservation work had to be carried out brick-by-brick. Because only materials which were close to the original specification had to be used, our project cost doubled. And because of the intricate decorations on the façade, renovation works added an additional four months to the project. When the renovation was almost completed, a bombshell was dropped on us. We were not allowed to use the main door of the building as our entrance but to use a small entrance door which we had created to supplement the building entrance. And as the agreement was that the renovated area was to be shared use, the management decided to rope off half the lobby area to be out-of-bounds to visitors to the shopping area, making the entire configuration very odd.

This and the many other issues, for example, switching off heat to the building when there were no scheduled concerts even though the shopping area was still in operation. We were only able to solve all these daily issues after we had agreed to pay a monthly salary to the Director-General of the concert hall. Hardly halfway through our lease, there was a change in management of the concert hall and a new DG was appointed; he had plans of his own. We had heard that he wanted to take over the area that we had renovated and lease it out himself. Despite our many offers to settle any grievances; he was not one to agree. He finally managed to get a court order to terminate our lease, based on small technicalities.

---

[4] I myself was in this very lobby area before and after the renovation and can testify that it was not a pleasant sight before renovation; thereafter, it was of course not only modern and clean but also attractive to the eye.

The lesson we learnt was that every project was not as straightforward as it seemed. Even the best-planned project would have to face regular surprises. There were many joint projects like ours where the foreign party brought in finance and expertise but was later booted out by their Russian partners, sometimes by force, and other times by bribing already-sympathetic judges."

The turbulent 1990s and beginning of stability under Putin made an impression on another Singaporean, Edwin Tham, who moved to Moscow in 1996 to work as a lawyer in a law firm. His views are outlined below in some detail for they represent the invaluable observations of an individual with long-standing legal experience in the ways of doing business in Russia.

Initially, experiencing a big culture shock — it was unlike anywhere else he had lived previously (he had studied in the UK and worked in London, New York and Singapore) — what struck him first was the palpable, viz. "grand architecture contrasted with the shocking air of decay. Public buildings were in desperate need of renovation, roads and pavements were crumbling, parks were overgrown, public toilets were unsanitary and the streets were dimly-lit. At the time, many Russians did not have the money to dress well, bestowing upon them a rather seedy look, which added to a feeling of menace (accentuated by all the stories about contract killings and murders which were indeed widespread in those days). The recent Soviet past was very much in evidence — most cars on the streets were still Soviet models from the 1980s and 1970s. Shopping was a challenge, as even supermarkets continued the Soviet practice whereby one had to tell the sales clerk what one wanted to buy and the quantity and would receive an invoice, whereupon one would have to pay at the cashier and only then when armed with the receipt, would collect the purchase from the sales clerk!"

Tham also commented on the attitudes of Westerners towards Russians then. He recalled that "there was quite a pervasive 'expat syndrome' at work. The other expats were Brits and Americans (with a few Europeans thrown in), and many did not treat Russia or their Russian colleagues with much respect. Many of them were constantly complaining about how awful Russia was, and the various shortcomings of the Russians (the Americans were the worst whiners). Some of the criticism may have been justified but it was often expressed in an arrogant way. Probably, there was this sense that the West had 'won' the Cold War and the Americans in particular treated Russia like a defeated country."

On the other hand, "the Russians were generally more sociable and interested in me (both as a person as well as a professional) and more genuine than either Brits or Americans. They were also very keen on self-improvement. I was extremely impressed, for example, that many of my Russian colleagues were learning a third or even fourth foreign language, or working on their doctoral dissertation! The other thing which I found sad was that there were people working in the office who had been highly-educated professionals in Soviet times but, when the Soviet Union collapsed, had to find work wherever this was available, often far below their original station in life — for example, as secretaries, receptionists, or even cleaners."

Tham feels that "in the 1990s the Russian government was dominated by the so-called 'Young Reformers' who thought that the most effective route from a command to a market economy was privatising everything overnight. It did not occur to them to consider whether Russia had the institutional and legal framework for this. Needless to say, the main result was to place large sections of the economy into the hands of oligarchs."

Like all those who had experienced first-hand Russia's development from the 1990s, Tham points out that the country "has changed and developed a great deal since the 1990s. The standard of living, especially in the big cities, has improved drastically. Public infrastructure has been significantly rebuilt, historical buildings have been beautifully restored, and people are more prosperous — better-dressed and better-fed. The law-and-order situation has also improved and Moscow is really like any other European city, indeed probably safer than most. Russia has become much more 'normal'. The nightlife is still good though, although not quite as decadent; the drugs and prostitution are much more discreet!"

Tham believes with merit that "the comparison between Russia in the 1990s and Russia up to 2014 couldn't be greater. By the time the crisis over Ukraine happened, Russia had enjoyed respectable GDP growth since 2001, the rouble was stable, it had over US$500 billion in foreign reserves, the level of corruption had fallen and the demographic collapse of the country had been halted. Living standards and personal consumption — at least in the main cities — rose steadily during the 2000s. Many new businesses catering to the growing middle class opened, suggesting optimism about the future. Most importantly, the power of the state was rebuilt (the 'power vertical', as the Russians call it) and the oligarchs were brought to heel. Russia started pursuing its independent interests. My guess is that in 1998, there was a fightback by nationalist elements of the Russian 'deep state' who saw that Russia was in grave danger of imploding. Ultimately, Yeltsin resigned (or, more likely, was persuaded to resign) and Vladimir Putin became acting president. When this happened, I was not sure what to expect. Initially, I was not a Putin fan — he was almost completely unknown, with no apparent political base, and I feared he would be another tool of the oligarchs (Berezovsky himself took credit for 'selecting' Putin, although this may be an exaggeration.) I was also sceptical when Putin said he wanted to reduce corruption and increase Russia's per capita GDP to the level of Portugal's. However, I must admit that he has more than delivered on these things. There remain many problems in Russia but they are not of an existential nature, unlike those of the 1990s. The problems for Russia going forward are now — (1) succession: there appears to be no one who can step into Putin's shoes; and (2) geopolitics: in particular how the current tensions between Russia and the West will be resolved, and how Russia will manage its relationship with China."

On the country's future, Tham assesses that "the government's main challenge has been to diversify the economy away from its dependence on the resource sector, especially oil and gas. Unfortunately, the results have been mixed and the main challenges are the following:

- Although the Soviet Union had a very strong science and engineering base, the universities and colleges were badly neglected during the

1990s and for most of the 2000s. The result is that currently, compared to the US and China, the number of research papers published and patents registered by Russians is tiny. Thus, despite the government setting up 'innovation hubs' like Skolkovo or Innopolis, my impression is that Russia currently underperforms in R&D and faces a struggle to rebuild its capabilities in hard and applied sciences. The situation is not helped by the fact that, for the past 20 years, the brightest Russian students have tended to migrate to careers in finance, law, or accounting, because those jobs are more lucrative.

- Bureaucracy and red tape are still burdensome and add to the overheads for businesses. As a related matter, many bureaucrats are still very rigid and inflexible.

- Ironically, the situation is worse in the big cities than in smaller towns! While huge resource companies are able to manage this burden, compliance costs represent a significant expense for SMEs. However, to be fair, the situation has improved slightly due to many government services being put online.

- Lack of depth in the domestic financial and capital markets. This became a major strategic liability after 2013 when Western sanctions cut Russian companies from international financing. That, combined with high domestic interest rates, have made it extremely difficult for companies to raise money for capital investment. The Russian government needs to find a way to repatriate Russian (i.e., oligarch) capital which is currently held offshore."

Every cloud has a silver lining and Tham cites the "few statistics and facts on business conditions in Russia during my 20 years there:

- In 1997, Russia was ranked in 128th place for corruption by Transparency International. By 2017, it was ranked 40th.
- In 2008, Russia was ranked in 118th place by the World Bank for ease of doing business. By 2017, it was ranked 35th.
- FDI into Russia was only US$3.75 billion in 1997. By 2007, it had increased almost 20-fold to US$52 billion according to UNCTAD.

(This number has obviously fallen significantly as a result of Western-imposed sanctions over Ukraine.)

- In 2017, Russia introduced extensive revisions to its Civil Code which makes the legal framework for business and finance much more commercially-oriented and aligned to international practice."

Finally, Tham argues that "the crisis in Ukraine has brought simmering geopolitical tensions out into the open and now I think the next five to 10 years will be highly unpredictable." He believes that the Western (primarily the US/UK) agenda has long wanted regime change in Russia and the restoration of a Yeltsin-type comprador government, possibly even the break-up of the country. The Ukrainian crisis provided the catalyst for the West to pursue this agenda in a much more overt and aggressive way by imposing sanctions designed to cripple the Russian economy followed by constant demonisation of the Russian leadership (MH-17, state-sponsored doping, the Skripal case, 'supporting a brutal dictator' in Syria, to name a few examples). It will be very difficult for Russia to pursue reforms and grow its economy, if its access to capital, investment and technology is limited. Russia will continue to move closer towards China but this is not an easy process given the historical mistrust between the two countries and a very powerful 'Atlanticist' tendency among the Russian elites."

Russian Perspectives

A Russian businessman, who wishes anonymity and had lived through the wrenching changes in the 1990s as well as the rise of Putin, had this to say:

"Post-Soviet Russia was a very difficult phase in the history of the country. On the one hand, poverty, lawlessness, even chaos appeared to be the order-of-the-day for the masses; on the other, and for me and many others (admittedly a minority) who plunged into business despite its uncertainties and even dangers, the 1990s also represented opportunities. As there were then either no laws or regulations or if there were, they were ill-defined, those who were enterprising and risk-takers, could and did take advantage of the situation to establish businesses to cater to the then nascent but growing demand for goods and services. These men invariably became wealthy or well-off compared to the majority who remained poor and miserable. As a trained engineer, I would have loved to practise what I had learnt but since there were no worthwhile employment opportunities, I did not have a choice but to go into business. I do not have any regrets. The road was difficult but it was worth the time, effort and risks. Businessmen in the 1990s had to contend with organised crime and the need to have a krysha (protection). That was the price of being a businessman. With Putin's rise to power, organised crime gangs' krysha was replaced by law enforcement officials. The Putin era saw the elimination of most organised crime gangs; if they had not been eliminated, they were co-opted by law enforcement officials. Official corruption while high during the Yeltsinite era, reached higher levels during the Putinite epoch simply because there was more money in the system, thanks to the large increases in energy prices in the 2000s. However, to be fair, Putin has cracked down on corruption which nevertheless, remains a significant challenge to Russian societal and economic development. Also, despite the instability of the Yeltsin period, it was he who brought freedom to Russia — for instance, for the first time in its history, people could freely travel abroad. Hence, Yeltsin couldn't be judged solely on the basis of the difficulties 'shock therapy' imposed on the country but also the freedom he introduced to it; for instance, the right to travel freely should be prized and not taken for granted."

Like a number of his fellow businessmen, he saw Russia's future at risk if wide-scale and much-needed structural economic and political reforms were not introduced and implemented. Putin's era, in his view, had been one of *zastoi* (stagnation); hence, the need to introduce reforms was becoming an urgent necessity. Russia had all the ingredients to become a successful economy — it had many talented people in science and technology and a vast land filled with mineral resources. It was a "myth" that Russians were lazy and uncommitted people. One necessary reform was to reduce the size of the state's role in the economy — this state of affairs had led to the squeezing out of the more vibrant private sector.

Russia's current issues with the West had made an already bad situation worse for the economy and Russian businessmen (for instance, it was becoming difficult for them to open foreign bank accounts or seek foreign loans).

Overall, this businessman hoped that the situation would change for the better sooner than later but did not sound optimistic on this note.

In the view of Mikhail Berger, Head of the Russian media holding Rumedia, and a prominent journalist in the 1990s and 2000s, during the 1990s "when the first large inflow of capital and companies began to form, the majority of the working-age population began to work in the private sector, there was a completely new reality, both economically and psychologically. While restrictions on wages in companies disappeared, a significant part of the population was below the poverty line. On the one hand, there was almost complete freedom of speech, on the other — the economy was in a very difficult situation."

Berger points out "the stratification of society increased rapidly. Many people were unprepared for market conditions, many were in a weak position. At the same time, it was a period of easy entry into the business. Market segments were free and entry barriers were low. The problem, however, was that the old social institutions had been destroyed and new ones had not been created."

While many families lived below the poverty line, and the most active and competitive people left the country, "large oligarchic capital began to form in the period 1994–1997, facilitated by the so-called collateral auctions and close relations between business and government."[5] He rightly recalls that "regional elites in the 1990s were very influential and constantly blackmailed the federal authorities with their growing sovereignty. However, with the rise to power of Vladimir Putin, business ceased to have a significant impact on power, and regional elites recognised the power of the Kremlin."

---

[5] Here, Berger is referring to the loans-for-shares scheme described earlier.

High oil prices of the 2000s contributed to the emergence of new large companies and "the period between 2000 and 2013 can be called the years of satiety; the incomes of the population grew constantly, the number of dollar billionaires too." Berger correctly assesses that "in this context, the issue of deep reforms in the economy lost its relevance for the government. This was and is the main challenge for the reformers who remained in the government."

It is not a surprise that Berger thinks that "in the next five to seven years, I do not expect significant changes in both foreign and domestic policy. At the same time, the geopolitical situation for Russia may deteriorate, its involvement in the global economy will decline."

While the business environment today had improved compared to the 1990s — the banking system, arbitration process, and tax administration have strengthened, "the share of the state in the economy is constantly growing and this reduces competition and efficiency."

Finally, Berger notes that "tension in relations with the West continues to grow and there are no visible factors that would change the situation. As a result, Russia loses an important sales markets and access to capital markets. These circumstances will put pressure on the economy and restrain economic growth in the coming years."

Finally, the standpoint of Sergei Markov about the Yeltsinite and Putinite era offers a workable framework of analysis.

According to Markov, who generously recorded his views for this book, Yeltsinite Russia found itself in a very difficult period of dramatic transformation which had few parallels in Russian history. There were essentially five "revolutions" during Yeltsin's term of office. First, there was a marked and quick change from the Soviet planned economy to a market economy "with no real plan". The outcome was the loss of jobs for the majority of the people. The second "revolution" came in the form of the change of the political system from the centralised one-party rule of the Communist Party of the Soviet Union (CPSU) to that of an open, competitive party politics. Russian voters, who up till then had become used to voting for a preferred candidate of the CPSU, had to choose between different candidates in the new political environment. Third, the Soviet collapse led to the establishment of new countries — 15 former Soviet republics — this was the "statehood revolution". Fourth, there was an "identity revolution". Thirty million ethnic Russians became citizens of the new countries of the former Soviet space and their rights were not respected — the Russian language was suppressed in many of these countries. Moreover, for those Russians who lived in the Russian Federation, the question of identity arose — were their fellow ethnic compatriots in the new countries to be considered Russian or foreigners? Finally, the geopolitical revolution took place after Russia lost its superpower status with the Soviet collapse. All these developments "made tremendous problems" for Russia.

Markov notes that Putin inherited the chaos, anarchy, and oligarchic rule from his predecessor. According to Markov, Putin's first main objective was to deal with the five revolutions, stabilise the country and bring it law and order. To achieve this goal, Putin had first to build a good and strong team. This team consisted of:

a) his former colleagues and friends from the KGB who had to deal with major governmental institutions and manage political transition;
b) liberal economists like Herman Gref and Alexei Kudrin, and liberal lawyers like Dmitry Kozak (a former Deputy Prime Minister) and Dmitry Medvedev; and
c) ideologized managers like Igor Shuvalov (a former First Deputy Prime Minister who now runs VEB, the State Development Bank).

All of them were part of his life — those in (a) were from his professional life in the KGB, and those in (b) and (c) were from his work in the St. Petersburg Administration.

With his team in place, Putin crushed Chechen "terrorists, criminals and jihadists" in Chechnya and neighbouring regions. It was not an easy task as the Russian Armed Forces were then not well-equipped, were undermanned, and under-financed. Putin also restored power to the government by removing oligarchs from their positions there as well as from their control of national television stations. The influence of Yeltsin-era oligarchs like Boris Berezovsky, Vladimir Gusinski, and Mikhail Khodorkovsky in Russian political life was removed. By introducing high taxes on the oil and gas industry, much needed revenue flowed into government coffers, while state control over the oil and gas sector was introduced by nationalising Yukos (Khodorkovsky's oil company) and having the largest shares in Gazprom. US and European advisers in the Russian government were also removed, restoring "Russian sovereignty" in the government.

Chapter 10

Encounters With Personalities

It was unfortunate that I did not meet as many members of the *dramatis personae* of post-Soviet Russia as I would have liked. It was not for lack of trying; one must always have either some concrete proposal to secure access to such people and/or the standing to make a request for a meeting. I did not have either in my position as the second man in the Embassy. However, I did have the good fortune of having met the following individuals in person, even if fleetingly.

Mikhail Gorbachev

He was the last Soviet leader; I first met him with Ambassador Kausikan in 1994 when he was reduced to leading the Gorbachev Foundation, a non-profit organisation (NPO) dealing with issues in Russian history and politics. My second and last encounter with him took place in 1996 when Ambassador Kausikan's successor, Mark Hong, met him.

During those two occasions, the focus of the meetings was on the developments in post-Soviet Russia. His account of the Soviet break-up and analysis of post-Soviet Russia's development did not reveal anything out-of-the-ordinary. What struck me was that he appeared to have lost the verve and force of personality as the former leader of a superpower. I left both meetings filled with some sense of sympathy for him. He cut a forlorn figure, and must have had difficulties reconciling his then relatively lowly position with the power he had wielded when he ran the Soviet Union from 1985 to 1991. The station that he had found himself — from an erstwhile figure of world-historical stature to the head of an NPO — was not one he could have relished. One must also note that Gorbachev was extremely unpopular with his people, many of whom blamed him for the Soviet collapse; this fact was reflected in his dismal performance at the polls for the highest office in the country in 1996. According to Wikipedia, he received only 0.5% of the vote.

Whatever place history will give him in the next 50 years, one cannot deny that without his role and the decisions he had made, the Cold War with the West might not have come to an end so fast and with relatively little bloodshed. In that regard, the West, and the nations of Central and Eastern Europe, were and remain grateful to him.

Vladimir Zhirinovsky

He was and remains a flamboyant political personality, having led the ultra-nationalist but incongruously named Liberal Democratic Party of Russia since its establishment in 1991. During the Yeltsinite epoch, he and his party appeared to be playing a serious oppositional role to the President but since Putin's rise to power, he has been considered part of the loyal opposition. The year before I first met him with Ambassador Kausikan (in 1994), his party had garnered 23% of the vote in the 1993 State Duma elections and achieved broad representation throughout the country. He has run in all presidential elections since 1996, with the exception of the 2004 election.

Since he would normally come across as boisterous, his critics did not take him seriously; however, during the meeting with Ambassador Kausikan, Zhirinovsky engaged us both with a quiet and earnest tone. Upon our departure, he presented the Ambassador with a bottle of vodka emblazoned with his name! It did not taste that bad!

It was obvious that his antics were meant for public consumption and appealed to his supporters who were attracted by his colourful and politically incorrect messages on the state of the country directed at the West or perceived internal opponents. He has been quite effective all these years, acting as a safety valve for the dissatisfied members of the electorate — they "blow off steam" through him.

I encountered Zhirinovsky at least another four times during my three tours of duty in Moscow, at diplomatic or other events, and exchanged a few words with him. Again, he would adopt, a different *persona* from that presented in public or on television, displaying a serious *mien* during our brief chats. This is not to say he was never serious in public discussions; rather, he knew how to tailor his behaviour to suit members of his audience, as well as the circumstances.

The fact that he has politically survived and, to some extent, politically thrived for almost three decades, show that he has had and still has a role to play in Russian politics. Obviously, Putin saw and still sees Zhirinovksky's value in the political system; had he not, Zhirinovsky would have long been consigned to the political wilderness. Zhirinovsky the private politician is not Zhirinovsky the public politician.

General Alexander Lebed

Just before the 1996 Presidential elections (in which he was a candidate), were held, I really believed that Lebed had a very good chance of becoming the next President. He had charisma, a presence by dint of his impressive physical appearance yet a disarming, husky voice, and appeal to many in the electorate who yearned for a "strongman" whom he embodied.

In the first round of the election in June 1996, he came in third place behind Yeltsin, and Communist Party leader, Gennady Zyuganov, with 14.7% of the vote. With Lebed's support, Yeltsin won the election in the run-off in July 1996 against Zyuganov. However, Lebed could not fit into the politics of Moscow and to the disappointment of his supporters, decided to run for the office of governor of Krasnoyrask, in Siberia in 1998, and won the office.

He came onto the political scene in the mid-1990s when it was believed Russia needed a strongman to right the wrongs that had befallen the country. He projected that very image with his background as a capable and no-nonsense military man. *The Economist* wrote on 2 May 2002, a few days after his tragic death in a helicopter crash in Krasnoyarsk, that he "was that rare Russian bird: a senior officer more or less in favour of democracy. Ordinary Russians liked his earthy, soldierly style."

Fate had dealt him and his country a cruel blow. Who knows how Russia would have developed had he chosen to remain a figure in national politics and had assumed the highest office in the land?

I met him with other diplomats at an event organised especially for us in late 1995; he gave us a talk on his vision of Russia. Thereafter, we all were given an opportunity to exchange a word or two with him. On being told I was a Singapore diplomat, his eyes lighted-up and he made some complimentary remarks about Singapore's success from which Russia could learn. He not only sounded genuinely interested but that sincerity came forth from his body language as well. A few months later, I arranged a meeting between one of his advisors and Ambassador Hong during which the Ambassador highlighted the lessons of Singapore's success. Unfortunately, there was no follow-up. I supposed then that Lebed must have had much more pressing concerns.

Alexei Mordashov

The only oligarch with whom I had ever come face-to-face in a small meeting was Alexei Mordashov, the main shareholder and chairman of Severstal, a Russian conglomerate with interests in metal, energy, and mining companies.

I accompanied Ambassador Simon de Cruz in a three-way meeting with him in 2009, after the financial crisis took hold in Russia. He was forthright yet did not come across as arrogant and self-assured as one would have expected of wealthy, powerful men. Unlike other oligarchs, he was not surrounded by aides and a retinue of his employees — only he, the Ambassador, and I were present at the meeting. Relatively fluent in the English language, he outlined his thoughts on how Russia would overcome the financial crisis which had hit it quite suddenly and relatively hard (GDP fell almost 8% in 2009).

Ambassador de Cruz and I left the meeting quite pleased, for it was not normal practice that an oligarch would set aside time to receive the envoy and his deputy of a small country with which he had little to do. His assessment of the economic situation was of interest.

Tall and good-looking, and impeccably well-dressed, one could be forgiven if one's first impression of him would be of a man-about-town. But behind that exterior lies a sharp and serious personality.

Alexander Lebedev

A debonair-looking and tall individual, Lebedev was one of Russia's wealthiest men when I first caught sight of him in the flesh during his attendance at a dinner for our then Foreign Minister, Professor S. Jayakumar in September 2002. Professor Jayakumar was then on a visit to Russia. Lebedev, who is fluent in the English language, was the cynosure of the evening's Russian and foreign guests. He was said to have been a KGB spy in the Soviet embassy in London in the late 1980s.

His presence at the dinner gave me an opportunity to size him up, even if it had been at some distance. He came across as a confident and extrovert individual. Unlike most wealthy tycoons, he did not make his fortune in raw materials or the energy sector but in the financial and banking sectors.

Valentina Tereshkova

Another personality I had the honour and pleasure of meeting was Valentina Tereshkova, the Soviet Union's and world's first female cosmonaut. It took place during a meeting between a Singapore parliamentary delegation and members of the State Duma some time in 2012. Tereshkova was and remains a ruling United Russia deputy. While she did not hold any high office, she was and still is revered as a hero, and to some, her importance in Russian space history is only surpassed by Yuri Gagarin, the first man to have travelled in space and Alexei Leonov, one of the first cosmonauts who trained with Gagarin and was the first man to have made the spacewalk.

It certainly took me back to 1963 when as an eight-year-old, I read with great interest *Straits Times* reports about her historic achievement. It was unimaginable for me then to think that one fine day, almost five decades later, I would get the opportunity to meet her in person.

I also met PM Medvedev, Finance Minister Alexei Kudrin, Foreign Ministers Igor Ivanov and Sergei Lavrov, Mayor Luzhkov, and his successor, Sergei Sobyanin, as well as Russia's foremost banker, Herman Gref, during their meetings with our leaders. They all exuded the charm, magnetism, articulation, confidence, and command of expertise expected of men in leadership positions.

Chapter 11

Singapore's Relations With Russia

Between 1994 and the end of the century, our relationship with Russia was one in which both sides had been feeling their way through, given the fact that they were more focused on developments in their immediate regions.

Growing Interest on Both Sides in Each Other

The relationship began to gain momentum with the September 2002 visit of Foreign Minister, Professor S. Jayakumar, the first to post-Soviet Russia by a Singapore Foreign Minister (FM), at the invitation of his Russian counterpart, Mr. Igor Ivanov. During his visit, he called on Ivanov as well as Finance Minister Alexei Kudrin and Yuri Luzhkov, the Mayor of Moscow, then a powerful political figure in his own right. An Avoidance of Double Taxation Agreement was signed during the visit and witnessed by FMs Jayakumar and Ivanov. FM Jayakumar was accompanied by a business delegation.

From then on, both countries took the necessary steps to raise the level of ties, thanks to the growing interest in both countries' business sectors and members of the political leadership. A major platform from which the relationship strengthened was the Russia–Singapore Business Forum (RSBF)[1] which was established at the initiative of Ambassador Mike Tay, in 2006.

---

[1] The website of a state body, the International Enterprise Singapore (IES) describes the RSBF as the premier platform for fostering investment, trade and thought leadership

Prior to that, there was no high-level platform for both countries to engage each other with a view to establishing and building links between the business sectors and top-ranking officials and ministers of both sides. The late Minister Mentor (MM), Mr. Lee Kuan Yew's keen support of the RSBF in its initial phase provided a boost to its subsequent success. MM Lee would regularly visit Moscow and Russia in the following years, not only as part of Singapore's efforts to reciprocate growing Russian interest in us, but also to establish and promote links with Russian political and business leaders.

There were three clear indications of Russian interest in Singapore.

Skolkovo Moscow School of Management

First, the Skolkovo Moscow School of Management (SMSM) invited MM Lee to join its International Advisory Board (IAB), chaired by Prime Minister Dmitry Medvedev. MM Lee was the first high-level foreign political personality to have been invited to join the IAB in 2006, when the School was established. The SMSM is said to be Russia's best.

MM Lee attended the IAB's first meetings in 2007 and subsequent meetings in 2008, 2009, and 2010. During his visits, he met Medvedev, Moscow Mayor Luzhkov, as well as the powerful Mintimer Shaimiyev, the President of Tatarstan, an autonomous constituent of the Russian Federation (in 2007), and in 2010, then Prime Minister Putin.[2]

Unfortunately, for me personally, protocol and other considerations did not allow me to sit in on MM Lee's meeting with PM Putin (only the Ambassador, MM Lee's Principal Private Secretary and the Embassy's interpreter had been present). However, I gathered thereafter that MM Lee did most of the talking, a measure of Putin's respect for him.

---

between Russia and Singapore and for having brought together top government officials and business elite from both countries to foster economic partnerships and raise global competitiveness.

[2] Putin stepped down from power in 2008, paving the way for Medvedev to win the Presidency that year. Putin sought and won a third term as President in 2012. Putin could not run for a third term in 2008 due to constitutionally-mandated term limits.

The respect MM Lee enjoyed in Russia on the whole and in Tatarstan in particular was also evident when Shaimiyev's then PM, Rustam Minnikhanov (he succeeded Shaimiyev in 2010), personally accompanied MM Lee on the flight to Kazan, its capital, from Moscow. Shaimiyev placed his presidential aircraft at the disposal of MM Lee and his delegation, of which I was a member. The very informal banter during the flight between Minnikhanov and MM Lee testified to the natural warmth between the two leaders. An outcome of MM Lee's visit to Tatarstan in 2007 was a long-standing relationship in which many Tatar officials have been trained in Singapore. A Singapore company, RSP Architects, was also involved in the master planning of the Innopolis satellite town; the satellite town includes the Innopolis Special Economic Zone and Innopolis University. According to a CNA report dated 23rd of June 2013, a Memorandum of Understanding was signed between Educare International Consultancy and the Ministry of Education and Science of Tatarstan to facilitate the delivery of training programmes and consultancy services by Educare until 2016.

Intergovernmental Commission

The second signal came in 2008 when the Russians proposed the establishment of an Intergovernmental Commission (IGC)[3] between our two countries. Upon receiving the proposal from the Russian MFA, I proceeded to work on it, and in consultation with Ambassador Tay, strongly recommended that we respond in the positive.

The RSBF and IGC have become a solid basis for both countries to raise the level of their relationship. The latest IGC, the 10th Session, was held in Vladivostok in September 2019, and headed by Senior Minister and Coordinating Minister for Social Policies, Mr. Tharman

---

[3] The IES's website states that the IGC was set up after then-Russian President Dmitry Medvedev visited Singapore in November 2009. The IGC is a high-level dialogue aimed at exploring and promoting broad-based cooperation between Russia and Singapore in various fields, including trade and investment, information and communications technology, transportation, health, education, people-to-people ties, culture and other areas of mutual interest.

Shanmugaratnam. He and Deputy Prime Minister, Mr. Maxim Akimov, witnessed the signing of six agreements which can be expected to further raise the level of the bilateral economic relationship.

More High-level Visits

A concrete sign of the upward trend of bilateral relations was seen in the increased frequency of high-level visits. The zenith of bilateral relations with post-Soviet Russia hitherto took place with the visits of MM Lee and Senior Minister (SM) Goh Chok Tong and a large business delegation to Moscow and other parts of Russia in 2008. MM Lee attended the annual SMSM IAB meeting while SM Goh gave the keynote address to the SMSM forum on "Doing Business in Russia".

From the Russian side, the first state visit by a Russian Head of State to Singapore took place in 2009 when then President Medvedev visited Singapore in November of that year, during which he met Singapore President S. R. Nathan and PM Lee Hsien Loong.

PM Lee made a working visit to Russia in May 2016 in conjunction with the ASEAN–Russia Commemorative Summit held in Sochi. He also visited Moscow on his first bilateral visit to Russia and met PM Medvedev, the Mayor of Moscow Sergei Sobyanin, and Chairman of the Eurasian Economic Commission, Tigran Sargsyan. PM Lee also met members of the Singapore community in Moscow. In Sochi, he called on President Putin.

The Singapore Model

Visits by Russian officials to ascertain whether they could take a leaf from Singapore's developmental experience illustrated Russia's increasing respect for Singapore's experience, which in essence was nothing new. Such interest and respect had been present since the 1990s and later during my first and second tours in Moscow. However, this time, attention from the Russian side was high-level, a clear manifestation of Russian seriousness to learn from Singapore.

The following examples testify to this — in September 2009, First DPM Igor Shuvalov visited A*Star[4] to better understand research work in A*Star, and was particularly interested in Biopolis and Fusionpolis; billionaire Viktor Vekselberg, Chairman of Renova Group and Head of Innograd Russian Initiative also visited A*Star in the same month, where he was briefed by Chairman Lim Chuan Poh on Singapore's investment R&D in One-North, as well as Singapore's integrated public R&D landscape that incorporates the research expertise of A*Star laboratories, universities, hospitals, and polytechnics. Vekselberg headed efforts to establish the Skolkovo Innovation Centre, Russia's answer to Silicon Valley. These visits were meant to explore how much Russia could learn for its own efforts to introduce high-tech into the Skolkovo Innovation Centre, first announced in November 2009 by then President Medvedev.

In March 2010, Anatoly Chubais, CEO of Rusnano (Corporation for Nanotechnologies) and a delegation visited A*Star as well, to learn more about its R&D policies, infrastructure, and commercialisation, and A*Star's role in supporting MNCs and start-ups. Rusnano also began to cooperate with Singapore. EDB's January–March 2011 issue of Singapore Investment News reported that Rusnano, EDB,[5] and 360ip, a Singapore-based global investment and fund management company, would collaborate on the development of nanotechnology projects through the Asian Nanotechnology Fund. A memorandum of understanding for establishing the Fund was signed by Chubais, Tan Choon Sian, Deputy Managing Director, EDB, and Glenn Kline, President and CEO, 360ip. The Fund would have a target capitalisation of US$100 million, of which RUSNANO and 360ip would each raise

---

[4] A government agency, the Agency for Science, Technology and Research (A*STAR) website states that it drives mission-oriented research that advances scientific discovery and technological innovation, plays a key role in nurturing and developing talent and leaders for its research Institutes, the wider research community, and industry.

[5] The Economic Development Board or EDB is a government agency that is responsible for strategies to enhance Singapore's position as a global centre for business talent and innovation.

half the amount. In addition, EDB would support the Singapore-based businesses of the Fund's portfolio of companies with grants totalling S$27 million. The Fund would focus on helping its portfolio of companies become more competitive in nanotechnology research, commercialisation and production.

Russia's interest in the Singapore "model" was also evident in former Economic Development Board (EDB) head, Mr. Philip Yeo's visit to the Russian Far East (RFE) in 2011. His objective was to assess the viability of Singapore helping to develop the port of Vanino,[6] in the Khabarovsk region. Mr. Yeo's visit was undertaken in response to a suggestion by the then Deputy Prime Minister, Sergei Sobyanin, who later assumed the post of Mayor of Moscow; Sobyanin is said to be close to Putin.[7]

I accompanied Mr. Yeo on his visit, together with David Lim, whose past roles included Group Chief Executive Officer of Neptune Orient Lines Limited and Chief Executive Officer (CEO) of the Port of Singapore Authority, among others. We toured Vanino and met the port's officials. While I was not familiar with the complexities surrounding developing any port, even my untrained eye could see that its old and rusted infrastructure would require much time, effort, and resources to not only turn it around but make its future development and prospects secure. Mr. Lim felt that while the port project for the Trans-Siberian railway had potential, there was no clear plan to develop it. Local officials were just hoping for some foreign investment to justify securing development funds from the federal government. He was of the view that for it to work, an overall plan on how the port would integrate into an end-to-end logistics system would need to be developed, but there was none of that.

Messrs. Yeo, Lim, and I also visited Russky Island, situated off Vladivostok; at the time, it was in the final stages of construction for

---

[6] According to Wikipedia, Vanino is an important port on the Strait of Tartary at the northernmost part of the Sea of Japan and is Russia's second largest coal port on the Pacific after Vostochny Port (near Nakhodka).
[7] Luzhkov was dismissed in 2010 by President Medvedev.

the 2012 Asia-Pacific Economic Community (APEC) Summit, hosted by Russia. It was a huge project, and we were informed that the site of the Summit would be handed over to the Far Eastern Federal University (FEFU) thereafter as its new campus.[8]

Mr. Lim's impression was that the attention and infrastructure that was being built significantly underestimated what was needed to make the RFE attractive and to create a sustained supply of good jobs. Projects like Russky Island had been developed for specific purposes, but connectivity to the overall Russian economy was not well demonstrated. While the government may have wanted to develop the RFE to tap growth in the Asia-Pacific, there were not enough good jobs to attract people from European Russia, or to retain the talent in the RFE. He felt that the loss of young people to Moscow and European Russia was a key concern and that was widely expressed during our visit.

This became evident too when we called on Alexander Levintal, the Deputy Plenipotentiary Representative of the Russian President in the Far East Federal District to which the Khabarovsk region belonged. Levintal's focus during our meeting was on the demographic challenges the RFE faced, given its very scarce population and low living standards in comparison to European Russia. In that regard, Levintal was appreciative of whatever role Singapore could play in helping the vast region to develop.

Another instance of Russia's interest in Singapore was seen in the suggestion of then Deputy Minister for Economic Development, Stanislav Voskresensky to Singapore to explore opportunities in Kaliningrad and to ascertain whether Singapore's model could be applied to it, since it too is a small region.

The former Koenigsberg, Kaliningrad lies between Poland and Lithuania. To that end, I was instructed to visit Kaliningrad in 2012 to "get a preliminary feel of the place". While there, I met some European diplomats, as well as foreign businessmen by way of introduction from my Moscow contacts. They provided me with a picture of Kaliningrad's economic situation and prospects. The situation there was not

---

[8] According to Wikipedia, in 2013, the FEFU opened its new campus there.

promising as far as I could discern from my short two-day visit. I was given to understand that the region was plagued by smuggling, organised crime, and a host of socio-economic issues, not unlike many regions in Russia. However, my own impression of the city of Kaliningrad was positive. It was comparatively clean, well-built, and organised — I was amazed to see residential districts whose buildings and homes reminded me of Germany. Indeed, Kaliningrad was German until 1945. German *Ordnung* (order) had left its indelible mark on the city.

The foreign businessmen I met as well as some local officials were justifiably confident that Kaliningrad's economy would benefit from the 2018 World Cup (which Russia hosted).[9] Indeed, federal resources to build the necessary infrastructure for the 2018 World Cup did provide a fillip to the city's economy.

Since my visit had been organised at rather short notice, and the Governor's schedule did not correspond to mine, I could not secure a formal meeting with him. As luck would have it, a Russian businessman whom I met there, invited me, at the eleventh-hour, to a charity auction event at which the Governor was to be the guest-of-honour, he assured me. And indeed, he was there; I was requested to sit next to him during the auction for pieces of amber jewellery. Given the fact that I was seated next to the Governor as well as being a Singapore diplomat on a first visit to the region, I felt obliged to participate in the auction although I had and still do not have any interest whatsoever in amber. However, I ended up purchasing an amber necklace for my wife to the tune of US$3,000! Since I did not come prepared with loads of cash, I had occasion to borrow about a quarter of the amount from the businessman (credit cards were not accepted), to whom I promptly repaid the debt the next day after finding an ATM. Nevertheless, the purchase of the amber necklace was not in vain as my wife loved it!

---

[9] It was one of the 11 host cities; the others were: Kazan, Moscow, Nizhny Novgorod, Rostov-on-Don, Saint Petersburg, Samara, Saransk, Sochi, Volgograd and Ekaterinburg.

Unfortunately, my encounter with the Governor at the auction event could not be translated into a substantive meeting for he was not in any way concerned about discussing any serious issues. In any event, I did make it known to him that I was in his region to look at any opportunities that might be available for cooperation between Singapore and Kaliningrad.

In between preparing for MM Lee's visits and work in connection with the annual RSBF event, the Embassy was busy with its outreach efforts and visits to regions like Krasnoyarsk, in Siberia.

I visited Krasnoyarsk in early 2009 to attend the Krasnoyarsk Economic Forum, an annual event said to be one of the most significant and anticipated economic events of the year not only in the Krasnoyarsk region, but also in Russia. The Forum provides a platform for discussion and constructive dialogue among members of the business community, government officials and civil society. The invitation to attend the Forum was extended to the Ambassador of Singapore. Since his schedule did not allow it, I went there in his stead.

I must say attending such an event in which hundreds, if not a few thousand, other participants are also present and in which one does not have a leading role, can take a toll on one's senses and patience. Thankfully, I met some of my contacts from Moscow, a number of whom I had not had the opportunity to meet often enough, due to their tight schedules and they readily shared with me their impressions of the event.

My impression of Krasnoyarsk, the third largest city in Siberia and an important junction of the Trans-Siberian Railway (the world's longest) and one of Russia's largest producers of aluminium, was not favourable. It was drab and dull. The streets were wide, like most Russian cities. Many buildings were large and in need of obvious repair. It was obvious that Krasnoyarsk needed domestic and foreign investment, and the fact that the Forum was held (and is an annual event) was a step in the right direction, for there were many participants from other parts of the world, including China as well as Western Europe and from Moscow as well.

Russian Cultural Centre in Singapore

The third indication of Russian interest in Singapore came during the visit of then Foreign Minister George Yeo to Moscow in March 2009 when he met the head of the Russian Orthodox Church (ROC), Patriarch Kirill. Patriarch Kirill expressed interest in building a Russian Cultural Centre (RCC) with a church, which Minister Yeo agreed to consider. (Subsequently, it was decided to grant the ROC's request.) Minister Yeo's trip to Sergiev Posad, not far from Moscow, to visit the Trinity Lavra of St. Sergius was greatly appreciated. The Trinity Lavra is the spiritual centre of the ROC. He was met by the monastery's top officials and shown around the holy site. Even though I had been there at least five times before, it was a pleasure to be there again. It is a must-see for any visitor to Moscow as it embodies the spiritual essence of Russia's religious and cultural traditions. I am not particularly religious but being a Catholic, I could not help but be attracted to and to feel the Lavra's spirituality whenever I visited it.

Work is proceeding on the RCC in Singapore. PM Lee echoed the sentiments of Singaporeans when he noted during his May 2016 visit to Russia that he looked "forward to the day when we see at least one golden Russian-Orthodox dome on the skyline of Singapore". The establishment of the RCC and a church on its grounds reflected Russian interest in Singapore which is not limited to politico-economic cooperation but also extends to the cultural sphere. By way of information, the ROC has become a very powerful force in Russian society. Putin and many leading members of the business and political elite support its activities and it is said that Patriarch Kirill has President Putin's ear.

President Putin laid the foundation stone of the RCC and planned Orthodox church during his first-ever state visit to Singapore in November 2018. This signalled Russian interest at the highest level to establish and promote links with Singapore and cater to the spiritual and cultural needs of the growing Russian community.

The impressive number of Russians living and working in Singapore speaks to Russia's growing interest in Singapore. A *TASS* news agency article dated 14 November 2018 on President Putin's visit to Singapore noted that more than 80,000 Russians visited Singapore while some 7,000 Singaporeans travelled to Russia in 2017; 4,000 Russians lived in Singapore on a permanent or temporary basis.

Singapore might see even more Russians coming to its shores in the coming years, should Russia's tense relations with the West force its businessmen to look for alternative markets.

Singaporeans Resident in Moscow/Russia

Singaporeans are an adventurous and enterprising lot and hence, one must not be surprised by the fact that they are found all over the globe, including Russia. There were some who adapted well to life and work in Moscow or other parts of Russia and stayed there longer than they had initially planned. Sadly, however, one of those "veterans" passed away in Moscow during my last tour of duty there.

It was, like most tragedies, unexpected. Out of respect to his family, and to his memory, I will not mention his name. He had lived and worked in Moscow for quite some time, running his own business and maintained regular contact with members of the Embassy. One weekend, he failed to turn up at one of our favourite spots for a drink as earlier agreed; friends of his and I with whom he was supposed to have met, believed that he could either have forgotten or changed his mind about meeting us. To my horror, I was informed the following Monday by a mutual friend that his maid had found his corpse upon entering his flat to do her daily chores. Since I was not only a friend of his but also the consular officer on duty (my consular colleague had been on leave then), I visited his flat and caught sight of his corpse. The local authorities deemed that he had died from natural causes.

I worked with his close friends and the local authorities to make arrangements for his remains to be repatriated to Singapore — his next-of-kin flew to Moscow to conduct the religious ceremonies and bring their loved one's remains back home. It was an experience any diplomat would have to go through whenever his/her citizens meet an unfortunate end in their host country — but for me, it was all the more poignant as I personally knew the deceased.

Another similarly unfortunate case took place when a Singaporean working in Moscow had a stroke in his workplace. After being informed by his employer, I hastened to the intensive care unit of the hospital where he had been taken; he was in a coma when I got there. I subsequently learnt he did not make it. This chap was also personally known to me.

On a lighter note, the Singaporeans resident in Moscow through my three tours in Moscow maintained good and close links with the Embassy; that was not only not surprising but perfectly normal. First, there were not many of us in Moscow/Russia.[10] Second, the Embassy was the focal point of social activities during the festive seasons and encouraged its citizens to keep in touch with it. With time and the growing links between Singapore and Russia, the number of Singaporeans in Moscow and other major cities will increase.

Economic Links on the Rise

Trade with a stronger Russia under President Putin, as well as Singapore business interest in Russia, grew by leaps and bounds. The following trade figures, provided by the Singapore Ministry of Trade and Industry (MTI) illustrate the trend: in 2000, the year Putin was elected President, bilateral trade between the two countries amounted to S$617 million; by 2004, the end of his first Presidential term, it reached S$1.1 billion. Between 2004 and 2008, his second term, bilateral trade rose to almost S$3.8 billion. Trade increased to over S$6 billion in 2012 during President Medvedev's term (2008–2012); between the time Putin was re-elected to the post in that year to 2013, when I left Moscow for good, trade had grown to S$7.1 billion. It reached a high of S$10.8 billion in 2014, and then decreased in 2015 to S$7.7 billion, in 2016 to S$4.5 billion before resuming an upward trend in 2017

---

[10] I believe not more than 20 at any one time lived and worked in Moscow when I was there; there were others who would visit Moscow often as part of their work. There must have been others who had business there but did not have any contact with the Embassy.

when total trade amounted to almost S$7.4 billion. It increased to S$8.5 billion in 2018, but decreased to S$7.1 billion in 2019.

As of 2017, 690 Russian companies were present in Singapore with Russia being Singapore's 24th largest trading partner. Singapore companies are active in Moscow, Tatarstan, and the Penza region. Singapore's stock of Direct Investment Abroad in Russia amounted to S$420 million as at the end of 2015; there are about 20 Singapore companies in Russia, in various sectors such as technology, consumer goods and services, infrastructure and trade.

Bilateral trade links could strengthen with the conclusion of a Free Trade Agreement (FTA) between Singapore and the Russian-led Eurasian Economic Union (EAEU) in October 2019 and with Russia itself. (The EAEU is composed of Russia, Belarus, Kazakhstan, Armenia, and Kyrgyzstan.)

It is also noteworthy that Singapore companies' interest in Russia have begun to show concrete results, particularly in the tourism sector. Changi Airports International (CAI)'s website notes that CAI marked its first foray into Russia in June 2012 by investing in four airports of the Krasnodar region, viz. Sochi, Anapa, and Gelendzhik, as well as Krasnodar itself. (I had visited these places earlier, as a tourist).

Through a joint venture with its local partners, Basic Element[11] and Sberbank of Russia, CAI set out to develop the airports into world-class aviation centres.

According to CAI, the Krasnodar region has an area of 76,000 kilometres square and a population of about 5.5 million. An established domestic tourism destination and an important agro-industrial centre, the region sits astride the main transit routes from Europe, Ukraine and central Russia to the Caucasus, and the trans-Asian territories south of the Caucasus and Central Asia. Its picturesque coastline and mountain range draw some 16 million tourists annually. The region was host to major international events such as the 2014 Winter Olympic Games, annual F1 Grand Prix and International Investment Forum. Also,

---

[11] Basic Element is owned by billionaire Oleg Deripaska; Basic Element is one of Russia's largest and most dynamic diversified business groups. Sberbank is Russia's largest bank and is led by Herman Gref, an open admirer of the late MM Lee and Singapore.

according to CAI, in February 2017, it together with its partners, Russian Direct Investment Fund (RDIF)[12] and Basic Element, acquired Vladivostok International Airport (VVO) in Russia's Far East. Vladivostok is the main city and administrative centre of the Primorsky Krai, the maritime province of Russia. With a population of 600,000, the port city is an important transport, industrial, trade, and financial centre for the county.

Recent High-level Visits

President Putin's first-ever state visit to Singapore in November 2018 marked the zenith of the political relationship, taking place nine years after that of Dmitry Medvedev. His visit, together with his participation in the Third ASEAN–Russia Summit and 13th East Asia Summit (held in Singapore) also marked an important step in Russia's effort to broaden its widely-publicised "pivot" to the East. Hitherto, it has been focused on China and Northeast Asia.

The Secretary of the powerful Security Council, Nikolai Patrushev visited Singapore in March 2016, meeting then Deputy Prime Minister and Coordinating Minister for National Security Teo Chee Hean, according to a Singapore MFA press statement dated 14 March 2016. Patrushev embarked on a second visit to Singapore in August 2019, and met Mr. Teo again. He also met Minister for Home Affairs and Minister for Law K. Shanmugam. According to a Singapore MFA press statement dated 30 August 2019, they discussed ways to strengthen bilateral cooperation in tackling common challenges such as terrorism, cybersecurity and transnational crime. They also had a wide-ranging exchange of views on regional and international issues. Following their meeting, they witnessed the signing of the Memorandum of Understanding on Security Cooperation between the Ministry of Home Affairs of Singapore and the Ministry of the Interior of Russia. The MOU will allow both sides to explore further cooperation in

---

[12] Established in 2011, the RDIF is a state-led fund charged with making equity investments in high-growth areas in the Russian economy, according to Wikipedia.

various areas including dealing with transnational issues, such as extremist activity and drug trafficking.

In October 2019, Mr. Teo visited Moscow and met the Special Presidential Representative for Environment Protection, Ecology and Transport, Mr. Sergei Ivanov and had a wide-ranging discussion in areas like smart city development, urban transportation, sustainable development, climate change, and cooperation in the Arctic. Mr. Teo also met the Deputy Mayor of Moscow for Regional Security and Information Policy, Mr. Alexander Gorbenko, and visited the Skolkovo Innovation Centre and Skolkovo Institute of Science and Technology.

We can expect more high-level visits in the years to come, if Russia's oft-declared pivot to the East becomes more than a slogan and as its economic orientation towards the Asia-Pacific assumes more substance.

Chapter 12

Russia's Significance to Singapore

That Russia is an important country we should not ignore is explained by the following reasons.

First, the country is the largest is the world, stretching from Europe to Alaska, from the Arctic to the Black Sea, and Central Asia, and shares a long border with China. No other country in the world, including trade-dependent Singapore, can ignore developments in the world's largest country, especially since Russia is economically, politically and territorially part of the Asia-Pacific.

Second, it is blessed with many natural resources — oil, gas, diamonds, precious metals, timber, and water, to name a few. The following figures speak for themselves. The Russian Business Consulting (RBC) news website reported on 14 March 2019 that the country's oil, gas, and other resources amounted to 60% of its GDP as of 2017. The website of the RBC, a leading business news multimedia holding company, quoted figures from the Russian Natural Resources and Environment Ministry. The Ministry estimated the market value of the country's oil reserves at US$1.2 trillion, double the figure in 2018, according to a RT report dated 20 September 2019. Even in an increasingly digital world, one would need the raw materials to build and power the physical sinews of a modern and organised society. Whatever the structural and other weaknesses the Russian economy and body politic suffer from, its wealth in natural resources more than makes up for it. It is not about to go bankrupt like many countries that are bereft of natural resources.

Russia is also a major food producer and exporter. President Putin himself in his February 2019 State-of-the-Nation speech pointed out that in 2018, Russia's agricultural exports increased by 19.4%, reaching US$25.8 billion; the goal, he stressed, was to reach US$45 billion in 2024. Again, being trade-dependent and with a very open economy looking for investment opportunities abroad, Singapore cannot ignore Russia's natural wealth as a source of commercial opportunities.

Third, its economy is one of the world's largest, with a GDP amounting to US$1.72 trillion. Singapore should continue to trade, engage in business as well as invest in Russia. In doing so, we must naturally be sensitive to and cognisant of the issues and circumstances surrounding Russia's current tense and difficult relations with the EU and the US for they are our longstanding and close friends in political, economic, social, cultural, historical and geopolitical terms. However, where there are opportunities which benefit both Russia and Singapore and which do not jeopardise our links with our Western partners or their interests, we should consider seizing them.

Fourth, it has a very talented and well-educated work-force, including and especially in IT. Singapore should attract some of this talent to its shores to upgrade its own skills.

Fifth, it is a founder-member of the UN and UN Security Council. Being a small country, our security and sovereignty are linked, to an extent, with the actions and decisions of the UN and the UNSC.

Sixth, with global warming, the Northern Sea Route (NSR), which borders Russia, might acquire more significance to trade between Asia and Europe. Russia is determined to develop the NSR, if President Putin's words are anything to go by. In his annual State-of-the-Nation speech in March 2018, he stressed that "the Northern Sea Route will be the key to developing the Russian Arctic and Far East. By 2025, cargo traffic along this route will surge tenfold to 80 million tonnes. Our goal is to make it a truly global and competitive transport route."

As a major global port with significant links to Asia and Europe, Singapore has an interest in devoting attention to developments in the NSR. Russia and Singapore also share some common interests in the Arctic. Russian Ambassador Andrei Tatarinov, in an address to the RSIS in December 2017, noted that Singapore had become a promising partner in the development of the Russian Arctic region, thanks to its vast experience in urban planning, transportation, and seaport infrastructure building. Russia is a major player in the Arctic through its membership of the Arctic Council (AC); Singapore became a Permanent Observer in the AC in May 2013, with the support of Russia and the other members.

Our interest in the AC was noted by a *Straits Times* report dated 16 May 2013 which quoted PM Lee Hsien Loong as saying the following: "I would like to thank the Arctic Council states for admitting Singapore as an observer. Singapore is not situated in the Arctic, but developments there — whether the melting of the ice cap or opening of new sea routes — will have important implications for Singapore as a low-lying island and international seaport. We look forward to contributing to the work of the Arctic Council."[1]

Seventh, thanks to its nuclear weaponry and growing conventional capabilities, it is the only country with the power to challenge the US nuclear arsenal. No country in the world can ignore developments in one of the world's two most powerful nuclear powers.

Finally, it is a growing power in the Asia-Pacific although thus far, it cannot challenge the US or China for supremacy or play a key role in the region's socio-economic development. While Japan, South Korea, and India play an increasingly significant role in the future development of the region as well, that does not mean that Russia will not become an important player. Hitherto, it has not, for reasons beyond the scope of this book. However, for all the reasons pointed out above, one

---

[1] (The AC's website states that it consists of the eight Arctic States: Canada, the Kingdom of Denmark including Greenland and the Faroe Islands, Finland, Iceland, Norway, Russia, Sweden and the United States. In 1996, the Ottawa Declaration formally established the Arctic Council as a high-level intergovernmental forum to provide a means for promoting cooperation, coordination and interaction among the Arctic States, with the involvement of the Arctic Indigenous communities and other Arctic inhabitants on common Arctic issues; in particular, issues of sustainable development and environmental protection in the Arctic.)

cannot rule out the possibility that Russia could become one of the Asia-Pacific's foremost powers with a say in the region's future.

Singapore's Image in Russia

Singapore must continue monitoring developments in Russia as well as its relations with the outside world, with a keen eye, even if Russia does not devote the same amount of attention to us. As a big country with a history of being a world power, Russia will always find it difficult to see small countries as real equals.

However, we have an advantage; despite our size, we have always had a good image in Russia, thanks to our success and the stature of the late MM, Mr. Lee Kuan Yew. His book, *From Third World to First*, was published in the Russian language and read widely by members of the Russian political and business elite, as well as by academics and journalists. Even during my first assignment in the 1990s, Singapore's success was noted by quite a number of the businessmen, academics and journalists as well as officials whom the Ambassador and I met.

I must add though that there was only one time when I was given to understand, in polite terms by a Russian official in the 1990s that Singapore was a "Western" country. He did not mean it in a negative sense but more that we were seen as being successful and modern. In the 1990s in Russia, having these attributes were synonymous with being "Western". The first time I was told that Singapore was a "Western" country was in Wroclaw, Poland in 1985. While walking the streets of its old town, a young man approached man and asked me, in halting English where I hailed from. Upon being told, he immediately pronounced Singapore as "a rich country, Western country", to my surprise but that comment hit a nerve of pride as well.

MM Lee and Singapore enjoyed the respect of many and his death accelerated the process. In an article dated 27 March 2015, Alexander Gabuev, Senior Fellow and Chair, Russia in the Asia-Pacific Programme, Carnegie Moscow Centre, observed that the Kaluga region governor "wanted to put a statue of the Singaporean reformer right in the centre of the region's capital. Officials in Tatarstan were reportedly interested in erecting such a monument as well. The national leaders also heaped praise on Lee. While speaking to his inner circle, (PM) Dmitry Medvedev loved to mention being counselled by the legendary prime minister. Reacting to the news of Lee Kuan Yew's death, Vladimir Putin's Press Secretary, Dmitry Peskov, publicly stated that the Russian president highly valued his contacts with Lee, who even reprimanded Putin on his excessively liberal economic agenda. Finally, the economics minister and later Sberbank president, Herman Gref, was one of the main enthusiasts of the Singaporean model."

News on Changi Airports International's (CAI) investments in a number of Russian airports has also strengthened our already established good image in Russia. According to a Channel News Asia report dated 28 March 2018, Sochi International Airport took the prize of Best Airport by Size and Region for airports in Europe, among those that handle five million to 15 million passengers per annum. It was also voted Best Airport in Europe among those that handle more than two million passengers per annum, at the Airports Council International's Airport Service Quality Awards.[2]

President Putin himself paid tribute to Singapore in his speech to the Supreme Council of the Russian-led Eurasian Economic Union (EAEU) countries on 29 May 2019 in Kazakhstan. Referring to the then ongoing Singapore–EAEU negotiations on a Free Trade Agreement, he noted that "the range of the EAEU's economic partners is continuously expanding. Today, we will adopt a decision to sign a free trade zone agreement with Serbia. The talks on a similar document with Singapore are nearing the final stage. *Today, Singapore has been recognised as the most competitive economy in the world.*" (Emphasis is mine).

It is not beyond the wit of Singapore's businessmen to take advantage of our good image in Russia, its large market and continuing efforts to improve its business climate, and to work towards building mutually

---

[2] CAI marked its first foray into Russia in June 2012 by investing in four airports which serve the resorts of Sochi and Anapa as well as the business centre and political capital of the Krasnodar region, according to its website.

beneficial commercial relations. The institutional framework for strengthening economic links between the two countries is present: Singapore has an existing Avoidance of Double Taxation Agreement (DTA) with Russia. The DTA was signed in September 2002 and came into force in January 2009; Singapore also has a Bilateral Investment Treaty (BIT) with Russia. The Singapore–Russia BIT was signed in September 2010 and came into force in June 2012. The potential for growth in Singapore's commercial relations with Russia is there and could be fully exploited.

Like most countries, doing business in Russia has its challenges. While there was and is no *vade mecum* on how to do business in Russia, there are broad patterns.

Months before the combined visits of MM Lee and SM Goh, I felt it was more than long overdue to examine the challenges, obstacles and perils of doing business in Russia, given the increasing Singapore business interest in the country. After meeting a wide range of contacts over a period of four to five months — Singaporeans, Russians, and Westerners in fields as diverse as business, media, diplomatic, academic — and consulting open sources in the Russian and Western media, I came to the following conclusions (outlined not necessarily in order of importance). While my on-the-spot research into the challenges of doing business in Russia was undertaken almost a decade ago, and the situation has improved by leaps and bounds since then, the challenges detailed below have not been totally eliminated, according to various open media and other sources I have consulted. Realistically however, these obstacles are structurally entrenched and would take some more time to fully eliminate.

First, red tape and bureaucracy were the bane of the small and medium-sized enterprises (SMEs). Unlike large corporations, foreign and Russian, they could ill-afford the time and expense of securing the many permits and licences to run their businesses. Moreover, large companies were more likely to have stronger links to the "right people" or have a strong *krysha*.

Second, SMEs were also more inclined to either cave-in or be subject to "inspections" by health, tax, customs, fire and other officials on a "regular" basis, given their weaker position when compared to large companies. While to be fair, inspections are part-and-parcel of any functioning economy, they could and did become an occasion to demand and receive bribes to overlook any perceived or alleged violation of the law. Russian media would report that Russian entrepreneurs would freely relate their experiences with "inspectors" from these government bodies. While they were obviously not happy with this state of affairs, they were resigned to having to deal with "inspectors" on a regular basis and pay them off, whenever it was necessary. My own Russian contacts would stress that it would never occur to entrepreneurs to seek redress as their standpoint was essentially that one could not successfully challenge the "*vlast*" (the authorities), unless one had a very powerful *krysha*.

Third, low and mid-level official corruption was then perceived as rife, including within law enforcement agencies. Hence, one had to have "friends" who would be practically one's "*krysha*" (unlike in the 1990s, in the 2000s, the *krysha* would embody powerful officials). Needless to say, most businessmen had to set aside a "fund" for such "friends". Corruption was and remains a sensitive yet widely debated issue. I would watch Russian TV stations and noted that all its anchors on popular socio-economic and political programmes would openly discuss official corruption and how and why it had to be dealt with.

In the 2000s, quite a few sources told me that corruption at all levels had become more widespread, since the pie had become bigger, with the growth of Russia's economy and its coffers. They did not think entrenched corruption could be totally eradicated, arguing with some merit, that all countries in a socio-politico-economic transition that Russia was in then, would have to deal with issues like corruption. Until and unless society stabilised so that the economy could grow in some predictable fashion and in the absence of strong checks and balances in the system, corruption could not totally be overcome.

No one can really give a reliable estimate of the level of corruption in dollar terms. All my years in Moscow I would read this or that figure but no one would categorically state that it was accurate or indisputable. In her book, *Putin's Kleptocracy: Who Owns Russia?*, the late Karen Dawisha, a Professor of Political Science in the Havighurst Centre for Russian and Post-Soviet Studies in Miami University in Oxford, Ohio, cited the figure of US$300 billion, quoting Transparency International estimates of bribery's annual costs to Russia.[3] As the saying goes, there's no smoke without fire, the only issue here being how large and dangerous the fire was and is for the country. Suffice it to say that corruption was a very delicate and controversial issue in the 1990s and up to the time I left Russia in 2013. It remains so today.

A recent comment by President Putin himself brings into sharp relief the continuing challenge that corruption poses to Russia's development. During a televised broadcast on Rossia 24 state television on 18 November 2019, he chided Cabinet members over the "hundreds of millions" that were being "stolen", referring to the ongoing construction of the Vostochny Cosmodrome, Russia's spaceport, in the Russian Far East. (Russia is still dependent on the Baikonur facility in Kazakhstan for its space programme.)

Fourth, the Russian judicial system was not perceived as objective and fair as it was believed that judges could be suborned. In this regard, I would hear of cases related to me by some contacts that this or that case that had been "bought". In other words, I had only anecdotal evidence of the corruptibility of Russian judges, no more, no less. The issue is, in the absence of concrete and incontrovertible evidence, whether one can give assumptions about the corruptibility of the Russian judicial system and its officials, full credibility. Having said that, the Russian judiciary was widely seen as corrupt at the time and this perception persists today.

I leave the reader to reach his/her own conclusions by reading an expert's assessments of the Russian judicial system.

---

[3] Karen Dawisha, *Putin's Kleptocracy: Who Owns Russia?*, p. 1.

The expert is Kathryn Hendley, a professor in the University of Wisconsin-Madison; in her book, *Everyday Law in Russia*, she challenges the widely-held notion that the system is corrupt and inefficient. Reviewed by an academic expert on Russia, Robert Legvold, who is Marshall D. Shulman Professor Emeritus in the Department of Political Science in Columbia University, in the September/October 2017 issue of the respected journal, *Foreign Affairs*, Hendley, according to him, "one of the most seasoned students of Russian law, would not deny that any country where the law is twisted to serve the political and venal interests of those with power, does not live under the rule of law. However, she estimates that in Russia, only three per cent of all instances of law enforcement involve such perversions. She does not question the damage done to democracy by such abuses, but she is more interested in the ways in which most citizens typically engage with the law: divorce proceedings, personal-injury suits, common misdemeanours, and so on. After two decades of close study, a good deal of it conducted in courtrooms, she paints an authoritative picture of how the law works for ordinary Russians and what they think of it. Russians normally try to resolve their problems out of court. But when they do seek legal recourse — and they increasingly do — they do so without misgivings. Hendley provides a fine example of how Russian reality is often much more complicated than those on the outside believe."

If one gives credence to her standpoint, then one must dismiss long-held notions that justice cannot be found in a Russian court. Indeed, in her contributory article, "Putin and the Law" to a book entitled *Putin's Russia, Past Imperfect, Future Uncertain*, edited by Dale R. Herspring, and published in 2007, Hendley similarly concluded that "justice is not out of reach in Russia; it is the likely outcome in most cases". However, she cautioned that "the continued willingness of those with political power to use law in an instrumental fashion to achieve their short-term goals means justice can sometimes be out of reach".

Fifth, there was a practice incongruously labelled as "raiders" by the Russian media and Russians in general. This essentially involved the takeover of a rival's business (though the rival might not necessarily be in the same business) with the help of "bought" officials and law enforcement officers. It might or might not include the physical occupation of a business' premises by more often than not, armed men and/or "bought" officers of the tax police. Also, in cases where there was a dispute over its ownership, the "raider" invariably would have the legal backing of a "bought" judge. This practice was widely-known and the Russian media, including Russian state TV, did not seek to hide it. I myself watched Russian state television channels almost daily and can say that they highlighted quite a number of cases involving such questionable practices. I suppose the authorities did not see any point in trying to suppress this already well-known "practice".

Some foreign observers call it "asset-grabbing".[4] It goes without saying that one had to have high-level backing and connections when it comes to major and long-term investment projects — the higher, the safer one is — or so ran the logic. However, even then that might not offer total protection from "raiders"; if a dispute arose between a foreigner and his Russian partner(s), the latter would appear to have all the cards, being on home ground, unless the foreign partner had a stronger *krysha*. A Singapore businessman found himself in such a situation; I had also heard of similar cases involving other foreign businessmen.

Finally, trust in the system by businessmen was lacking. This grave problem persists to this day, judging by the comments of Finance Minister, Anton Siluanov. According to him, "business doesn't trust the state and therefore doesn't want to put this money into the economy". By this money, he meant the roughly 30 trillion rubles currently sitting in businesses' bank accounts; instead of reinvesting it into growth, Russian companies had elected to pay out record dividends.[5]

While these challenges appeared discouraging, the gains to be made were well worth the effort and risks. That was the sense I garnered from all the foreign and Singaporean business sources who stressed that profit margins were invariably higher in Russia than in their home countries.

---

[4] See article entitled *"Reiderstvo: Asset-Grabbing in Russia"* dated 1 March 2014 by Professor Philip Hanson, Former Associate Fellow, Russia and Eurasia Programme, Chatham House, for a comprehensive view of the issue.

[5] See *Intellinews* report dated 15 October 2019 by Ben Aris.

Chapter 13

Some Final Thoughts on Russia

I have never had either a roseate view of Russia or one filled with doom and gloom; in this book, I have tried to forge as realistic a picture as possible of the country. This book would not be complete without examining Russia's future. While domestic politics obviously influences its future development, the role its foreign relations plays in this process cannot be understated.

To a large extent, Russia's development and future prospects depend on the state of its relationship with the West, the EU, and the US. The EU and Russia are linked geographically, culturally, economically, and historically. While most of its territory lies east of the Urals, the majority of its people live and prefer to live in European Russia where living standards are higher than in Siberia and the Russian Far East, which are very sparsely populated.

Russia's relations with the US are important too for strategic and defence reasons; their economic interaction is limited, compared to Russia's links with the EU. Nevertheless, relations with the US will always be uppermost in the minds of Russia's leaders, given the fact that the US is considered its most formidable threat since it is the only other nuclear superpower.

While relations with the West are paramount in Russian calculations, its strengthening links with China must also be taken into account by Russian leaders in any major decision which has foreign policy and/or economic policy or defence/strategic ramifications.

Russia's Euro- and US-centric Orientation

By far, Russia's leaders and people are more concerned about their relationship with the West than any other region of the world, despite their oft-repeated protestations to the contrary.

The current tensions in Russo-Western relations have not and will not significantly alter the factors which account for Russia's deeply-entrenched Euro- and US-centric outlook.

First, the historical context must be considered. Russian history has been and still is inextricably linked to European history. From the rise of the Russian political entity, the introduction of Christianity, subjection to Mongol/Tatar rule, wars against the Teutonic Knights, the Poles, Swedes, its major roles in the Napoleonic war, the Concert of Europe, in the Crimean war against England and France, in wars with Turkey in the 1760s and over the Balkans in the 1870s, in World Wars I and II, and the 1945–1991 post-war world — all these major developments tied Russia to Europe. The major fault line and front in the Cold War between the Soviet Union and the US/Western Europe lay in divided Germany and in Europe, with the rest of the world being sideshows or areas of proxy wars.

Moreover, intellectual thought in 19th-century Tsarist Russia was divided between the Slavophiles and Westernisers, with respect to Russia's place in Western civilisation. According to Columbia University Press Encyclopaedia, the Slavophiles were of the view that Russian civilisation was unique and superior to Western culture, supported autocracy and opposed political participation, but favoured the emancipation of serfs and freedom of speech and press. On the other hand, the Westernisers felt that Russia's development depended on the adoption of Western technology and liberal government.

These strands of thought did not entirely perish with the establishment of Communism in Russia. Communism itself was a Western ideology, adapted to Russian realities by the Bolsheviks. Russia, as the world's first Communist state, faced Western hostility. Its own actions, in reaction to Western intervention in the Russian Civil War, in preaching world revolution, and opposing the West, especially the US after World War II, on the global front on a host of issues, caused its relationship with the West to be marked by decades-long mutual tensions and suspicions. This state of affairs did not end until the Soviet collapse.

Russia thereafter aspired to become the European country it had been before 1917. Under President Yeltsin, it sought to return to the "civilised world", two words bandied about by its intellectuals and leaders very often in the 1990s and even today. The "civilised world" continues to capture the imagination of Russia's leaders, businessmen and intellectuals. In the 1990s and early years of this century, Russia's membership of the G-8, its declared intention of joining the OECD, membership of the Parliamentary Assembly of the Council of Europe, Putin not ruling out joining NATO (in an interview with the BBC's David Frost in March 2000) — represented attempts to *join the civilised world*" (my emphasis). They were in vain.

The factors that explain the West's "rejection" of Russian membership in its "club" are examined later in this chapter.

Second, the cultural/ethnic factor, cannot be underestimated. Broadly speaking, Russians of all stripes and political persuasions, even those who live in Siberia and the Russian Far East, which are geographically closer to Asia, associate themselves more with Europe than Asia. They would prefer to spend their holidays in Rome, Paris, London or New York to Beijing, Tokyo or Seoul. They would feel more at home in the West than in Asia, prefer emigration to Western countries and on the whole, would rather work and live in Western societies. That was and still is my impression after living and working there and chatting with many a Russian in European Russia, Siberia, and the Russian Far East. One cannot blame the Russian, who might not say he is a European but is more familiar and comfortable with European traditions, customs, habits and cuisine as well as history than with any other region. There are obviously exceptions to this rule.

Although Russians believe theirs is a unique civilisation, neither Western nor Eastern, they have always looked upon the West, specifically Europe as a standard either to emulate or to reject while still considering the West as the "civilised world". One of Russia's leading observers, Andrei Kortunov, Director-General of the Russian International Affairs Council (RIAC), rightly argued in an article in the

RIAC dated 25 April 2018 that "Russians continue to apply for and to receive more Schengen visas than any other country of the world. The EU remains the main point of destination for Russian students seeking education abroad. Cross-border cooperation clearly survived the 'no business as usual' pattern. In sum, it seems that the European-Russian divergence since 2014 has not yet reached the point of no return and nothing is already predetermined for years and decades to come."

Russian scholars have also highlighted Russia's cultural proximity to the West; Mikhail Remizov, President of the Moscow-based Institute of National Strategy told a Canadian academic in an interview in November 2017 that "…if we understand civilisation in terms of its roots: antiquity, Christianity, a certain component through Biblical thought, plus Slavic, Celtic, German, Indo-European roots, myths, then we (Russia) are quite close to Europe."

A leading academic, Professor Sergei Karaganov, Dean of the Faculty of World Economy and International Affairs in the National Research University-Higher School of Economics in Moscow, and Honorary Chairman of the Presidium of the Council on Foreign and Defence Policy, pointed out in a paper in September 2017 that "it is essential to emphasise the preservation of cultural affinity with Europe and readiness to go with it to Asia. Vladivostok is Asia's most European city." (His paper revolved around Russia's turn to the East.) I had made Karaganov's acquaintance during my final tour of duty in Moscow. He has a breadth of vision which is unmatched by many in his profession and his views on many issues are respected.

No less than President Putin himself has alluded to Russia's European roots (see below).

Despite building, in recent years, a close relationship with China and striving for stronger links with the rest of Asia, Russia cannot and will not simply weaken or discard centuries of close contact, let alone its own ethnic, cultural, religious, and historical links, and geographical proximity with Europe. Asia was and is still seen as alien.

The words of Dr. Vyacheslav Nikonov, spoken at the ASEAN–Russia Conference, organised by the Institute of Southeast Asian Studies in April 2011 in Singapore, reveal to a large extent the Russian perception of Asia. According to him, Russia "is an Asia-Pacific country too although it has not been very aware of this capacity. The main obstacle which has been hard to surmount is the Russians' — and particularly the Russian political and economic elites' — disdainful attitude towards Asia as a secondary region of the world." His remarks were made in his keynote address entitled "Russia and ASEAN" to this conference on 26–27 April 2011.

While 2011 is almost a decade ago, Nikonov's assessment is authoritative, given that his many important positions.[1] Old habits die hard, as the saying goes. I doubt that core attitudes with respect to Asia could have drastically changed since 2011.

In any case, the different perceptions and expectations that the West and Russia have of each other are major, but not insurmountable obstacles to a relaxation of tensions. If during the 1990s, one had hoped (and if this hope is still cherished) that Russia would adopt Western liberal political culture as a whole or even in small steps, it is obvious today that Russia is not headed in that direction. Liberal political parties in Russia since the 1990s have not had much success in making a lasting and indelible impact on the country's political scene and among its voters. The strongest and longest-lasting liberal party, Yabloko, has not had a presence in the Duma (Parliament) since 2007, while its candidate for the Presidential elections in 1996, 2000, and 2018, Grigory Yavlinsky, managed to garner only 7%, 6%, and 1% of the vote respectively, according to a BBC Monitoring report dated 6 April 2018. The report added that Yavlinksy was quoted as saying at a meeting of Yabloko's party bureau on the same day that he would no longer be standing in future Presidential elections.

The reasons for the failure of liberalism to take root in Russia are varied and have been examined to some extent, earlier in this book. Professor Alexander Lukin, Head of the Department of International

---

[1] He is Chairman, Committee on Education and Science in the State Duma; Dean at the School of Public Administration, Lomonosov Moscow State University; President of Polity Foundation and Unity for Russia Foundation think tanks; and Chairman of the Executive Board of Russkiy Mir Foundation.

Relations in the National Research University–Higher School of Economics, Moscow, in an article in *Strategic Analysis* (2018: p. 145), entitled "Putin's Political Regime and Its Alternatives", rightly points out that "the main danger of Russian liberalism is that it runs contrary to the views of the majority of the population", and adds that most public opinion polls "show that most Russians do not want their country to take a subordinate role to the West. They view Western policies as inimical to Russia's status as an independent state. Russians also do not support 'liberal' economic ideas. While not opposing a market economy, they are quite satisfied with a paternalistic government that looks after their well-being and security".

While there are obviously objective factors that explain the current state of Russo-Western relations, perceptions of one another have played and continue to play a significant role. The Western predilection is to hold Russia up to Western standards. A Russian academic hit the nail on the head when he related to me during a lunch almost two decades ago that unlike China, Westerners could not understand why Russians could not or did not think or behave like they did, although "we look like they do", his point being (Slavic) Russians are ethnically whites but did not share Western values. This academic knew whereof he spoke, having had a very distinguished background in international as well as domestic affairs. He remains a fairly prominent personality.

I strongly believe Russia sees itself and is seen as potentially as part of the West, given its history, religion, traditions and ethnicity as well as geographical proximity to Europe. One can argue that it is a multi-ethnic and multi-religious state but no one can convincingly maintain that Russia is an Asian country. Its core culture, religion, as well as ethnicity and language are European. Russians (of Slavic descent who comprise the majority and who run the country) are Europeans, their religion is Orthodox Christianity of the Eastern branch, and their language is Indo-European, like most of the rest of Europe. From this standpoint, Russia cannot be considered anything other than a European country.

Putin himself and leading Russian intellectuals have never tired of making this point. During the 2017 World Festival of Youth and Students held in Sochi, he stressed that while Russia was a "Eurasian space", its "culture, language group and history" is "undoubtedly a European space as it is inhabited by people of this culture".

Putin's standpoint on Russia's European roots has been consistent all these years — in the book, *First Person: An astonishingly Frank Self Portrait by Russia's President Vladimir Putin*, by Nataliya Gevorkyan, Natalya Timakova, and Andrei Kolesnikov, (2000: p. 169), he stressed that "of course, Russia is a diverse country, but we are part of Western European culture. No matter where our people live, in the Far East or in the south, we are Europeans." His view is shared by many an elite member, in both the political and business as well as academic establishments, even if they have not openly expressed themselves to that effect.

Third, economics plays a significant role. Despite sanctions, the EU remains Russia's largest trading partner, a point stressed by Igor Ivanov, Foreign Minister of Russia (from 1998–2004), in an article dated 27 March 2018 in the *Moscow Times*, an English language daily. Prime Minister Medvedev, in an interview with Russian television channels on 5 December 2019, focused on the losses to both sides, due to the current tensions and sanctions. According to him, before the current tensions began in 2014, "our trade with the EU was considerable, US$417 billion, but later it slumped to some US$250 billion."

Moreover, despite the EU's long-standing desire and efforts to reduce its dependence on Russian gas, Russian gas exports to the EU are still of significance. American political scientist Thane Gustafson in his book on the EU–Russia energy relationship, *The Bridge: Natural Gas in a Redivided Europe,* (Harvard University Press, 2020), argues that each side seeks to exploit gas and oil to influence the other in the big game of power politics but Russia seems to have the upper hand. The European Union now imports nearly 40% of its natural gas from Russia.[2] And according to *Intellinews'* 3 December 2019 analysis, "Russia relies on Europe for the vast bulk of its gas exports, with volumes totalling just under 200 bcm annually."

---

[2] See review of his book in Nature.com dated 2 December 2019, by Professor Andrew Moravcsik, Professor of Politics and International Affairs and Director of the EU Programme, in Princeton University.

It is also noteworthy that Germany, the key EU member, remains committed to the Nord Stream 2 gas pipeline project, which will run from Russia to Germany across the Baltic Sea, in the face of US opposition.

The US fears that Europe would become more dependent on Russian gas. President Trump has consistently complained about Germany's purchase of Russian gas, arguing that the US "is protecting" Germany while "it is paying billions to Russia". He reiterated his stance in a June 2020 rally in Tulsa, Oklahoma, saying: "We're supposed to protect Germany from Russia, but Germany is paying Russia billions of dollars for energy coming from a pipeline. Excuse me, how does that work?"

The Russians believe the US wants to eliminate competition to its gas exports to the EU. A *Deutsche Welle* report dated 18 December 2019 quoted Kremlin spokesman Dmitry Peskov as saying that the US was preparing sanctions to maintain its "artificial domination of European markets" and push EU members into buying more American over Russian gas. Peskov reiterated his standpoint about the alleged commercial motives behind US sanctions against the project: a *Bloomberg* report dated 16th July 2020 quoted Peskov as saying that US sanctions were "an attempt to force Europeans to buy more expensive gas under less attractive conditions."

Fourth, geography is a constant factor: European Russia borders on EU and NATO member states. While it is a huge transcontinental landmass, with most of its territory lying east of the Urals, the majority of its people lives and prefers to live west of that mountain divide, in European Russia, which is more developed and economically stable. Russia's challenge is to develop its sparsely-populated but vast Siberian and Far Eastern territories.

Fifth, Russia's security and major geopolitical interests in the first instance are centred in Europe. In Russia's modern history and within living memory, threats to the country emanated from the West. They were embodied in the invasions by the Poles in the 17th century, Napoleon in the 19th century, intervention by the Western powers (and Japan in the Russian Far East) in Russia's civil war after the

Bolsheviks seized power in 1917 and the Germans in 1941, the last having left an indelible mark on Russian consciousness for it was the most brutal war fought in history and caused a huge loss of Russian/Soviet lives. (The Soviet victory over Nazi Germany on 9 May 1945 is celebrated with much fanfare and sentiments every 9 May). The Mongol/Tartar yoke is too distant historically to play a role in modern Russian psyche.

This preoccupation with the West has security considerations as well. They explain Russia's deeply entrenched antipathy towards NATO, in particular, its eastward expansion and the very fact that NATO still exists long after the Soviet collapse. Commenting on NATO's 70th anniversary summit in London, President Putin was quoted as saying by *Interfax* news agency on 3 December 2019 that NATO was established in 1949 "as the main component of the Cold War being unfolded at the time and a way to oppose the Soviet Union". He added that "as is well known, there is no Soviet Union now, and there is no Warsaw Pact, which was a military pact created in response to NATO's establishment, while NATO still exists and is developing". He also stressed that the number of NATO members had grown from 12 at the moment of its inception to 29 today.[3]

Finally, the West's relative decline is not seen as final in some influential quarters of Russian intellectual circles. An astute observer, Dmitry Trenin, head of the Carnegie Moscow Centre, correctly pointed this out in a think-piece dated 18 February 2019. Noting the West's current challenges and problems — Brexit, a divided US, France's challenge in the streets of its cities, etc., Trenin noted that:

"a few Russians are quite giddy at this view. They should sober up. Western economies, even if they may be facing yet another recession, are fundamentally strong. The United States still basically controls global finance and leads the world by a huge margin in both technology and innovation. For all the talk of fake news and Russian propaganda, mainstream Western media continue to dominate the

---

[3] North Macedonia joined the Western Alliance as its 30th member in March 2020.

information landscape across the globe. Migration waves to Western Europe and North America testify to how attractive Western living standards remain for the masses of less fortunate people all over the world. And, of course, the Pentagon wields phenomenal military power. So, unlike what happened to the Soviet Union and the communist system in the late 1980s, the West will live to see another day, even if it will have to transform itself in the process. So, how should Russia deal with America and Europe in their present condition? Above all, one needs to accept that while the West is altering its structure at the national, international and supranational levels, it is not withering away. The United States will continue to be in the lead, even if its leadership looks less benevolent and less altruistic. Europeans and other allies will have to accept the new regime, even if begrudgingly, and protect some of their own interests… In any case, the bonds that tie Europe to America will not disappear."

Trenin's realistic assessment of the West's strengths and weaknesses clearly indicates the Euro-centric and US-centric *Weltanschauung* of Russian academia.

While Russia's ties with the West are likely to stay strained in the foreseeable future, they will not become a long fixture on the global stage, like the US–Soviet Cold War. The current tension in the relationship over a host of unresolved issues — the Ukrainian crisis, the annexation of the Crimea, Russia's role in Syria, perceived Russian interference in the US presidential elections and other Western elections and the Skripal affair — would appear at first glance, to justify the conclusions of some experts. However, Russia and the West do not have a choice but to eventually find a *modus vivendi* to regulate and place their relationship on a stable, predictable and long-term basis.

Russia and the West, especially Europe, are closely linked, as pointed out above. They will not be able to live side-by-side in a permanent state of tension and hostility. The Europeans would not want an unresolved hostile and tense relationship with an important and large neighbour whose market and energy resources they desire and require. Europe, especially Germany, does not want any unnecessary tension with Russia that would jeopardise not only commercial links but more importantly, might become a *casus belli* for open hostilities. The outcome of the 1941–45 war with the Soviet Union on Germany's post-war life, remains imprinted on its leaders' minds.

On his part, President Putin is unlikely to make any more moves to further strain the relationship with the West.

He will have become Russia's longest-serving leader since Stalin, when his current term ends in 2024. He is keenly aware of his legacy — bringing stability and economic growth, and restoring Russia's place among the great powers — and would not want to endanger it by engaging in a long-drawn out contest with the West. Ever the pragmatist, he remains interested in normalising relations with the West. Putin is aware that Russia still needs Western management skills and investments to modernise its economy. This is a point which economic liberals like former Finance Minister Alexei Kudrin and the head of Sberbank, Russia's largest bank, Herman Gref, have long argued. They have his ear.

Putin might execute a *volte face* in Russia's relations with the West, at a time of his choosing and when one least expects it. One can expect the unexpected from Putin. The last several years have shown that he is adept at making moves and decisions which stunned and surprised both his supporters and critics. After all, he offered the US assistance against the Taliban and international terrorism after the 11 September 2001 attack, reportedly against the advice of his military and intelligence officials. His action was unexpected.

Moreover, he has never closed the door to the West, despite his hard-line tone *vis-à-vis* the US/West. He has made it clear that Russia would not engage in an arms race, a reflection of his awareness that a major reason for the Soviet collapse was the arms race with the US/West. In his February 2019 State-of-the-Nation speech, he made it clear that "we are not interested in confrontation and we do not want it, especially with a global power like the USA."

I do not see the current tense state of the Russo-Western relationship going beyond the end of his current Presidential term in 2024. Russia would eventually return to its European "roots" and normalise relations with Europe. On what basis this could take place is another issue and beyond the scope of this book.

*T*he China Factor

The US might not follow Europe's lead but it too cannot afford a permanent/semi-permanent state of hostility with Russia in the face of China's growing power. President Donald Trump's well-known disposition towards Russia ensures that the US would also not want a conduct a long-term hostile relationship with Russia. Even if he is not re-elected, the US' deep-seated suspicion of China will ensure the need for a more balanced relationship with Russia, in order to ensure that the latter does not move any closer to the former that it already has.

The deterioration of the US-China relationship in the aftermath of the spread of COVID-19 into the US, has presented Russia with a strategic dilemma.[4]

In the current confrontation between the US and China, Russia's role is key to maintaining the strategic balance among the three great powers. Russia today appears to be in the position China had been during the Cold War, when the US' relationship with China was close, and together, they worked to contain and weaken the Soviets. Russia today is closer to China than it is to the US. The question is how long this state of affairs could continue.

While it values its links with China for economic, political and geopolitical reasons, it is also an open question whether it would want or can afford to be seen to be fully on China's side in the years ahead, should US–China tensions come to open blows over, for instance, the South China Sea.

Being one of the world's two nuclear superpowers, Russia is keen on maintaining strategic parity with the US and would like to extend the New START treaty, which limits the number of strategic nuclear

---

[4] Hitherto, Russia has been the only major power to have vociferously supported China against US' allegations of Chinese responsibility for spreading the virus abroad. Russia's relationship with China has not been openly affected, in spite of COVID-19's deleterious impact on its economy and well-being of its citizens.

weapons the US and Russia may deploy; it expires in 2021. The US has not shown the same level of enthusiasm, and would like to include China into the negotiations for a new treaty. The US has been pressing Russia to persuade China to join them in negotiating a new treaty; however, since its nuclear arsenal is smaller than the US' and Russia's, China is unlikely to do so.

The US' announcement of its intention to withdraw from the Open Skies Treaty, alleging Russian violations, has alarmed Russia. The Treaty came into force in 2002, and currently has 35 participant states, mainly European countries and Canada. It establishes a programme of unarmed aerial surveillance flights over the entire territory of its participants and is designed to enhance mutual understanding and confidence by giving all participants a direct role in gathering information about military forces and activities of concern to them.

Earlier, the US withdrawal in 2019 from the Intermediate Nuclear Forces (INF) Treaty with Russia, had also caused consternation in Moscow. Concluded in 1987, it banned both countries' land-based ballistic missiles, cruise missiles, and missile launchers with short medium-range and intermediate-range. The US accused Russia of non-compliance as reasons for its withdrawal.

To Russia, these US' actions and coolness towards an extension of the New START Treaty are of concern, not only for national security but also reasons of national prestige; in the dialogue on arms control, Russia engages the US as an equal and is recognised as such by the US. Hence, Russia remains keen on having a "normal" relationship with the US, which would preserve the arms control dialogue.

Even before COVID-19's emergence, President Putin took measures to ensure that not all Russian eggs were placed into the Chinese basket and that he did not intend to burn his bridges to the West.

First, he invited major Western leaders to attend the 75th anniversary celebrations of victory in World War II on 9 May 2020 in Moscow. President Emmanuel Macron accepted the invitation. More significantly, he also invited President Trump (although he declined it in March 2020). Chancellor Angela Merkel and President Xi Jinping had likewise been invited to the event. In April 2020, it was postponed due to concerns about COVID-19, to the third week of June 2020. No Western leader, let alone China's, was represented at the event; one assumes COVID-19 must have played a significant role in their decision. Most of the political leaders present at the event, hail from the former Soviet republics, as well as from Serbia.

Victory Day, as this annual celebration is described in Russia, is a very important day in the history of post-Soviet Russia. Attendance by any major Western leader at this event would be a significant symbolic boost to President Putin's standing with his people and to Russia's prestige — it would be seen as the weakening of Western isolation of Russia.

Second, the Russo-Ukrainian exchange of prisoners in early September 2019 helped pave the wave for the revival of the Normandy Four format — Russia, France, Germany, Ukraine — to resolve the separatist conflict. France hosted the meeting on 9 December 2019 in Paris. It was the first time the leaders had met in more than three years. President Putin has long been aware that the current state of Russo-Ukrainian relations is a major obstacle to normalising Russia's relations with the EU.

Third, in January 2020, he suggested holding a summit of the leaders of Russia, China, the US, France, and Britain (the five Permanent Members of the UNSC) in 2020 to discuss world affairs. He maintained that such a meeting would be symbolic in 2020, the 75th anniversary of the end of World War II and the establishment of the UN. All the other four members of the UNSC have agreed to this suggestion. Apart from signalling to China that Russia is not totally isolated from the US/West, his proposal serves two other goals: to maintain face-to-face contact with the three Western leaders of the UNSC and, in the process, help improve the atmosphere in the relationship with them, and to show his domestic audience that he and Russia still enjoy the respect of world leaders.

Fourth, since the start of the year, he has held a series of telephone calls with President Trump to discuss issues ranging from oil price stabilisation to the fight against COVID-19 and arms control.

Finally, Russia's assistance to Italy and the US during the height of the pandemic in March and April 2020 was calculated to improve the atmosphere between the two sides. The US reciprocated Russia's gesture in May with similar assistance in the fight against COVID-19.

Some Western leaders, on their part, would also like to avoid alienating Russia irrevocably. President Trump, for instance, intimated a day before the G7 Summit in France in August 2019, that Russia might be re-admitted into the Western Club known as the G8, from which Moscow was expelled, following the annexation of the Crimea. Trump was supported by President Macron, the host of the Summit. Japanese Prime Minister Shinzo Abe was also reported to have said at the Fifth Eastern Economic Forum held in Vladivostok from 4 to 6 September 2019 that he supported Russia's return to G7. The US is the host of the 2020 G7.[5]

Had President Putin at the time no real interest in re-joining the G7, he would not have minced his words to reject it outright. Instead, he expressed readiness to host a G8 summit with China, India, and Turkey.

Recently, President Trump suggested that Russia, Australia, India, and South Korea be invited to the 2020 G7 scheduled for September 2020. Thus far, Canada and the UK have rejected Russia's return to the G7.

As of this writing, Russia itself has not totally rejected the US invitation. A *Reuters* report dated 1 June 2020 quoted President Putin's spokesman, Dmitry Peskov, as saying that "President Putin is a supporter of dialogue in all directions, but in this case, in order to respond to such initiatives, we need to receive more information, which we unfortunately do not have."

To assuage probable Chinese concerns, the next day, *TASS* news agency quoted Russian Foreign Ministry Spokeswoman Maria Zakharova as saying that President Trump's initiative to hold an

---

[5] The G7 consists of the US, Canada, the UK, France, the FRG, Japan and Italy. Russia joined the G7 in 1997 — its membership was suspended in 2014 following its annexation of the Crimea.

expanded G7 summit, involving Russia and some other countries, was a step in the right direction. However, it would not ensure universal representation without China's participation. She stressed that "it is hardly possible to implement serious undertakings of global significance without China's participation."

To reassure China, Konstantin Kosachev, Chairman of the Foreign Affairs Committee of the Federation Council, emphasised that he was against building any bloc or coalition aimed at a third country, in reference to President Trump's invitation to Russia, and the other three countries to attend the 2020 G7 meeting, without China. He made this comment in a video conference with Indian journalists, according to a *Times of India* report dated 10 June 2020.

China has become a major factor in European calculations towards Russia. Like President Trump, though perhaps to a lesser degree, President Macron has his reservations about China. According to a *Financial Times* article dated 11 September 2019, he was quoted as telling a gathering of his country's ambassadors in August that "pushing Russia away from Europe is a profound strategic error, because we will push Russia either into an isolation that increases tensions or into alliances with other great powers such as China," adding that Europe "will never be stable or secure if we don't pacify and clarify our relations with Russia."

The growing Russo-Chinese relationship has obviously become too close for comfort for Europe, what with Russia's prodigious natural wealth, military technology and strength, as well as large market. The worsening state of US–China and US–Russia relations is also not in the overall EU interest, including and especially in economic terms. US sanctions against Russia and tariffs against China have negatively affected the EU as well. These facts cannot be ignored by its politicians.

The West is also keenly aware that no sustainable and long-term resolutions of the Syrian conflict and Iranian nuclear issue can be achieved without Russian support. Russia has become a crucial factor in the Middle East with its intervention on the side of President Bashir Assad and relatively close links with Iran.

President Putin also has domestic political reasons to consider for seeking normalisation with the West. That would lead to the lifting of sanctions and help strengthen the economy. Normalisation of relations with the West would also help to diffuse growing domestic dissatisfaction with him over the state of the economy and other issues.

Russia is not the Soviet Union which was essentially a closed society. Soviet citizens, by and large, did not have a choice but to live in their closed society. By contrast, since the Soviet collapse, many Russians have travelled all over the world and to the West, and with the Internet, are fully aware of the outside world. Even President Putin cannot isolate his people from the outside world, especially the EU, which is geographically close and culturally, historically and traditionally linked to Russia.

While he would like to restore normality to Russia's relations with the West, he does not want a repetition of the relationship like that of the 1990s in the aftermath of the Soviet break-up. It is worthwhile examining the nature of Russo-Western relations in the immediate post-Soviet era.

Just a few years after the Soviet collapse, Russia's relations with the West could be described as unrequited love: President Boris Yeltsin hoped that Russia could be somehow integrated into the West. It sought not only Western economic assistance but also entry into the G7 in 1993. The West however, did not or could not, for its own reasons, fully bring Russia into its "club". Both sides had monumental obstacles to overcome in their dichotomy of views with respect to the Soviet collapse and how to manage post-Soviet Russia's relationship with the West.

To most Russians, the Soviet break-up was the outcome of their own choice and actions, and not due to Western military or politico-economic pressure. Hence, post-Soviet Russia could neither be equated with Weimar Germany nor with Nazi Germany and Imperial Japan. Having freed themselves from Communism, Russia expected to be welcomed into the Western world.

Why Post-Soviet Russia Could not Join the West

While the West subsequently integrated many former Warsaw Pact (WP) members and the Baltic states into the EU/NATO, Russia was left out. The West could not simply forget (but perhaps could forgive) the erstwhile dangerous existential rivalry and relationship with Moscow between 1945 and the Soviet collapse. Undoubtedly, the former WP members and Baltic states could have played a significant role in moulding the overall Western perception of a resurgent Russia which could threaten their newly-found independence from Moscow.

Having witnessed directly the tensions between the West and the Soviet Union over the deployment of the Cruise and Pershing II missiles in the West Germany in the early 1980s when I served in Bonn, I wondered whether Russian leaders themselves realistically expected the West to "bring them into its club" just a few years after the declared end of the Cold War.

Russian leaders failed to see that four decades of the Cold War and seven decades of Communism had effectively meant that Russia was an "outsider" and the rest of Europe and the larger West continued to look it at it from this angle. Moreover, they should have known that Western distrust and fear of a revanchist Russia could not totally disappear just a few years after the fall of the Soviet Union. That was a point I had really wanted to convey to all my Russian contacts and friends at the time, but never did. I did not believe they would accept my standpoint as worthy of thought. I was keenly aware that the assessment of a junior diplomat from a small country, far removed from the complexities and experience of the long Soviet/Russian competition with the West, was not likely to be treated with any seriousness.

Russia's failure to join the Western "club" after the Soviet collapse is connected with the deeply-rooted fear of the Russian colossus in the European psyche. A chequered history is one reason (on the part, especially, of the Eastern and Central Europeans as well as the Balts, and to an extent, the Nordics) on the one hand. The long domination of Eastern and Central Europe by the Soviet Union and military standoff between NATO and the WP left a lasting, suspicious residue in European and American minds about post-Soviet Russia's place in a

Europe freed from the Berlin Wall and the fall of the Iron Curtain. The fear, distrust, and suspicions of former WP members as well as the Baltic states which were then clamouring to join the West, and had support in their quest, also put paid to any Russian hope of becoming a member of the "club".

On the other hand, Russia has long been considered an "Asiatic" power by its European neighbours. Europe's somewhat jaundiced views of Russia have deep-seated historical roots. The Marquis de Custine's "*Letters from Russia*", a fascinating account of his journey across Russia in 1839, in which he described Russia in rather unflattering terms, bears testimony to this fact. In short, there was and is some prejudice, justified or not, in the European and, by extension, US perception of Russia. Historically, Tsarist Russia's own relationship with Western Europe had been clouded by episodes of bad blood and distrust, the 1854–1856 Crimean war being an example.

Moreover, post-Soviet Russia was simply too large to absorb or integrate into the EU, let alone NATO. Who would lead a larger West with Russia in it — the US or Russia? I did not believe at all that Russia would or could submit to US leadership of the West, given its own sense of empire and erstwhile status of a superpower.

Also, were Russia ever to join NATO or become a member of an "enlarged" West, China could be expected to react to such a development with alarm. Even at the time, it was clear that China was on the way to becoming a world power and hence its views on issues like Russia joining the West in some shape or form, could not be simply brushed aside or ignored by either Russia or the West. The West also certainly did not want to inherit Russia's existing challenges in directly facing China.

Finally, the speed with which the collapse of the Iron Curtain and the Soviet Union took place could have strengthened the somewhat cock-a-hoop sentiments in intellectual and political circles in the West over this historic development. In this atmosphere, the notion of Russia joining the West would not have been of importance.

In retrospect, one should also not have harboured any illusions that Russia, as the successor state to the Soviet Union, could have, so soon after the Soviet collapse, realistically adopted a totally calm and emotionless approach to its relationships with the former WP countries or ex-Soviet republics in the Baltic states. This is especially so since Moscow felt that its security interests and sense of *amour propre* (being a Great Power for centuries on the world stage and a superpower during the Soviet period) had not been taken into account by the West, in relation to NATO's eastward expansion and other issues. That was the nub of the issue.

Both Russia and the West, in particular the EU, had to content themselves with the 1994 Partnership and Cooperation Agreement (PCA), in place of any institution or attempt to bring Russia into the European fold. The PCA essentially defined relations between Russia and the EU in political, economic, financial, social, and cultural terms without any commitment by the EU to integrate Russia into its Union.

War with the West?

This issue deserves some attention. The current tension in Russo-Western relations has led to speculation in some quarters of the Western academic and media world about the possibility of Russia becoming militarily aggressive and willing to risk war with NATO by invading the Baltic states, or a Central and Eastern European (CEE) country like Poland, which are NATO and EU members. Russia's annexation of the Crimea and continued support for the separatist regions of the Ukrainian eastern regions are seen as evidence by its critics of its willingness to use force to achieve its politico-strategic objectives. Moreover, President Trump's apparent lukewarm attitude towards NATO is said to be a possible factor that would invite Russian aggression against the Baltics or CEE countries.

There can be no doubt that the West will neither provoke nor initiate hostilities with Russia but will defend any NATO member-state that comes under an unprovoked military assault by Russia. Since my book is about Russia, I will focus on the factors which explain why initiating war with the West is also not in Russia's calculations or vital interest.

First, if I may reiterate, President Putin and members of the ruling elite are cognisant of the fact that Russia requires Western investments, technology, and markets for its energy and other exports, and to develop its economy. China is a growing and important market for Russia but in the foreseeable future, it cannot totally supplant the EU. Moreover, Russia does not want to be totally reliant on the Chinese market for its energy and other exports.

Second, unless Russia could be certain of Chinese backing to the hilt (political, economic, as well as military) in any military action against a NATO member state, it would not make such a dangerous decision to attack a NATO member state. China would not support any such Russian move, unless it itself becomes a victim of US and Western military aggression.

Third, Russia is aware that war with the West would weaken both sides and the only major power that would benefit from this situation would be China. Russia would not undertake any action that would further strengthen an already strong neighbour with which it has had a long, difficult, and tense relationship until only the last few decades.

Fourth, as long as NATO remains united and all its members are committed to help each other in the event of external aggression, Russia would be foolish to launch an open military attack on any NATO member state. Its regular military exercises in the last few years since 2014, have signalled clearly to Russia that NATO is willing, able, and ready to counteract any Russian military move against any of its member-states.

Fifth, the long history of bad blood between the CEE countries/ Baltics and Russia ensures that they will offer determined and stiff resistance to any Russian invasion and subsequent occupation. Such a scenario would not be like the annexation of the Crimea, which was generally free of violence. Russia certainly cannot afford militarily, economically, politically, and from the standpoint of national morale overall, to have an Afghanistan in Europe, literally at its front-door. In this regard, it is worth noting an article published in the *Military Times* (MT) published on 24 April 2019 on the issue of a possible Russian attack on the Baltics. It quoted Stephen J. Flanagan, a senior political scientist at the Rand Corporation, who co-authored a new study on deterring Russian aggression in the Baltics for the Pentagon. The study, which was supported by the US Pentagon and conducted within the federally-funded Rand National Defence Research Institute, devised a multitude of scenarios under which Russia could interfere in the Baltic states — ranging from attacks below the threshold of armed conflict to flagrantly annexing the land of neighbouring states. The worst-case scenarios are unlikely, the *MT* quoted Flanagan as saying; he added that "our general assessment is we don't believe, and many of the Baltic leaders don't believe, that the Russians would make a land grab and sue for peace". He however stressed that "…they are opportunistic. If they think they can cause a crisis in NATO and make NATO look feckless or unable to respond quickly, that may be something they would risk".

It would therefore make sense for NATO member-states to continue showing resolve and make clear to Russia that it would respond forcefully to any Russian attack on a member-state. Increasing and maintaining their defence expenditures to reflect this resolve have this deterrent effect.

Sixth, launching a hostile, military assault against a NATO member-state would also open the possibility of the overthrow of the government by internal instability and oppositional forces, should hostilities not go in Russia's favour. The events of 1917 would definitely be on the minds of Russia's leaders if they must make decisions involving war and peace with the West.[6] Russia's people, since the end of the Cold War, have had more contact with the outside world, either directly through travel or indirectly thanks to the Internet, than they ever have had between 1917 and 1991. While they are patriotic, they are no longer as pliant as they might have been during the seven decades of Communism. Hence, President Putin does not have an iron-clad guarantee that his people would wholeheartedly support open military aggression against a

---

[6] The Romanov dynasty was removed, due to a series of military setbacks at the hands of Germany and consequent war fatigue, stoked by the Bolsheviks and other forces opposed to the dynasty and continued hostilities.

NATO member country and war with the West, and would not turn against him, if hostilities were not to evolve in Russia's favour.

Seventh, the modern history of Russia since 1917 shows that it feared Western aggression but did not openly resort to war to either thwart it or meet it head-on, by making the first move. The prime example was Stalin's apparent belief that Hitler would not launch Operation Barbarossa, even as his agents like the well-known Richard Sorge in Tokyo, were reporting the opposite. Stalin permitted shipments of food and raw materials to Nazi Germany almost up to the eleventh hour.

Of course, this does not mean Russia would not resort to force to defend its security interests, if it believes it has been pushed into a corner. Indeed, according to an analysis dated 12 December 2019 done by the *International Institute of Strategic Studies*, "in October 2019, Russia carried out what was probably its largest nuclear forces exercise since the collapse of the Soviet Union in 1991." The analysis noted that:

> "unlike other nuclear exercises in recent years, the Russian Ministry of Defence briefed Russian media about *Grom*-2019 and released selected official information about the exercise. The intention, at least in part, may have been to demonstrate to a domestic audience that Russia remains a 'strategic' power capable of meeting any threat posed by an external aggressor, and that Putin continues to lead a strong, militarily capable country that demands respect and its rightful place on the world stage. The scale of the exercise was probably intended to convey to international observers that, even though some of its systems are ageing, the Russian armed forces retains a formidable nuclear capability that is operationally fit for purpose."

Unsurprisingly, the analysis assessed that "in an uncomfortable echo of the late 1970s and early 1980s, when Washington and Moscow confronted each other in Europe with theatre nuclear weapons, the involvement of these weapons in Russian exercises raises the alarming spectre of Europe once again being considered a potential theatre for a limited nuclear exchange".

However, this does not mean that Russia is contemplating an open and unprovoked military attack on a NATO member-state.

Eighth, President Putin and Russia's military leaders are fully aware that NATO and the West are economically and militarily stronger than Russia. To lend verisimilitude to any speculation of a Russian attack on the Baltics or a CEE country, one might wish to consider the relative strengths of Russia and the NATO member countries. Russia's military and economy are much smaller than that of the US and NATO countries and logically and rationally, it would not make sense to start an open conflict with a stronger opponent. According to an article dated 15 February 2019 by Lucie Beraud-Sudreau, Research Fellow for Defence Economics and Procurement with the *International Institute for Strategic Studies*:

> "the nominal increase in US defence spending (US$44.5 billion in 2018 dollars) was the largest increase in the world in 2018 — far above China, which was the second largest at US$16.7 billion. It almost amounted to Germany's total defence outlays in 2018. However, European nations also contributed to the global trend. After years of reduced spending after the end of the Cold War and in the wake of the financial crisis, NATO's European member states increased their defence budgets by 4.2% in real-terms in 2018. Their total spending would — if the aggregate figure of US$264 billion were considered on its own — amount to the second largest defence budget in the world. It would be equivalent to 1.5 times China's official budget (US$168 billion), and almost four times Russia's estimated total military expenditure (US$63 billion)."

In any case, Russians know what war with a stronger West could mean for their country. Their experience in World War II had brought untold death and destruction not only on the Soviet Union's infrastructure but more so, on its people, including civilians, unlike the much kinder fate that the Western allies like Britain and France, as well as the US, had to bear.

Finally, members of the country's ruling elite and those who serve them, unlike their Soviet counterparts, prefer the Western way of life to anything else. Remember that those who have been running the country after Yeltsin must have been living relatively frugal, if not deprived lives during the Soviet period with little or no access to *la dolce vita* in the West. A holiday in Rome, Paris, or London was considered heavenly at the time. The last 30 years of freedom to travel to and live in the West, once largely forbidden fruit, is still very much cherished, by both the members of Russia's elite as well as ordinary people.

The current tensions with the West have had an effect on their attitudes; however, that does not mean Russians would no longer be keen on visiting or living in the West. If I may repeat myself, Russians, despite their oft-repeated protestations to being Eurasians or having a unique civilisation, are, after all, ethnically Europeans. Those with the means, as like as not, would rather make for Europe or the US for a holiday while many wealthy Russians have properties, not to mention having their children schooled in London and elsewhere in the West, than in Asia; all this speaks to the fact that they are more at home with Westerners than with Asians. I chatted with so many Russians across their large country in all my years there about the West and travel and almost with no exceptions, all of them expressed the wish to see the Eiffel Tower or the Coliseum or just visit the West, if they had not been there. Asia and the rest of the world were simply an afterthought, if a trip to the West was not financially within reach.

An open military conflict with the West would close all this off to them totally, including their leaders. It would require very extreme circumstances for them to make the harrowing decision to launch an unprovoked attack on a NATO member-state.

If anything, war between the West and the Soviet Union would have been more likely since the latter's leaders and their families as well as their own people had relatively little contact with the West, unlike the situation since the Soviet break-up.

President Putin has shown in the last two decades at the helm of Russia that he is a pragmatist. War with the West is not a sign of any pragmatic Russian leader.

Russia's Relationship with China

This topic has been touched upon in some detail in the preceding section. Other factors in this relationship are considered here.

Russo-China relations have been on the uptrend in the last decade or so, even before Russo-Western ties underwent serious strains over the annexation of the Crimea and the crisis in Russia's relations with Ukraine. It is therefore debatable whether Russia's declared "pivot" to the East, essentially focussed on China, was the direct outcome of its strained relationship with the West over the Crimean and Ukrainian issues.

In this regard, the standpoint of Sergei Strokan, a leading commentator on domestic and international affairs with *Kommersant*, a prominent Russian daily, is noteworthy. He rightfully argued before an RSIS audience on 8 February 2018 that Russia's "pivot" was more focussed on China than on the rest of Asia, let alone ASEAN. Russia had no alternative but to turn to China as it was a powerful neighbour and major consumer of Russian energy; also, President Putin could show the world and his own people that Russia was not internationally isolated. The Chinese had exploited Russia's strained relations with the West for instance in negotiations for the supply of gas to China which had been hampered by years of disagreements over price. Russian gas would be supplied at a lower price.[7]

Russia also supplied China with higher level military technology like the latest Sukhoi fighter aircraft. Moreover, Russia's initial reservations about the BRI (Belt and Road Initiative — China's ambitious infrastructure project to link it with Europe through Central Asia, as well as maritime Asia) were shelved when Presidents Putin and Xi agreed in 2015 to cooperation between the Russian-led Eurasian Economic Union (EAEU) and the BRI. Both countries also agreed on energy cooperation in the Arctic as well as China's construction of a high-speed railway between Moscow and Kazan. A total of 32 bilateral

---

[7] The agreement to supply China with gas over 30 years, worth US$400 billion, was finalised in a May 2014 agreement.

agreements were signed in 2015 — they bound Russia to China for a long time. Russia was the junior partner in this relationship. It was ironic that the Russia–US relationship had floundered on the refusal of the US to treat Russia as an equal, among other factors — now Russia was the junior partner with China. President Putin was the main factor here as he wanted the relationship to be strengthened, Strokan maintained.

Strokan also argued that the idea of a pivot to the East was originally conceived by the late Foreign Minister and subsequently Prime Minister Yevgeny Primakov in the late 1990s with his Russia–India–China triangle (RIC) which later became the BRICS (Brazil, Russia, India, China, and South Africa). Strokan labelled the BRICS a "paper tiger". Since India and China could not get along, the RIC and BRICS could not serve as the pivot to the East — China became the most obvious alternative. With respect to the pivot towards ASEAN, Russia had an uphill battle to overcome in order to build-up its current modest relations with ASEAN. He placed the onus on Russia to do its homework in this respect. ASEAN was "undiscovered terrain" — Russian businessmen had to overcome cultural barriers and get out of their comfort zone to gain access to ASEAN's markets, he stressed.

Dr. Alexander Lukin, one of Russia's foremost scholars on China, also put forth the argument that the "pivot to Asia" was not a response to a worsening of relations with the West, but to two purely objective challenges: the need to establish relations with a region that is gradually becoming the centre of world economics and politics, and to Russia's strategic goal of developing its Siberian and Far Eastern regions.[8] Lukin admits in his book that "progress has been slow in accomplishing those goals". He cites a number of internal domestic and social reasons.

In vogue among Russian leadership and academic circles is the concept of a "Greater Eurasia" (GE) in which Russia, due to its large size spanning Europe and Asia, would play a leading role, alongside China. According to Lukin, the GE's "foundation is Russo-Chinese

---

[8] See Alexander Lukin, *Pivot to Asia: Russia's Foreign Policy Enters the 21st Century*, Vij Books India Pvt Ltd., p. 39.

closeness, propelled by the rise of China, the collapse of the USSR and strengthening of a new Russia, and the active stimulation by attempts of the US and its allies to contain the development of both states within the rubric of the international system under Western domination".[9]

The GE concept envisages Russia and China working with other states in Central Asia, India, even including ASEAN, and linking the Russian-led EAEU with the BRI, to form a vast region of economic and political cooperation.

President Putin himself called attention to the interest of the EAEU in the BRI. Addressing the opening ceremony of the Second Belt and Road Forum for International Cooperation in Beijing on 26 April 2019, he noted that "Russia has emphasised on numerous occasions that PRC President's Belt and Road Initiative rhymes with Russia's idea to establish a Greater Eurasian Partnership". He added that "the 5 EAEU states[10] have unanimously supported the idea of pairing the EAEU development and the Chinese Silk Road Economic Belt project".

However, there are obstacles to its realisation. A leading Russian academic recently assessed the difficulties ahead to "harmonise" the EAEU and BRI. In an article dated 2 May 2019 published by the *Valdai Discussion Club* (VDC), one of Russia's foremost think-tanks, Timofei Bordachev, the VDC's Programme Director, stressed that it would be "a challenging task as the expansion of infrastructure implies compatibility between leaders, mutual security guarantees, new rules and regulations for the common economic space, and supranational political structures to oversee trade, tariffs, foreign investment and immigration".

Analysing the GE concept is beyond the scope of this book. However, logic dictates that grand visions involving not only two great powers, Russia and China, but also other large countries like India and many other diverse countries, and stretching over great distances,

---

[9] Source: "Alternative Scenarios — Positive Scenario II", by Alexander Lukin, p. 9 in *The Asan Forum*, 12 April 2019.
[10] The five states are Russia, Armenia, Belarus, Kazakhstan, and Kyrgyzstan.

require much time, effort, and energy, political will, and above all, vast material resources before they can be fully realised, not to mention be sustained over the long-term for the benefit of all parties concerned.

It is difficult to see the GE concept replacing Russia's Euro/US-centric focus in its foreign policy, let alone weakening its still relatively strong and important economic, social, cultural, and political links with the EU in the short- to medium-term. Whether and if the GE concept would eventually become reality in the long-term (say 20 to 30 years) is anyone's guess.

Lukin's description of "Russo-Chinese closeness" does not totally reflect certain realities on the ground, especially in the Russian Far East (RFE) and Siberia.

During a visit to Tomsk in Siberia in 2007, local officials gave the impression to Ambassador Tay and me that they would prefer Singapore to Chinese investments, without seeking to elaborate their reasons other than to praise Singapore's reputation. Even during my earlier visits to Vladivostok and Khabarovsk in the mid-1990s, the impression I garnered then was that China was an unwelcome shadow, ever present on the horizon. A Singapore company which was then based in Vladivostok had issues securing work permits for some of its Chinese workers even though it would have liked but could not get enough locals to carry out the necessary tasks. Of course, much time has elapsed since then but that is not to say that Siberia's and the RFE's inhabitants' ingrained prejudices against China have dissipated.

Ever since the Soviet collapse, the disparities in the living standards of Russian cities close to China have become more and more apparent. A close Russian personal friend who has lived in Europe for the last two decades or so, was born and raised in Blagoveshchensk in the Amur region (opposite the Chinese city of Heihe). She would regale my wife and me about stories of obvious Chinese prosperity in Heihe compared to her home town in the mid-1990s (she still has relatives and friends there whom she visits). She could recall the Soviet period when Heihe was known to be poor and underdeveloped; roles have reversed today. Like most Russians who live east of the Urals, she has a visceral fear of China's growing power.

Fear and resentment of China come alive especially when it revolves around Chinese purchases of land. The following example speaks volumes. According to an article in 4 January 2018 issue of the *Financial Times*, "a sleepy tourist town on the shores of Siberia's Lake Baikal has become an unlikely lightning rod among Russian nationalists after Chinese investors bought up properties on the town's lakefront." Russian newspapers have inflamed public opinion over the town of Listvyanka, running headlines about a Chinese "invasion", "conquest", and even China's "yoke" — a reference to the Mongol invasions of the Middle Ages. An online petition with 55,000 signatures (Listvyanka has a population of less than 2,000) claims that Beijing is seeking to transform the area into a Chinese province, and asks Russia's President Vladimir Putin to ban land sales to the Chinese there. The petition has received wide coverage in newspapers including in *Moskovsky Komsomolets*, a national tabloid. "The people are in a panic! The authorities are inactive, but if this situation will not change, we will continue to lose our underbelly! Our property!" reads the petition on the website Change.org published by Yulia Ivanets, who is identified by her page on Russian social media site Vkontakte as being from the neighbouring town of Angarsk. "We have let the goat into the garden," she wrote.

The *New York Times* article by Neil MacFarquhar on 2 May 2019 on the issue surrounding unpopular Chinese investment in the Lake Baikal area, deserves mention as well.

There have been other instances of open reservations about the increase of China's presence in the RFE and Siberia but I do not think it is necessary to list them all to make the point.

While the leadership especially in distant Moscow might rave about the country's links with China, it is clear that those on the ground might not fully share their optimism. Professor Oleg Barabanov, Programme Director of the VDC, Professor of MGIMO (Moscow State Institute of International Relations) and Professor of the Russian Academy of Sciences rightly assessed the issues facing Russian leaders in preparing their people to accept China's rise. In an article dated 14 May 2019 in the VDC, he noted that:

"another challenge for Russia in the context of the rise of China is related to the perception of China by Russians. Despite all the great work in the sphere of soft power to strengthen the positive image of our nations and states, a portion of the Russian public has adopted, to put it mildly, a reserved attitude to China and its residents. The echo of the notorious "Chinese threat" is tenacious. Importantly, the scepticism of China shows itself both in the liberal and conservative-patriotic segments of Russian public opinion. This can be seen quite clearly in the media and in statements by opinion leaders. For example, during the top-rated daily political talk shows on Russian television, whenever they talk about China, the anti-Chinese horror stories come from both liberal- and patriotic-minded opinion leaders. As a result, a surprising anti-Chinese consensus takes shape before the viewer, which brings together political forces which hold diametrically opposed views on all other matters. Such an attitude occasionally goes beyond social stereotypes and becomes part of economic decision-making. This can be seen in the sometimes cautious attitude to Chinese investment in Russia, especially local projects. Sometimes, the locals in Russia are biased towards Chinese tourists."

Barabanov also argued that for the "consolidation and unity of Greater Eurasia is the key value of the SCO (Shanghai Cooperation Organisation) and the EAEU–BRI association), not only diplomatic work outside of Russia is required, …but also a lot of work inside the country."

Remarks by a top official reveal some unease at the growing links between the two countries. On the eve of President Xi Jinping's state visit to Russia on 5 June 2019, President Putin's spokesman, Dmitry Peskov in an interview with RT (Russia Today) aired on 3 June 2019 stressed that "China is not our partner number one yet. Still, the EU countries are number one for us and I cannot agree with those who say that Russia is turning eastward". His subsequent remark was just as telling: "No, I hope Russia will never turn eastward. The Russian eagle looks to both sides — to the West and to the East, that's the nature of every policy of Russia, be it political and diplomatic or economic activities."

Yet, while relations with China today are a declared top priority for Russia, the hitherto hoped-for economic windfall from China has yet to materialise. Indeed, in an article dated 28 February 2018, Paul Stronski, a Senior Fellow at Carnegie's Russia and Eurasia Programme, argued convincingly that despite strong rhetoric and political will on both sides for cooperation in the Russian Far East (RFE), "there are serious doubts surrounding the realisation of pledged investments". Russia's Achilles heel is the RFE and Siberia in terms of socio-economic development.

Stronski's conclusions are also borne out by data compiled by Professor Olga Alexeeva, Professor of Chinese History in the History Deparment, University of Quebec, and Professor Frédéric Lasserre, Professor of Geography in the Geography Department in Université Laval, Quebec, in their article entitled "The Evolution of Sino-Russian Relations as seen from Moscow: the Limits of Strategic Rapprochement" published in *China Perspectives* (2018/3).

According to them, "in 2009, to stimulate the development of regional Sino-Russian relations, Moscow and Beijing adopted a 'Programme of Collaboration between the regions of the Russian Far East and Eastern Siberia and the North-East of the PRC', which gave details of 160 joint projects to be implemented by 2018, 94 of which were to be on Russian soil. Although remaining highly ambitious on paper, this collaboration programme did not manage to produce significant economic results as a result of back-pedalling by the Kremlin, which did not wish to confirm its intentions by releasing the financial and institutional support needed for the realisation of the planned initiatives. Consequently, at the present time, only 22 of these are under construction whilst the others have been suspended or abandoned for various reasons."

The perceptive academic, Sergei Karaganov himself pointed out in an article dated 12 March 2018 in *Rossiskaya Gazeta* that "Russia and China have proposed a big Eurasian Partnership, a 'One Belt, One Road' and 'a community of common destiny'. But it needs to be specified and developed further". His standpoint reveals Russia's ongoing reservations about whether its close political relationship with

China can and will materialise into tangible and long-term benefits for Russia.

Some Russian experts on China have also ascertained that the BRI has thus far not lived up to expectations. In their joint article dated 17 January 2019 in Russia in *Global Affairs*, Alexander Gabuev, Senior Fellow in the Carnegie Moscow Centre, and a China scholar, and Ivan Zuenko, Research Fellow, Institute of History, Archaeology and Ethnography of the Far Eastern Department, Russian Academy of Sciences, noted that "…Russia's participation in the 'Belt and Road' initiative has so far produced quite modest economic results".

The level of Chinese investments has apparently not lived up to Russian expectations. Another China expert, Professor Alexei Maslov, from the prestigious Higher School of Economics in Moscow, told the Chinese television network CGTN host, Tian Wei, in an interview aired on 6 June 2019 that since 1991, Chinese investment in Russia totalled only about US$30 billion, which was less compared to Chinese investment in the US and Europe.

This is not to say, however, that Russo-Chinese economic relations are weak. Trade has increased; in 2018, China became Russia's top trading partner with turnover at US$108.3 billion; trade increased in 2019, amounting to US$110.79 billion. President Putin pointed out at the June 2019 annual St. Petersburg International Economic Forum (SPIEF) that to reduce currency fluctuations and instability (and dependence on the US dollar), both countries plan to "develop the practice of conducting financial transactions in our national currencies". He added that there was "tangible success" in investment with about 30 projects worth a total of US$22 billion underway.

Russian energy supplies to China can be expected to increase with the completion of the Power of Siberia natural gas pipeline to China — it was officially opened by Presidents Putin and Xi via teleconference on 2 December 2019. In May 2014, Gazprom and the China National Petroleum Corporation signed a 30-year agreement for gas to be supplied to China in the amount of 38 billion cubic metres per year.

China is also involved in Russia's LNG sector, owning almost 30% of the Yamal LNG project. In April 2019, two Chinese state oil companies acquired each a 10% stake in the Arctic LNG 2 project, according to *Intellinews* report dated 6 June 2019. According to a *Nikkei Asian Review* report dated 24 May 2020, Russia and China in 2019, entered into a deal that saw state-owned companies from both countries team up to ship LNG from the Arctic. Russia's major LNG producer, Novatek and state-owned shipping company, Sovcomflot partnered with two of China's state-owned enterprises, COSCO Shipping and Silk Road Fund, to manage a fleet of dozens of ice-breakers to transport the fuel from Novatek's plants, including Yamal LNG.

Russia is also building nuclear power plants in China. Planned cooperation in other sectors include projects in aircraft and helicopter manufacturing, space exploration, biotechnology, pharmaceuticals, and other knowledge-intensive industries. Noteworthy is Huawei's agreement with MTS, a Russian telecoms company, to develop a 5G network in Russia. According to Chinese automaker, Great Wall Motor, its production plant in the Tula region, with a manufacturing capacity of 80,000 cars a year, rising to 150,000 cars by 2020, is "the largest investment project of the Chinese manufacturing industry in Russia", estimated at $500 million.

Russia might also be able to play a role in meeting Chinese demand for food, in the face of the US–China trade war. According to a *RT (Russia Today)* report dated 7 June 2019, Russian agricultural exports will continue to grow and are expected to reach US$45 billion within the next five years, according to Agriculture Minister Dmitry Patrushev. Boosting sales of agricultural products abroad is currently one of Russia's top-priority tasks. Earlier, he said that Russia would soon become one of the world's 10 leading exporters of agricultural products. The country's producers managed to expand into a number of strategically important markets in 2018. The surge was reportedly due to the growth of grain, fish, and meat exports. China might become one of the major importers of Russian poultry and dairy products, if US–China trade tensions continue to affect US agricultural exports to China.

Military-to-military links have also been strengthened. According to Dmitry Trenin, Director of the Carnegie Moscow Centre (CMC) in his article dated 2 December 2019 in *Outlook*, President Putin, in his remarks in October 2019, for the first time, publicly confirmed that Russia was assisting China in creating an early warning system that should alert the Beijing leadership to missile launches that might be directed at China, thus making sure that no attack against China would come as a complete surprise. Trenin assessed the decision, in an interview published by the CMC on 19 November 2019, as one which "would strengthen Beijing's deterrence capabilities and complicate a potential adversary's calculations" and that "their cooperation allows Moscow to partially balance a relationship that is increasingly tilted toward Beijing". He also noted that both countries' forces have been training together for a decade, raising the level of joint exercises from anti-terrorism exercises to China's participation in Russia's major strategic drills in 2018 and 2019, conducting war games on land; naval manoeuvres in the East and South China Seas, the Mediterranean Sea, and the Baltic Sea; and joint air patrols over the Sea of Japan.

There is no doubt that links between the two countries will continue to grow since both share a common position on the need to stand up to what they perceive as US global dominance and interference into their domestic affairs.

However, a difficult history filled with tension, distrust, and open hostility, not to mention the vast cultural, racial, and religious distance between Russia, a European country and China, a very different civilisation, ensure that Russia and China will not be able to settle down into a really close and comfortable relationship. Being the only European country sharing one of the world's longest land borders with China cannot but be uncomfortable for any European state, much less one like Russia with an imperial past, messianic political and economic ideology and superpower status, not to mention a tense relationship in the 1960s and open hostilities in 1969. One must also recall that Tsarist Russia's relations with Asia, including China, its now-declared close partner, were not one of equality. Together with the Western powers, Tsarist Russia participated in the carving-up of China in the 19th century, while Central Asia was incorporated into its empire. Tsarist Russia had also acquired vast areas of Siberia and subsequently the Russian Far East.

The Soviet predicament with respect to its territories east of the Urals and in Central Asia was described to me by a German expert on the Soviet Union from the Bundesinstitut für ostwissenschaftliche und internationale Studien in Köln (Federal Institute for Eastern European and International Studies in Cologne) in the mid-1980s. I met him during my assignment to Bonn. According to him, unlike the Western powers, the Soviet Union could not retreat to the mother-country during the post-war decolonisation process. To do so would have meant giving up hard-won, strategic, and, in some areas, economically significant territory in the Russian Far East, Siberia and Central Asia. The Soviets would not allow their Communist rhetoric that their system was anti-colonial, just and noble, to take precedence over these more significant *Realpolitik* considerations.

In my view, Russia, as the successor state to the Soviet Union, inherited this dilemma, willy-nilly.

Both countries today choose for their own reasons, not to publicly harp on the past but their tortured history cannot be conveniently swept under the carpet. While they no longer have open differences over their certain sections of their lengthy border, history has long memories.

To their credit, both sides concluded a border demarcation treaty in 2008 that finally settled past disputes over their frontiers. Nevertheless, the tortured past can rear its head, even in the face of purportedly close relations between the two countries. A recent example makes this point clear.

According to a *South China Morning Post* article dated 2 July 2020 by Eduardo Baptista, "the Russian embassy in China has been pilloried on social media by Chinese diplomats, journalists, and internet users after it held a celebration of the founding of Vladivostok — because it is on land that used to be part of China. The modern-day territory of Primorsky Krai, whose capital is Vladivostok, was formerly part of the Qing's Manchurian homeland but was annexed by the Tsarist empire in 1860 following China's defeat at the hands of Britain and France in the second opium war." The report said that when the Russian embassy posted a video on Weibo of a party held on 2 July to celebrate the 160th anniversary of the city's founding, it prompted an online backlash. It added that "Shen Shiwei, a journalist for state-owned broadcaster CGTN, tweeted that the post "recalled people's memories [of] those humiliated days in 1860s". It also quoted Zhang Heqing, a Chinese diplomat working in the embassy in Pakistan, as commenting "isn't this what in the past was our Haishenwai?", referring to the Chinese name for the area before its annexation."

Even if the border is officially no longer a bilateral issue, two regions in which both countries have a keen interest, for economic, political, and geostrategic reasons and where they currently work together, could become contentious bilateral issues in the future.

The former Soviet republics of Central Asia, historically, a Russian sphere of influence since the Tsarist era, have in recent times, increasingly fallen under China's shadow. Their economic links with China have grown by leaps and bounds, to Russia's chagrin. For now, both countries appear to be content with the roles that they are playing in the region, with Russia assuming the dominant role in providing security while China buttresses the region's economic foundations with investments in infrastructure (principally to support its BRI initiative) and increased trade as well as imports of energy from Kazakhstan and Turkmenistan as well as Uzbekistan. How long this arrangement can be sustained without open tensions developing between the two countries remains to be seen.

The Arctic is the other region where Russia and China now cooperate but also has the potential to become a bilateral issue in the future. Russia has economic and geostrategic and military–security interests in the region. First, Russia is keen on developing the NSR between Europe and Asia. Second, the region boasts immense energy and other resources which Russia wishes to exploit. These two factors play an important role in Russia's plan to develop the relatively underdeveloped region. From the geostrategic and military-security angles, Russia jealously guards its sovereignty over the region.

Dmitry Trenin, Director of the Moscow Carnegie Centre, points out in his 31 March 2020 article on the Arctic that "Russia's Arctic strategy views the region as a strategic resource base for the country, and seeks to bolster it. While aiming to maintain peace and develop cooperation with its Arctic neighbours, the Russian strategy provides for the expansion of its military presence and installation of a border control system in the region. Moscow believes that any international system of governance in the Arctic should recognise Russia's role and significance. This concerns not only the protection of the region's unique ecological system, but also the use of resources and regulation of navigation." However, as Trenin points out, the Chinese strategy is to offer an inclusive system of managing the Arctic, with China playing a leading role in this system. He argues that "this is where the main conflict between the Russian and Chinese strategies lies."

Russian suspicions about China in the Arctic have been made plain with the arrest in June 2020 of Valery Mitko, President of the Arctic Academy of Sciences in St. Petersburg, for allegedly spying for China. His arrest showed that Russia is closely watching Chinese non-commercial activities in the Arctic. Nevertheless, Russia needs Chinese investments to open up its Far North and Far East regions for economic and social development and it does not have much choice but to continue working with the Chinese to achieve its socio-economic objectives in the region.

China's interest in the region lies in helping Russia develop the NSR, as part of its Polar Silk Route, a possible alternative or additional trade waterway to the current longer route that flows through the Straits of Malacca and South China Sea (and which in a crisis or war with the US, are vulnerable to interdiction by the US Pacific Fleet). China is also keen on exploiting the region's energy resources as seen in its involvement in Russia's LNG sector (details are found above in this section).

One must also note the apparent lack of Russian expertise and interest in China. This state of affairs does not bode well for the future development of closer Russo-China relations. Anatoly Karlin, a blogger who lives in Moscow, but who had spent most of his life in the UK and the US, wrote in November 2017 about the sad state of Sinology in post-Soviet Russia after the Soviet fall till the present-day. Quoting research done by Alexander Gabuev, a leading Sinologist in the Moscow

Carnegie Centre, his article noted that salaries for top Sinologists dropped from a comfortable 400–500 rubles during the 1980s to US$30–$50 by the mid-1990s. This low figure corresponds to what I had then been told about the sad state of wages in Russia for academics.

Gabuev himself confirmed with me in an e-mail exchange for this book that there are not enough experts on China. It says quite a lot that Russia does not have much expertise on China.

Indeed, Professor Su Ge, S. Rajaratnam Professor of Strategic Studies in RSIS, Co-Chair, Pacific Economic Cooperation Council, Chairman, China National Committee for Pacific Economic Cooperation, and a former diplomat, is of the view that both countries do not know each other well enough to establish any alliance-type relationship. He pointedly stated that he was optimistic about the future of Chinese relations with the US, as both countries knew each other very well; for instance, there were "many Chinatowns" in the US, in contrast to none in Russia. Hence, Russia and China needed to deepen their people-to-people links and diversify their economic relations into more non-energy sectors. Both countries had become close, into a "warm embrace", thanks to the US' hostility to both of them.

Professor Su Ge's comments were made in answer to my question on his assessment of Russo-Chinese relations in the current face of tensions between the US and these two great powers, after his speech for the RSIS Distinguished Public Lecture entitled "International Order and the Historical Journey of China's Diplomacy" at RSIS on 1 October 2018.

His views are echoed by Russian academic, Ivan Timofeev, Programme Director of the Valdai Discussion Club (VDC) and Director of Programmes at the Russian International Affairs Council. In an article dated 26 November 2019 in the VDC, he correctly pointed out that while "…Moscow and Beijing have developed unprecedented constructive relations at the political level…human contacts between the Russians and the Chinese are not yet comparable with those with Western countries. The same applies to most other non-Western countries. Without growing into the fabric of human and professional ties, Russia's turn to the East will just remain on paper".

In my view, Timofeev has fully hit the nail on the head.

Russia's Euro- and US-centric orientation for all the factors outlined earlier, ensure that Russians are very likely to remain more at home dealing with Europeans and Americans than with Asians and other non-Western peoples. Russians are, after all, I reiterate, a European people.

Ultimately though for Russia, it is not only a geopolitical necessity to remain independent of China's momentous weight but also has socio-economic and cultural considerations, in its search for an alternative economic model. In the words of Professor Andrei Kortunov, a leading Russian academic of the RIAC in a recent article: "Russia would not be able to copy China's model, because we just do not have that kind of demographic and cultural background. In this case, Russia's only option would be the Western one, because culturally and psychologically we are simply closer to the West."[11]

There are indications that China might not consider Russia a fully trustworthy partner. This perspective was quite obvious in a commentary in the *Global Times (China)* on 9 December 2019 by Wang Wen, Professor and Executive Dean of Chongyang Institute for Financial Studies and the Deputy President of the Silk Road School, Renmin University of China. In his opinion piece, he pointed out the need for both countries to "have a strategic reassurance so that their current strategic mutual trust is sufficient to ensure that their relations will not be affected by any third party in the future and can withstand uncertainties".

Professor Wang added that "having entered a new period, both countries should look beyond history and earnestly find each other's merits. China cannot guide Russia, nor does it need to. To China, Russia has many aspects to learn from, but Russia should also open its arms to its neighbour more widely". The *Global Times (China)* is said

---

[11] See his interview by Jaanus Piirsalu in the Estonian *International Centre for Defence and Security, Paper Issue* dated 15 May 2020.

to be a nationalist-looking daily which reflects the ruling Chinese Communist Party's views.

The recent border clashes between China and India in May/June 2020 also illustrated the limits of Russian trust and confidence in China. Despite their oft-touted close relationship, Russia chose to accelerate its S-400 air defence system deliveries to India by a year, the *Moscow Times* reported on 26 June, quoting the *Kommersant* business daily. The next day, the *Business Standard,* one of India's largest English language dailies, reported that Russia had suspended delivery of the same defence system to China. *The National Interest* also published on 30 July an article by Mark Episkopos, who serves as research assistant at the Centre for the National Interest, which echoed the weapons system's suspension.

Finally, President Putin's consistent praise of President Trump and vice versa must have been taken note by China. It is difficult to see President Putin becoming an open critic of President Trump. If President Trump is re-elected in 2020 and if current US policy towards China remains largely unchanged, with Presidents Putin and Trump continue openly expressing praise for each other, China might consider it a source of concern and even trepidation, especially if concrete policy changes, which signal some level of rapprochement, are made by Russia towards the US and vice versa.

President Putin therefore has balanced his open praise for President Trump by regularly keeping in touch with President Xi and reaffirming continued support for their close ties. This was evident in their telephone conversation on 16 April 2020. According to the Kremlin website, both leaders had "an in-depth discussion of the developments in the coronavirus pandemic"; it was stressed that "mutual support in countering this global threat is further evidence of the special nature of the Russian–Chinese comprehensive strategic partnership. The two leaders reaffirmed their commitment to further strengthening their cooperation in this area, including the exchange of experts and medical equipment, medicines and protective gear." The website added that President Putin "praised the consistent and effective actions of Russia's Chinese partners, which helped stabilise the epidemiological situation in the country" adding that he stressed "that it was counterproductive to accuse China of releasing information to the global community on this dangerous infection in an untimely manner."

Speculation about an alliance or entente between them must be treated as such. It is obvious that Russia does not seek an alliance relationship with China for that would mean a junior status, by virtue of the imbalance in their relative strengths. More importantly, Russia would not agree to such a position, given its own sense of *amour propre* as a great power. Racial, cultural, and religious considerations will also not allow Russians to accept such a status in relation to China, a totally different civilisation. Strategically, an alliance relationship with China would bring the full weight of the US against Russia.

Nevertheless, the poisoned atmosphere in US–China relations is of profound concern to Russia. Hence, Russia has been making carefully conducted moves, to retain Chinese confidence in their hitherto mutually beneficial relationship, while not totally burning its bridges with the US/West.

In the foreseeable future, it is likely that Russia would try to balance both superpowers. Indeed, in an interview with the *Nikkei Asian Review* (Japan) published on 12 June 2020, Konstantin Zatulin, deputy chairman of the State Duma's Committee for Relations with the Commonwealth of Independent States and Russian nationals abroad, stressed Moscow does not want to be "played as a card by either China or the United States" in their geopolitical race to the top. He stressed that while Russia did not support any proposal "to surround China with a 'sanitary fence' and create problems for it," Russia would not "... adopt an unconditional pro-Chinese position on all issues, just because we have a difficult relationship with the United States." He added that Russia did not want to become dependent on either the US or China; hence, Russia's role should be "to restrain both sides from extremes rather than to become an appendage to either China or the United States."

Overall, Russia cannot but ensure good, stable, and close relations with China. Mutual visits by both Presidents Putin and Xi have been taking place quite regularly in the last several years. It is a signal to their peoples that relations between the two countries must be strengthened and raised to the highest levels possible.

Russia's Other Challenges

Its future development also depends on how and whether it addresses or at least manages its large size and related demographic, as well as socio-economic and political challenges.

Large Size

Russians are very proud of their country's large size and are given to blowing their trumpet about it. I would hear that point being made so many times, by intellectuals, government officials, businessmen, journalists, taxi drivers, and even street vendors, all over the country.

Being the world's largest country for the better part of the last 400 years with much of the globe's natural resources, Russia has enjoyed strategic depth (witness the wholesale transfer of many of its war-making facilities east of the Urals at the height of the threat posed to Moscow and European Russia by Operation Barbarossa). A major contributory factor to the inability of Nazi Germany's powerful war machine to overwhelm and defeat Russia was the fact that the country is too large to conquer, let alone pacify and occupy.

Russia also has never had to concern itself with making a living, unlike resource-poor and territorially small countries like Singapore. On the other hand, the world's largest country would find it difficult, if not impossible to defend every square inch of its territory in a conventional war, with its relatively small population. Therefore, Russia will never forsake, let alone weaken its nuclear arsenal. Historically, it had attempted to secure strategic depth by territorial expansion.

Also, the fruits of economic development would not be able to be widely spread in such a large landmass. Moreover, meaningful development itself cannot be undertaken, let alone achieved within a relatively short span of time, in such a vast expanse of land.

Finally, large parts of the country, particularly in Siberia and the Russian Far North are simply inhospitable to habitation. Technology can only go so far to conquer vast distances and physically challenging and demanding environments.

In other words, Russia's large size carries with it both advantages and disadvantages. On balance, Russia's tremendous size without a proportionally large population to develop and defend it, is not to its full advantage.

Demography

Since President Putin's assumption to power, the economy has grown by leaps and bounds and his people's lives have improved tremendously. Nevertheless, the fall in population growth has not appeared to be manageable. More than a decade ago, a Russian academic whose research focussed on Russia's demography painted to me a rather gloomy picture of the country's future population trends, maintaining that it would continue to fall and measures to arrest this development would not reverse the trend.

Writing in the 5 February 2018 issue of the *Rossiskaya Gazeta*, a Russian government daily which publishes official decrees, statements, etc., Leonid Radzikhovski, a well-known independent Russian political analyst, cited the latest statistics on Russia's population as 146,877,088; if one compares it with 148.5 million in 1995, according to World Bank and US Census Bureau, Russia's population loss has not been as dramatic as some observers had believed. However, trends into the future are not encouraging. According to a *Moscow Times* article dated 17 May 2018, the UN Department of Economic and Social Affairs said in a report released on the same day that Russia's population would decline to 132.7 million by 2050.

The latest figures on its population challenge are not hopeful. Russia's Audit Chamber (AC) reported that the total population declined for a fourth consecutive year in 2019, according to a *Moscow Times* article dated 7 November 2019. The article quoted the AC's report as saying that "the natural population decline accelerating for the fourth year in a row creates serious risks for Russia's national goal of ensuring sustainable growth". Macro-Advisory Eurasia Strategic Consulting (MAESC), a leading consultancy on Russia assesses that the demographic challenge has serious economic repercussions in the immediate future. In a May 2019 study, MAESC estimates that the Russian workforce is expected to shrink by two million between 2020 and 2025.

Falling or low population growth has not only economic but also security implications for any country, more so for Russia, since it is a major global power and wishes to remain so.

I do not wish to jump on the bandwagon of quite a few observers of Russia who argue that Russia's future as a major power is questionable because of its demographic challenge. It is still too early to tell how this problem will sort itself out. But it is a grave challenge to Russian policymakers.

President Putin himself pointed out this problem in a major speech on 1 March 2018. Speaking before the Federal Assembly (composed of the Duma, the lower house, and Federation Council, the upper house) in the annual State-of-the-Nation speech, he pointed out that "the working-age population declined by almost 1 million in 2017. This tendency toward reduction will continue in the next few years, which may become a serious handicap for economic growth; there are simply no workforce resources", *Interfax* news agency reported him as saying in a report dated 1 March 2018. To ensure a sustainable and natural population growth in the coming decade, he announced that "we will have to allocate at least 3.4 trillion rubles for demographic development measures and for the welfare of mothers and children within the next 6 years", according to the same Interfax report.

On 20 February 2019, in his State-of-the-Union speech, President Putin devoted the lion's share of it to domestic issues and began his speech by acknowledging that "Russia has entered an extremely challenging period in terms of demographics. As you know, the birth rate is declining". He correctly noted the causes of Russia's demographic challenge, stressing that "this is caused by purely objective reasons, which have to do with the immense human losses and deaths experienced by our country in the 20th century, during the Great Patriotic War and the dramatic years following the dissolution of the Soviet Union". His reference to "the dramatic years following the dissolution of the Soviet Union" was evident during my first tour of duty in Moscow. Millions of people found themselves in poverty and unable to afford medical care, let alone food. Many took to drink. Suicide rates rose. According to an article written by Francis Notzon, Yuri M. Komarov, Sergei P. Ermakov, *et al.*, dated 11 March 1998 in the *Journal of the American Medical Association*, "age-adjusted mortality in Russia rose by almost 33% between 1990 and 1994. During that period, life expectancy for Russian men and women declined dramatically from 63.8 and 74.4 years to 57.7 and 71.2 years, respectively".[12]

President Putin however was confident that as Russia had "succeeded in overcoming the negative demographic challenges in the early 2000s", it could return "to natural population growth by late 2023–early 2024." He therefore announced a series of measures to support families with children by raising income levels, lowering their tax burden, as well as mortgage rates. Healthcare too would be improved — an additional 1,590 outpatient clinics and paramedic stations are to be built or renovated in 2019 and 2020.

His message was reiterated by Prime Minister Medvedev; in his annual report on 17 April 2019 to the State Duma, he stressed that "unfortunately, not many people were born in the 1990s. We need to prevent another demographic collapse and increase the average life expectancy to 78 years by 2024, taking it to 80 years by 2030", *TASS* news agency quoted him as saying in a report dated the same day.

However, there is some scepticism about the government's declared measures to tackle this challenging issue. Referring to Rosstat's

---

[12] I take the liberty of reiterating an earlier source on this issue. David Satter, a long-standing observer of Soviet and post-Soviet Russia, cites the figure of five to seven million people who "died prematurely during the Yeltsin period" on pp. 75 and 76 of his book, *The Less You Know, the Better You Sleep.*

statement that Russia's population as of 1 January 2019 stood at 146.8 million while the population had declined by 93,500 to 2018, a Russian expert, Professor Igor Nikolayev, felt that the figure of 93,500 people was a "substantial loss", equivalent to the population of towns like Magadan (in the Russian Far East). In an article dated 17 March 2019 in *Moskovsky Komsomolets,* a Moscow daily, Nikolayev of the prestigious Higher School of Economics in Moscow, wrote that the government's targeted measures to deal with the demographic problem "...will not work if the overall standard of living does not rise".

President Putin's announced measures in his last two State-of-the-Nation speeches clearly point to his determination to raise the living standards of his people; whether they will bear fruit, only time will tell.

The demographic challenge is serious enough to have elicited a response from the head of the powerful Russian Orthodox Church, Patriarch Kirill. A report dated 20 May 2019 on the website of *RT* quoted him as saying that if Russia gave up on abortion, its population would increase to 156 million by 2029 and 166 million by 2039. He also felt that demographic problems would not be solely solved through monetary bonuses given to families with children. However, his standpoint did not find resonance with Deputy Health Minister, Tatyana Yakovleva; *RT* reported on 6 June 2019 that according to her, the demographic problem would not be solved "...with restrictive measures, but only make it worse".

Related to the demographic challenge is life expectancy, which like demography, had fallen drastically during the tumultuous post-Soviet and Yeltsinite era. Latest figures, however, are encouraging.

The *Moscow Times* reported on 21 April 2020 that life expectancy reached a record 73.4 years in 2019, citing the country's Health Ministry as saying in an Interfax report. The increase from 2018, when average life expectancy stood at a little over 73 years, is attributed to a 3.5% decrease in male mortality and a 2.1% decrease in female mortality among working-age Russians. "Thus, Russia was able to save the lives of an additional 13,600 working-age people," the Health Ministry's press service was quoted as saying.

New Economic Model

In the economic sphere, Russia must find another model to carry it forward into the next few decades of the 21st century. The hitherto natural resources model (principally but not only energy) and its downstream effects have served it well and brought a real measure of prosperity to the country. However, experts believe rightly that this model has run its course, not only given the current low energy prices but also because of the rapid changes in the global economy due to the tech revolution and more global emphasis on increasing the consumption of non-fossil fuels.

I do not wish to go into further detail on this aspect for it is beyond my competence. Suffice it to say that President Putin and his government are keenly aware of this challenge.

He himself has seen the necessity of setting a new economic course, as seen by his annual State-of-the-Nation speech in February 2019. In it, he stressed that:

> "to achieve high growth rates, it is also necessary to resolve systemic problems in the economy. I will highlight four priorities here. The first one is faster growth in labour productivity, primarily based on new technologies and digitalisation; the development of competitive industries and, as a result, an increase in non-primary exports by more than 50 percent in six years. The second one is to improve the business climate and the quality of national jurisdiction, so that no one moves their operations to other jurisdictions, to ensure that everything is reliable and runs like clockwork. Growth in investment should increase by 6–7 per cent in 2020. Achieving this level will be one of the key criteria for evaluating the Government's work. The third priority is removing infrastructural constraints for economic development and for unlocking the potential of our regions. And the fourth thing is training modern personnel, of course, and creating powerful scientific and technological foundations."

Only time will tell if he and his government will succeed fulfilling these declared objectives. One should not, however, simply dismiss them out of hand as mere talk. Russia's relative isolation from the West will only make its leaders and Putin himself even more determined to ensure that their country succeeds against all odds, even in the face of the negative impact on the economy brought about by COVID-19.

The Brain-Drain

Related to the economic challenge is possible brain-drain. The *Moscow Times* issue of 24 January 2018 cited a RANEPA[13] report published the day before as saying that each year, an estimated 100,000 Russians emigrate to the developed world, around 40% of whom have a higher education. A total of 2.7 million Russians currently live abroad, of which 1.5 million have kept their Russian citizenship; however, only about 800,000 who have a higher education, live abroad. This figure does not appear to be large, when compared to the size of Russia's population. Nevertheless, if more highly-educated Russians move abroad, that would present a real problem.

According to figures cited by Gordon Hahn, Expert Analyst at Corr Analytics and a Senior Researcher in the Centre for Terrorist and Intelligence Research, Akribis Group, San Diego, California, in his article dated 13 May 2018, between 2012 and 2016, over a million people left the country. His assessment is that "the Kremlin's failure to provide competitive opportunity and lifestyle for Russian youth is driving a massive Russian brain drain abroad".

He adds that:

> "the exodus is more likely to weaken rather than strengthen Russia's already weak pro-democracy movement. In sum, instead of voting for pro-democratic forces and/or fomenting unrest, Russia's discontented, highly educated, highly skilled university graduates tend to move abroad to find suitable work. The departure of these 'best and brightest' removes the most talented potential organisers and leaders of revolution. This is especially true when many young Russian emigres are computer technology, Internet marketing, and

---

[13] RANEPA is the Russian Presidential Academy of National Economy and Public Administration.

social network specialists — an important cadre for making revolution in the information age."

Indeed, the brain-drain remains a significant challenge for policymakers, if a 27 March 2019 Stratfor.com report is anything to go by. According to it:

"the continued fall in population will undermine Russia's economic position, particularly as the people most likely to leave are young, educated professionals in sectors like technology and the military. Rosstat, too, has noted the increased brain drain: In 2017, 22 per cent of emigrants from Russia possessed advanced degrees, up 5 per cent from 2012. The fall will make maintaining tax revenues and sustaining the pension system challenging for Russia, something that prompted the government to raise the retirement age effective this year. The change will also alter Russia's demographic composition, as migrants from faster-growing countries in the Caucasus and Central Asia are likely to migrate to Russia in greater numbers to make up for the population loss. This, in turn, could foment more ethnic tensions in the country and increase political instability."

The Russian preference to emigrate to the West is made evident from a *Deutsche Welle* report dated 20 April 2019; it cited the findings of the independent Levada Centre pollster which state that many of Russia's young people would like to live in the West, with over 40% of Russians between the ages of 18 and 24 looking to moving permanently abroad. An article dated 10 April 2019 by a leading expert, Yaroslav Lissovolik, Programme Director at the Valdai Discussion Club, and Member of the Government Expert Council on the development of Russia's human capital and "soft power" reveals the extent of Russian brain-power in the West.

In his article, Lissovolik notes that more than 70% of Russia's entire research diaspora is concentrated in Western Europe and the US, while "Asia accounted for almost 15% of Russia's entire scientific diaspora". A noteworthy point is that "of the key areas in the Russian scientific diaspora, it is necessary to set aside physics, biology and mathematics which account for almost two-thirds of Russia's total intellectual diaspora. On the whole, the fundamental and technical sciences account for the overwhelming majority of the Russian diaspora, whereas social and humanitarian sciences add up to little more 6% of the total." He adds that the distribution of the Russian academic diaspora in major research areas in percentages is as follows:

Research Area	Percentage (%)
Physics	33.6
Biology	22.8
Technical Sciences	12.7
Mathematics	9.3
Chemistry	6.1
Social and Humanitarian Sciences	6.1
Earth Sciences	5.2
Medicine	3.6
Agricultural Science	0.6

Lissovolik's regional distribution of the Russian scientific diaspora, in percentages, is also worthy of note and is as follows:

Research Area	Percentage (%)
Post-Soviet States	2.3
Western Europe	42.4
Scandinavia	5.2
Eastern Europe	1.1
North America	30.4
South and Central America	1.9
Asia	14.7
Africa	1.2
Australia and New Zealand	0.8

Singapore is one of the beneficiaries of Russia's brain-drain to Asia. According to the National University of Singapore (NUS) website, Nobel Prize-winning physicist Professor Konstantin Novoselov joined NUS as Distinguished Professor of Materials Science and Engineering on 8 April 2019. He is the first Nobel-prize winner to join a Singapore university. Novoselov had been an international scientific advisor to the NUS Centre for Advanced 2D Materials since 2015. The website adds that Novoselov and Professor Sir Andre Geim were awarded the Nobel Prize for Physics in 2010 for their ground-breaking achievements with the two-dimensional material graphene. Professor Novoselov was the youngest Nobel Laureate in Physics since 1971 and the youngest overall since 1992.

I have already written about some scientists whom I interviewed in connection with the visa applications to Singapore. During my second tour in Moscow, I also met a young journalist, when he applied for a visa to Singapore in order to participate in some courses in INSEAD, Singapore. He conveyed an impression of being a brilliant, focused, and articulate chap and while I neither directly asked nor did he volunteer any extra information, the impression I garnered was that he was not particularly pleased with the prevailing situation in his country. Not surprisingly, I learnt years later that he had emigrated to the West and is now gainfully employed in a very prestigious American news agency. He is one of those highly-educated Russians who has been lost to the country.

Socio-Economic-Challenges

More of Russia's energies will be channelled into addressing domestic issues in the next few years. President Putin made that crystal clear in his 7 May 2018 inauguration speech. He stressed that:

> "Russia is a strong, active and influential participant in international life; the country's security and defence capability are reliably assured. We will continue to pay the necessary, close attention to these issues. But now, we must use all the opportunities available to us primarily

to address the most vital domestic development objectives, to achieve an economic and technological breakthrough, and to enhance competitiveness in the spheres that determine the future. A new quality of life, wellbeing, security and health are what constitutes our main goals and the focus of our policies. Our reference point is Russia for the people, a country of opportunities for self-fulfilment for each person."

His emphasis on domestic issues was reiterated in his January 2020 State-of-the-Union address. The absence of any harsh language about or criticism of the West in his speech was also indicative of his continued desire to lessen tensions while focusing on domestic challenges. This focus will not change, more so, since COVID-19 has exacted damage on the economy (GDP in 2020 might fall 6.6% according to the IMF). That would only exacerbate the gap between the haves and have-nots, and it has been a recurring problem for Russian leaders.

Ben Aris, an expert on the Russian economy, noted in his article in *Intellinews* dated 8 May 2018 that the independent pollster, *Levada* published the day before its findings that Russians were most unhappy with President Putin over wealth inequality. He himself is not unaware of this challenge, including growing poverty in the country. His 2018 State-of-the-Nation speech pointed out that 20 million Russian nationals lived in poverty, less than the 42 million in 2000, "but it is still way too many." He reiterated this challenge in his 2019 State-of-the-Nation speech, citing the figure of 19 million people living below the poverty line, and announced measures to combat poverty. They include a five-year support programme that would benefit more than nine million people.

Moreover, according to the Kremlin website dated 8 May 2018, during Putin's address to the State Duma the same day, he noted that he had signed the previous day "an Executive Order on the National Goals and Strategic Objectives of the Russian Federation to 2024". This document talks about an active demographic policy and a steady growth of the population, a breakthrough in technology and science, high economic growth rates, new living standards for Russian citizens, an increase in their real incomes, and a drastic reduction of poverty. Implementation of this decree would require the government to spend 8 trillion rubles (US$126 billion), as President Putin himself informed the State Duma.

The wide gap between the haves and have-nots was also reflected in the Credit Suisse Research Institute October 2019 report (on Global Wealth). It states that "according to our estimates, the top decile of wealth holders owns 83% of all household wealth in Russia. This is a high level, above the figure of 76% for the United States, which has one of the most concentrated distributions of wealth among advanced nations. Interestingly, it is also higher than the top decile share of 60% in China".

Related to this problem is that of falling incomes. According to a report dated 22 April 2019 in *Intellinews*, real incomes in Russia fell slightly in 2018, down for the fifth year in a row, and extended their fall between January and March, dropping by 2.3%. Nominal monthly incomes were up to RUB 45,000 (US$705) per month or a 5.2% increase year-on-year. The report assessed that the stagnation in real disposable income had led to a slow deterioration in the quality of life for ordinary Russians and was feeding a growing propensity for social unrest. It added that the Kremlin was aware of the problem and launched RUB25.7 trillion (US$390 billion) investments planned for 12 National Projects (NPs), from social spending to infrastructure investment as a way to boost growth and improve prosperity. The first beneficial effects of this programme are not expected to be apparent until 2021, when GDP growth is supposed to rise to 3%.

However, this goal is unlikely to be accomplished, thanks to COVID-19's negative impact on the economy. It has made the problem of falling incomes worse; quoting research from Moscow's Higher School of Economics (HSE), the *Moscow Times* of 1 June 2020 reported that more than 60% of Russians had seen their earnings drop as a result of the pandemic.

Even without COVID-19's adverse impact, the economy has long been seen to be headed towards stagnation; former Finance Minister, Alexei Kudrin expressed the view that to increase growth, the government must invest more in education and health. According to a RFE/RL report dated 11 July 2020, in a speech, he said if GDP fell 5% this year as expected, then the economy would have averaged just 1% annual growth over the past decade, which he described as very low. Russia had the potential to grow 3% to 5% annually but the government had not taken the steps needed and Russia was now in stagnation, he added. Russia had to increase current spending plans on "human capital" such as health and education by 1% percent of GDP; Russia also suffered from poor state administration and high regulatory barriers and must reform how government workers were trained and motivated.

Hence, President Putin must focus his attention and energy on domestic affairs in the remaining four years of his current presidential term. With the additional challenge posed by COVID-19, he does not have any choice.

Russia's Future Global Role

Russia's challenges do not render it powerless to mould and become master of its destiny and to play a significant role in global affairs. No one can doubt its vast potential, given its huge landmass and plenitude of raw materials as well as very highly-educated, talented and hardy people. *Nolens-volens,* Russia as a major power is here to stay, even if it would not be as strong as China or the US. Even a democratic Russia in the Western sense of the term will not relinquish its claim to be and to remain a great power.

Since Russia is integrated into the global economy, isolation from international economic and global affairs cannot be a viable course of its foreign policy, even were Russia to relinquish any pretensions to great power status. Exactly what role Russia could play in the future where the US and China as well as the EU, Japan, India, Brazil, Indonesia, and perhaps a united Korea will be the major powers, remains an open question. Possibly, the answer lies in the vision of Ambassador Extraordinary and Plenipotentiary of Russia, Nikolay Spasskiy. His views were articulated in his article dated 19 March 2018 in the journal, *Russia in Global Affairs,* where he argued that Russia "must understand that despite its 140-million population, it cannot become a superpower, yet it can be strong enough to be on its own and live better than many other countries do, although not all of them — we must be realists after all".

He thinks Russia cannot become a superpower because of its "insufficient population", a standpoint most experts would share. But Russia's large size and mineral resources' wealth, as well as strong armed forces still make it a power to be reckoned with. In the future, Russia would not need to join the EU or enter into an alliance with the US or China, but could position itself "as an independent centre of power — not as a superpower, but as a great country capable of standing up for itself (not only against Georgia) and having power not for its expansionist projection in the world but for guaranteeing a better material and spiritual life for its people".

While this vision does not assume Russia taking an aggressive posture towards the outside world, it does postulate Russia remaining a great power. Indeed, no rational mind can deny Russia this role.

On the other hand, Professor Sergei Karaganov believes that between the US and China, "Russia will be able to be useful in both cases either as a balancer between two potential hegemons and a guarantor of a new non-alignment, or as one of the active creators of the new partnership, turning from the outskirts of Europe and Asia into Northern Eurasia, one of its key centres." By "new partnership", Professor Karaganov feels the Greater Eurasia (GE) concept could become a reality in which Russia would find a leading role.[14]

My views of the GE have been outlined earlier. While I do not think it can be realised in the foreseeable future, if at all, Russia's future role in global affairs, in whatever form it might take, will be significant.

The Succession Issue

Until early 2020, the succession issue had been a subject of much speculation. It was not entirely a foregone conclusion that President

---

[14] For details, please see his article dated 29 June 2020 in *Russia in Global Affairs*, entitled "The future of the Big Triangle".

Putin would seek to remain in office after his current term ends in 2024. However, a train of events, beginning in January 2020 set in motion what is believed to be his plan to hang on to power beyond 2024.

In his not uncharacteristic way, he surprised observers as well as his inner circle (reportedly) by proposing major constitutional amendments during his January 2020 State-of-the-Nation speech. To ensure broad public support, he suggested putting the entire package of proposed constitutional changes to a referendum. Following President Putin's speech, Prime Minister Dmitry Medvedev resigned from his post. He was subsequently appointed Deputy Head of the powerful Security Council.

The PM-designate was Mikhail Mishutin, a capable technocrat who ran the tax service. His appointment was expectedly approved by the State Duma. Mishutin is credited with having established an effective and well-run tax system. While one might have believed even then that Russia after 2024 might see another leader, the denouement finally unfolded on 10 March. Addressing the State Duma, he supported a proposed amendment by Valentina Tereshkova, the well-known cosmonaut and a government deputy, who called for either removing the current two-term limit for presidential office or resetting the clock so that the law would not apply to President Putin's time in office. In so doing, he laid to rest long-held speculation about his political future.

The State Duma, Federation Council, and Constitutional Court all approved the proposed amendments. The whole package of constitutional amendments was to be decided upon by referendum on 22 April 2020; however, it was postponed to 1 July 2020, due to the outbreak of COVID-19 in Russia.

The most significant amendments revolved around the removal of the "in-a-row" clause which regulated the maximum number of presidential terms; in effect, the deletion of this clause allows President Putin to contest the 2024 presidential elections.

Others include the Russian Constitution taking precedence over international law and the State Duma having the right to approve the Prime Minister's candidacy, and those of the Deputy Prime Ministers and Federal Ministers.

Noteworthy also are clauses relating to social welfare viz. the minimum wage cannot be lower than the subsistence minimum and there is to be regular indexation of pensions. Equally significant is the clause defining marriage as a relationship between a man and a woman.

Indeed, these social welfare clauses are targeted at the majority of voters, given the social protection and guarantees these clauses offer to the working class. Moreover, the clause on recognising traditional marriage satisfies the conservative moral values of most voters as well as the powerful Russian Orthodox Church.

These three clauses ensured that President Putin's package of constitutional amendments would secure the support of the majority of voters. Almost 78% supported the amendment package while a little over 21% voted against it; turnout was 65%. The outcome was expected. If one compares it with his 2018 presidential election victory (68% turnout, 77% of the vote), it shows his widespread popularity has not been as dented as observers had believed.

President Putin could now theoretically, run for office again in 2024, for another two terms, till 2036. Of late, he has not ruled out running for re-election. A *TASS* news agency report dated 21 June 2020 quoted President as saying that "I have not made any decision so far. I'm not ruling out that I will stand for [election] if this emerges in the Constitution. We'll see." The report added that he cautioned Russian officials against searching for a successor to him now, saying that they should rather focus on their work. "They need to work rather than search for successors," he was quoted as saying. He made these comments in an interview for a film "Russia. Kremlin. Putin" on Rossiya-1 state television, according to *TASS*.

In my view, his purpose in putting forward the constitutional amendments package is not so much to prolong his political future to 2036 but to ensure that he will not be reduced to a lame-duck President, as his comments above clearly show. He has also recently remarked that it was not healthy for Russia to have a system like the Soviet era when leaders died in office.

He has taken this unprecedented step to ensure that he could turn over the reins of power to a hand-picked successor without too much worry, perhaps after re-running and winning the presidency in 2024. At this point in time, his likely successor is Prime Minister, Mikhail Mishustin.

Mishustin has the technocratic credentials to fully and successfully implement the important National Projects as well as raise the economic growth rates; so do the new and current members of his Cabinet. COVID-19's negative impact on the economy has placed an additional obstacle to Mishustin but he and his technocratic team are more than competent to handle the challenge. His fluency in the English language could not but have been noticed by President Putin. Such a facility would mean easier access and direct communication with the US, regarded as the most important country (despite oft-repeated protestations of close and vital links with China) and "main opponent" of Russia.

Second, Mishutin does not have any known links to Russia's powerful interest groups such as the *siloviki* or top security establishment officials and heads of powerful state corporations. Hence, President Putin need not balance the interests of these groups; were he a member of either of them, Putin would have to spend political capital and time on such a task.

Moreover, Mishutin would not be seen as "old wine in a new bottle" by the electorate. In this regard, he fits the bill of having new faces at the helm of power.

Fourth, being a political unknown without any expressed political ambitions, he is not considered a threat by either President Putin or the powerful interest groups. In that regard, he would be more at ease handing over power to Mishutin who would be expected to protect him from any political retribution.[15]

Ultimately, whether he does re-run for office in 2024 depends on the following factors.

---

[15] On assuming power, Putin granted his predecessor total immunity from prosecution, as well as financial benefits including a pension. It is logical to assume he would expect the same treatment from his successor.

Much would revolve around how the economy develops, and in the immediate term, how Russia manages the COVID-19 crisis and the effects of the oil price fall on its economy.

Secondly, should the non-systemic opposition leaders (those outside the loyal opposition in the State Duma) become a real alternative to him, then he might be forced to seek re-election. At this stage however, it is unlikely that his political opponents could mount a real challenge to his power and position. They are not united, lack a coherent policy programme, are weakened by official pressure, and do not enjoy widespread popular support.

Third, the state of his health is obviously a factor; he is still in fine fettle and can be expected to remain so, given his spartan habits and love for sports.

Fourth, the rise of competent leaders within the system who might prove capable of running for his office or whom he trusts and might seek to elevate, cannot be totally ruled out.

Finally, the state of relations with the EU and the US as well as China, is key. Should relations with these key actors deteriorate or enter into a crisis, he might choose to run for re-election.

Only time will tell if he would seek to remain in power till his eighties. He has a keen sense of destiny and would not relinquish power if he believes that it would endanger his legacy and the country's well-being.

Envoi

Some final words about the current socio-economic situation in Russia would be in order. Russia today is still quite a distance from Western Europe, North America, Japan, Australia, and New Zealand in terms of its socio-economic development, but it has come quite a long way from the 1990s and early 2000s, as seen from the following indicators.

First, the business climate appears to be improving by leaps and bounds in the last several years. In the World Bank's 'Doing Business 2019' ranking, Russia is rated 31 out of 190. It did not succeed in achieving the goal set by President Putin in 2012 to enter the top 20 countries by 2018 (it occupied the 120th position in 2011). Whether this ranking translates into real gains in the economy is another issue.

Second, as of 31 May 2020, Russia's international reserves stood over US$566 billion, according to the Central Bank of Russia. With such large financial resources, Russia is no longer an economically weak country, and is a far cry from the 1990s and early years of the 21st century. It also has relatively low foreign debt (about 15% of GDP).

Third, Russia's GDP has grown the last few years, in the face of Western sanctions. In 2015, GDP stood at US$1.36 trillion, while in 2018, it amounted to US$1.650 trillion, and in 2019, US$1.722 trillion (estimated), according to Macro-Advisory Eurasia Strategic Consulting (MAESC), in its December 2019 Macro Monthly report.[16]

Economic growth into the future is modest but encouraging. According to *Interfax* news agency report dated 30 June 2020, the Russian Economic Development Ministry projected in the latest version of its forecast that GDP would contract by 4.8% in 2020, and then grow by 3.2% in 2021, 2.9% in 2022, and 3.1% in 2023. The IMF however, has estimated a decline of 6.6%, due to the adverse impact of COVID-19.

Fourth, the middle class in Russia has grown. In an interview conducted by *TASS* news agency and published on the Kremlin website in March 2020, President Putin claimed that:

> "The middle class is different in different countries. There is a relevant methodology of the World Bank. The middle class is estimated using the number of households, of people whose incomes are 50 per cent above the minimum wage. This year's minimum wage is, if I remember correctly, 11,280 rubles, while the average wage is far higher. There are a lot of such people, well above 70 per cent."

One can dispute his figures but cannot doubt that the middle class is larger than in the past; there was no middle class to speak of in the

---

[16] For comparison, its GDP in 2013 was US$2.2 trillion, before the imposition of Western sanctions; they and low energy prices, etc, did take a toll on its economy but did not lead to its collapse, as some observers had expected.

immediate years following the break-up of the Soviet Union and in the early Putinite era. On the other hand, COVID-19's impact on the economy can be expected to adversely affect the middle class' fortunes and numbers.

Fifth, according to MAESC, Russia has 90 million internet users, the largest in Europe. Then PM Medvedev in a report to the Duma in 2018, said that internet coverage reached 72.5%; moreover, 30 types of government services and 150 municipal services could be accessed with a one-stop shop arrangement.[17]

Finally, exercise and sports have become entrenched as a way of life. According to a *Financial Times* article dated 13 March 2018 by Kathrin Hille, 50 million Russians, or more than 36% of the population aged between three and 79, practise sports regularly, an increase from 22.5% in 2012 (quoting Sports Ministry's figures). *TASS* news agency reported in an article dated 31 January 2018 that the total mortality rate in 2017 was 12.4 per thousand people, a 6.8% decrease compared to 2012 and 3.9% less than in 2016. The relative prosperity of the 2000s has definitely led to this trend; moreover, life expectancy reached 73. Compared to the 1990s, this is certainly an achievement.

Russia's future is assured, regardless of its political system. Its people have undergone a great many trials and tribulations. They endured political repression and material hardship, thanks to the excesses of Stalinism in the 1930s and then went on to fight and helped to defeat the tremendous war-making powers of Nazi Germany and thereafter rebuild their war-torn country. They sent the first man and woman into space. The Soviet Union lasted seven decades when one would have thought it could have disintegrated or imploded earlier, due to its economic inefficiency, political and social repression and costly arms race with the US, as well as financial and material support of its Warsaw Pact allies and many other "socialist brothers" in the Third World. The

---

[17] This breakthrough definitely reduces corruption at these levels of bureaucracy. In the past, many of my contacts and acquaintances would frequently complain of the red tape involved in securing such basic services and should one desire faster service, one had to reckon with a "fee".

break-up of the Soviet Union in December 1991 brought in its train untold suffering for the people of Russia, its successor state, with socio-economic and political chaos and instability. Yet Russia itself did not break-up like many observers in the 1990s and into the early years of this century had believed it would. The Russian people have also lived through the last six years of Western sanctions. Nevertheless, the country's socio-political system and its economy have not collapsed; all that is a tribute to the strength, resilience, fortitude, hard work and diligence as well as patience of its people.

That Russia exists in its current form and had not broken-up in the immediate post-Soviet and Yeltsin eras, like Yugoslavia in the 1990s, is to be appreciated, for otherwise the political, economic, and social, not to mention the geopolitical and geostrategic consequences and ramifications on its neighbours and the world at large, would have been too catastrophic to contemplate. President Yeltsin prevented the possible break-up of Russia by violently crushing the Chechen bid for independence; President Putin had undoubtedly gone one better than his predecessor in restoring order and stability and bringing a measure of unprecedented prosperity to the country, in the aftermath of the poverty and systemic chaos of the 1990s.

During my stay in Moscow, most Russians I knew were inclined to compare their country to the West and would lament that it was not a "normal" country. It might not have the living standards of Germany, the UK, France, or the US, but it is certainly striving to reach those standards. One cannot simply dismiss as pure talk the oft-expressed determination, resolve, and will of President Putin and his supporters to further develop Russia into a "normal" country.

As like as not, he/they would succeed. Failure would have grave consequences for the country. The only question is the time-frame. In the light of Russia's many challenges and problems, its transition into a "normal" country is likely to take at least another generation.

End

CPSIA information can be obtained
at www.ICGtesting.com
Printed in the USA
FSHW020151011220
76377FS